Environment '90

The Legislative Agenda

Environment '90

The Legislative Agenda

Congressional Quarterly Inc.
Washington, D.C.

Major contributers: Chuck Alston, Bob Benenson, Peter Bragdon, Robert Clayton, David S. Cloud, Beth Donovan, Pamela Fessler, George Hager, Kenneth E. Jaques, Phil Kuntz, Philip Marwill, Mike Mills, Sharon Perkinson, Alyson Pytte, David Rapp, Karine Roesch, Barry S. Surman, Pat Towell
Production Editor: Jamie R. Holland
Graphics: S. Dmitri Lipczenko
Index: Steve Moyer
Production: I.D. Fuller, Michael Emanuel, Jhonnie G. Bailey
Cover Photo: Jack Auldridge

Congressional Quarterly Inc.

Andrew Barnes Chairman
Richard R. Edmonds President
Neil Skene Editor and Publisher
Robert W. Merry Executive Editor
John J. Coyle Associate Publisher
Michael L. Koempel Director of Information Services
Robert E. Cuthriell Director of Development

Book Division

Patrick Bernuth General Manager

Library of Congress Cataloging-in-Publication

Environment '90: the legislative agenda.
      p.   cm.
   ISBN 0-87187-578-0
   1. Environmental law--United States. 2. Environmental policy--United States. I. Congressional Quarterly, inc.
KF3775.E465 1990
363.7'056'0973--dc20
                                                    90-1841
                                                      CIP

Contents

Part I

Part II

Editor's Note:

Congressional Quarterly Inc., an editorial research service and publishing company, serves clients in the fields of news, education, business, and government. It combines Congressional Quarterly's specific coverage of Congress, government, and politics with the more general subject range of an affiliated service, Editorial Research Reports.

Congressional Quarterly publishes the *Congressional Quarterly Weekly Report* and a variety of books, including college political science textbooks under the CQ Press imprint and public affairs paperbacks on developing issues and events. CQ also publishes information directories and reference books on the federal government, national elections, and politics, including the *Guide to the Presidency,* the *Guide to Congress,* the *Guide to the U.S. Supreme Court,* the *Guide to U.S. Elections, Politics in America,* and *Congress A to Z: CQ's Ready Reference Encyclopedia.* The *CQ Almanac,* a compendium of legislation for one session of Congress, is published each year. *Congress and the Nation,* a record of government for a presidential term, is published every four years.

The *Weekly Report* magazine was and still is CQ's basic periodical publication. Its January 20, 1990, special issue on the environment makes up the first half of this book, while four in-depth articles on the environment written and published by Editorial Research Reports (ERR) make up the second half. The names and dates of the ERR stories are "Setting Environmental Priorities," December 9, 1988; "Not In My Back Yard!," June 9, 1989; "America Turns to Recycling," November 17, 1989; and "Free Market Environmental Protection," September 8, 1989.

In conjunction with other organizations Congressional Quarterly publishes reference books that have become the staples of political science research.

Part I

Power of the Earth

*'The environment' is back, and this time the result
may be the greening of Congress*

**"The environment
belongs to all of us."**

—President Bush

Thirteen years after
Congress passed its last
major anti-pollution legislation — and 20 years after
American citizens demon-
strated their urgent con-
cern in a nationwide Earth
Day — "the environment"
is back. The watchword of
1970 has become a byword
for the 1990s.

This time, the move-
ment has reached far into
mainstream society, and
an extraordinary surge of
public anxiety is rever-
berating throughout the
world. Soviet President
Mikhail S. Gorbachev
makes the environment a
theme of his address to the
United Nations. Britain's
Margaret Thatcher talks
about the responsibility of
holding a "full repairing
lease" on the Earth. Pope
John Paul II sends out an
environmental prayer on
Christmas Eve.

And President Bush,
heir to the overtly non-
environmental Reagan ad-
ministration, adopts the
mission as his own.

As a result, business
and industry are being
forced to show proof of their ecological responsibility. State
and local governments are finding out that voters want
firm assurances that their air, water and soil will be protected for this generation and well beyond the next.

Caught in the middle of this political upheaval is the
U.S. Congress — and in particular, the 101st Congress,
which is about to experience an unrelenting session of
environment- and energy-related business.

Beginning with long-awaited showdowns in the Senate
and House over Clean Air Act amendments, and proceeding
to the overdue extension of federal solid- and hazardous-
waste laws, Congress will spend much of 1990 reworking two
of the most sweeping environmental laws of the past 25 years.

As it does, a constellation of smaller but equally salient
environmental issues will emerge. Recurring issues, such as

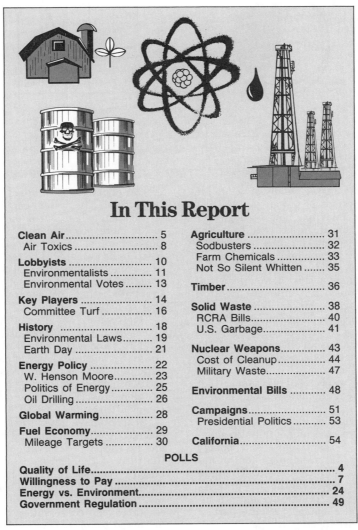

whether to preserve the
national forests and wil-
derness areas from oil and
logging development, will
compete for members' at-
tention with such burgeoning questions as how to
deal with global change.

In the meantime, the
Bush administration has
decided that the way to
craft a new (and lasting)
energy policy is to build it
around environmental
themes. That strategy will
get early tests this year on
legislation dealing with increased conservation and
the use of alternative fuels.

And that is not all.
There are other, seemingly
unrelated legislative priorities this year — ranging
from the farm bill to arms
control — that will assume
decidedly environmental
casts. At nearly every turn,
Congress will encounter the
"environmental question."
And it should be increas-
ingly clear that the answers
arrived at will chart a policy
course for this country —
and probably the world —
for the 1990s.

Indeed, with all the leg-
islation and policy ques-
tions on the agenda, this
second session could well
become known as the
"Environmental Congress."

Why has this one idea suddenly taken hold on politicians?
What is behind the pressures on Congress and the Bush
administration to reassert themselves in environmental pol-
icy-making? How do geographical, partisan and special interests on Capitol Hill coincide or collide on environment issues?

And what is the "reality check" on this surge of environmental interest in the United States and on the desire — or
even the ability — of Congress to respond effectively to it?

The New Politics

Clearly, a new attitude has entered Washington since
Ronald Reagan effectively iced the environmental movement of the 1970s with his anti-government, anti-regula-
tory fervor. In much the way his "Sagebrush Rebellion"
gained strength from perceived excesses in industrial regu-

3

lation and land-use controls, the new environmental movement has been revived by perceived industrial and business abuses on the land, air and sea. The *Exxon Valdez* oil spill in Alaska's Prince William Sound and warnings about a global "greenhouse effect" have been translated into an unmistakable message from the voting public: Clean it up.

The growing power and savvy of the "environmentalists" — conservation and advocacy groups whose memberships now number in the millions — have given vent to the public's outrage. These organizations have also developed strong political and financial ties to a new generation of members in Congress, many of whom are only now coming into key positions of power.

Most important, the movement has now been given a pulpit in the White House, where Bush has tried to preach moderation to his old oil, industrial and business benefactors, as well as to a still-skeptical environmental congregation.

By his actions as well as his words, Bush has shown not only how powerful the environment is with American voters, but how a presidential voice can alter the political dynamics of the issue in Congress. His introduction of a wide-ranging anti-pollution measure has transformed a 12-year stalemate into a seeming inevitability: passage of a clean-air bill. His imprimatur has itself empowered the very political forces that Bush's predecessor in the White House sought to disenfranchise.

As a result, there is a new, widespread acceptance that federal action on all kinds of environmental issues is both necessary and called for.

But there is an obverse reaction, too: that the federal government itself is to blame for environmentally irresponsible actions — on the part of the Defense and Energy departments, whose environmental mismanagement of nuclear weapons plants and even military bases will require billions of dollars in cleanup expenses; on the part of farmers, whose farm-subsidy programs practically require intensive application of artificial chemicals; on the part of timber interests, whose intensive logging practices on federal lands could endanger wildlife.

Reality Check

These are almost self-evident problems for Congress and the Bush White House to deal with. But here is the rub. The same competing interests that have made it virtually impossible to rewrite the Clean Air Act, craft a long-term energy policy or withdraw agriculture subsidies all remain in force and ensconced. The re-emergence of a strong environmental faction in Congress has, in many instances, only added to the panoply of special interests competing for dominance.

And even with the president's public support, the very nature of environmental legislation — it is unusually complex and highly technical, and almost by definition pits one geographical or economic faction against another —

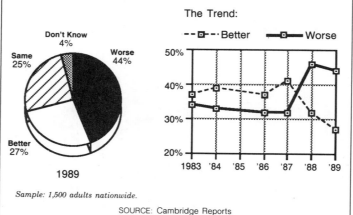

Quality of Life

Question: Overall quality of the environment around here: better or worse than it was five years ago?

Don't Know 4%
Same 25%
Worse 44%
Better 27%

1989

The Trend:

- - □ - - Better   ▬□▬ Worse

50%
40%
30%
20%

1983 '84 '85 '86 '87 '88 '89

Sample: 1,500 adults nationwide.

SOURCE: Cambridge Reports

BARBARA SASSA-DANIELS

presents contradictory messages to members of Congress. On the one hand they are being told to exact tough new restrictions on auto emissions, acid rain and toxic air pollutants, if only for the sake of saving human lives; conversely, each proposed "solution" promises to exact enormous sacrifices, not least of which are lost jobs.

Even where there is a potential for consensus, the sheer magnitude of such problems as dwindling landfill space or global warming requires solutions that may go far beyond Congress' institutional capacity to respond. Congress, by nature of its Balkanized committee structure, often creates policy either in broad brush strokes or in minimalist quick fixes. The system can work to its own detriment.

So then, where is the environmental movement of the 1990s more powerful than its precursors? Foremost, the public impulse for *improvement* appears (to politicians, at least) to be palpable. The fading fearsomeness of Cold War and economic apocalypse has left room for environmental anxieties to reassert themselves. And these facts cannot be overstated: that real environmental problems exist, and that something has to be done about them.

Thus voters are demanding at least a commitment to action, if not the action itself. The trends developing in California and other hotbeds of environmental action demonstrate that an appreciation of global ecological values is just as important today as the appreciation of international economic relationships was in the decades following World War II. And like all politics, these values are local. They revolve around the common desire for a better life — for quality of life.

Scholars have noted the similarity between the postwar emergence of environmental activism in the United States and an earlier "conservationist" movement, begun around the turn of the century. But as the University of Pittsburgh's Samuel P. Hays has written, the conservation movement that inspired Theodore Roosevelt and others was really an effort to make more *efficient* use of natural resources; soil conservation techniques, for instance, were promoted to increase crop yields, not preserve the Earth's surface. The new environmental movement, says Hays, involves values that stress the "quality of human experience and hence of the human environment."

This impulse, in the end, could form a new political geography in Congress, one where middle-class, consumerist — and essentially suburban — desires for safety and tranquility compete as strongly for political attention as the more established economic engines of peace and prosperity. The consequences could be pervasive. Back in 1974, Congress acknowledged its influence on the economy and decided that every bill should have a statement assessing the budget impact. It is not hard to foresee a time when Congress will respond to a similar concern and require every bill to show its impact on the environment.

—David Rapp

CLEAN AIR

The 'White House Effect' Opens A Long-Locked Political Door

*But George Bush, the would-be environmental president,
won't find it easy to live up to his campaign goal*

It was the summer of 1988, the presidential race was tightening and polls showed California shaping up as a tossup state whose huge bloc of electoral votes might go either way — George Bush or Michael S. Dukakis. Bush's strategists were scrambling for a "hot button," an issue that would galvanize voters.

The traditional concerns that had worked so well for Ronald Reagan — jobs, inflation, the economy — were "falling off the radar" for lack of interest, says Vince Breglio, a director of polling for the Bush-Quayle campaign. So "it was down the issue agenda that we began to look."

Down among second-tier issues such as health care and education, Bush's pollsters found what they were after: the environment.

Already an important issue in outdoors-conscious California, pollution fears were also generating big polling numbers on the East Coast, where the beaches, Breglio notes, were enduring "a summer of sun, surf and medical waste."

Bush embraced the issue with a vengeance. Although he had few environmental credentials and was still serving a president regarded as an environmental pariah, he set about building his environmental bona fides and distancing himself from his boss.

Bush, a onetime Texas oil executive, had already come out for a delay in offshore drilling off Northern California. He followed that with a pledge to do more about acid rain than just study it. He then talked about countering the greenhouse effect with "the White House effect." He went to polluted Boston Harbor to aggressively challenge Massachusetts Gov. Dukakis' own commitment to the environment. And in the dead of a hot summer, he went to smog-ridden cities and vowed to clean the air.

"I have been an environmentalist

By George Hager

CHECKLIST

Issue: Air pollution.

Legislation: Clean Air Act reauthorization.

Need for action: Previous law expired in 1988.

Main venues: House: Energy and Commerce Committee; Senate: Environment and Public Works Committee.

Outlook: House committee action in March. Senate floor action imminent.

since I first entered Congress in 1966," Bush insisted. "And I will be one as president."

Once in office, Bush followed through. He offered Congress a comprehensive proposal (HR 3030) to reauthorize the Clean Air Act and set new controls on smog, acid rain and toxic air pollutants.

Overall, it was a comparatively moderate measure that made neither industry nor environmentalists ecstatic, but that wasn't the point. The bill was a textbook example of the unique power of the presidency to alter the dynamics of an issue in Congress.

Bush jump-started the long-stalemated congressional clean-air debate, bringing the myriad geographical and economic interests to the table and forcing the most obstructionist and dogmatic players to sit down and deal.

Even the most partisan Democrats concede him that much. For the first time in 13 years, clean-air legislation is set to go to the floor of the Senate when Congress reconvenes Jan. 23. Congress is widely expected to finish a mammoth rewrite of the nation's clean-air laws by the end of the year.

But that may have been the easy part.

In the coming weeks and months, bitter disagreements between industry and environmentalists will have to be resolved, and unpleasant realities of the legislation will have to be confronted. Obscured by feel-good rhetoric about clean air and quality of life are potentially wrenching trade-offs: increased costs, altered lifestyles and lost or relocated jobs. The large majorities of Americans who tell pollsters they expect to have to pay something for clean air and an improved environment will likely find they have been taken at their word.

This comes when Bush, having played his trump card, has already shrunk to less heroic proportions, making his potential influence on the rest of the process much less dramatic. Unlike Reagan, Bush did not come to Congress with the rare, agenda-shaping mandate that Reagan brought to his tax and budget proposals, so he will not be able to logroll Congress.

Since introducing his bill, Bush has confined his public participation in the debate largely to news conference complaints that Congress is dawdling on his legislation. Meanwhile, his top aides have sent contradictory lobbying messages to the Hill, and his chief House allies have felt free to jettison key parts of his bill for provisions they like better. Bush's defenders on the Hill and in the White House say this is business as usual, and that the president is harboring his strength for a time when — on the House or Senate floor, or in conference — he can once again make a major difference.

But for now, although the administration remains a force, the power in this debate has clearly shifted back from the White House to the Capitol.

A Stagnant Debate

When Bush entered the process in 1989, Congress had been deadlocked over clean air for more than a decade. Since last amending clean-air laws in 1977, environmentalists and their Hill allies had failed repeatedly to update the legislation.

A chief reason was Reagan, who consistently cold-shouldered clean-air initiatives on the grounds that the science was shaky, that the need was unproven or that business and industry had done more than enough already.

That resistance from the Republican White House strengthened the already powerful congressional Democrats who opposed further tightening of clean-air laws.

In the House, John D. Dingell, D-Mich., chairman of the Energy and Commerce Committee, controlled the avenue through which most clean-air legislation had to travel, and he exercised his clout and legislative skills to kill outright or stall to death virtually everything that came his way. Dingell's mission was to protect the auto companies (Ford Motor Co.'s headquarters is in his district), which he felt had already been asked to do more than their share of air pollution cleanup.

In the Senate, it was the majority leader himself, Robert C. Byrd, D-W.Va., who stood in the narrow gap to block repeated ambitious proposals by the Environment and Public Works Committee to redraft clean-air law. Like Dingell, Byrd was driven in large part by a home-state agenda: He feared that acid-rain proposals would destroy the market for the high-sulfur coal mined in West Virginia and throw thousands of miners out of work.

With Reagan, Dingell and Byrd hostile to clean-air initiatives, Congress settled into a seemingly endless deadlock, as bill after bill died without emerging from the House Energy Committee or without reaching the Senate floor. Capitol Hill's environmentalists had long claimed strong support in both the House and the Senate for new clean-air law, but they

ASSOCIATED PRESS/WIDE WORLD

At polluted Boston Harbor, in his opponent's home state, Bush set about trying to establish his environmental bona fides.

lacked the legislative power to force the issue to either floor to prove it. Neither the Senate nor the House voted on a comprehensive clean-air bill in the 12 years that followed passage of the 1977 amendments.

Loss for Dingell Signaled Shift

But even during this long deadlock, there were signs that opponents of new clean-air legislation might be in the minority.

One of the starkest portents came in December 1987, when the House, given a rare chance to vote on anything connected to clean air, rose up against a Dingell-backed amendment to extend clean-air deadlines into 1989, which would have taken all the urgency out of trying to produce new

clean-air legislation before the 1988 elections.

Instead, the House voted for an amendment backed by environmentalists to push the deadlines only to August 1988, which kept the heat on Congress to write new law by that time.

Ultimately, the issue became moot because the Environmental Protection Agency (EPA) signaled that it would let even the extended deadline pass without invoking sanctions against most of the cities that had not yet met clean-air goals.

But for pulse-takers starved for some measurable indication of the House's mood on clean air and Dingell's clout on the floor, the vote against Dingell was revealing. Dingell and industry lobbyists had been confident that they would win comfortably; they came out badly beaten and publicly embarrassed, on the losing end of a 162-257 vote. *(1987 CQ Almanac, p. 299)*

Emboldened by their success, Capitol Hill environmentalists such as Henry A. Waxman, D-Calif., chairman of the House Energy Subcommittee on Health and the Environment, said they had more than enough votes on the floor to write tough new air pollution law — if only they could get it there.

In the Senate, Maine's George J. Mitchell, the leading Democrat among that chamber's environmental activists, managed to work out an eleventh-hour compromise with Byrd in fall 1988 that might have brought a substantial clean-air bill to the floor. But the deal fell apart under criticism from a disparate group of environmentalists, utilities and Western senators.

There was optimistic talk that the Mitchell-Byrd deal was a good omen for progress in the new 101st Congress, especially after Byrd stepped down as majority leader. Mitchell succeeded him, giving backers of a new clean-air bill a clear shot at the floor.

In the House, Speaker Jim Wright, D-Texas, included clean air among his announced priorities for the new Congress, but little else in the House appeared to have changed by early 1989. Without a push from the White House, it seemed possible that Congress could remain stuck in its familiar

12-year quagmire, hemmed in by tough demands from environmentalists on one side and implacable opposition from business and industry on the other.

Enter President Bush. In June, the administration announced a broad new clean-air bill, and the dynamic shifted overnight. Suddenly, it was widely assumed that there would be a bill. *(1989 Weekly Report p. 1460)*

Until then, the game had been industry's to lose. Obstructionist procedural tactics had been effective and risk-free, and the operating presumption had long been that legislation would never be passed, except in the unlikely event that environmentalists could somehow overpower the opposition. But with Bush pushing the bill, business and industry now had to scramble to make sure it was a moderate one.

Dotted With Legislative Pitfalls

Both Bush's proposed legislation (HR 3030) and the sprawling 431-page Senate bill (S 1630) have been compared to the tax code in their complexity and in the far-reaching effects they could have on business, industry and the average person's lifestyle.

Each of the bills' three broad sections — smog, acid rain and air toxics — is land-mined with the sort of intractable conflicts among jobs, the economy, health and quality of life that have paralyzed members of Congress until now.

For example:

● The bills' smog sections set out plans to bring urban and rural areas into compliance with clean-air goals for ozone, carbon monoxide and fine-particle pollution. There are serious disagreements over how tough the compliance methods should be and how severely to penalize an area for not meeting clean-air deadlines.

Despite a surprise House agreement last fall between archenemies Dingell and Waxman on auto emissions, the tailpipe controversy is very much alive in the Senate. And both chambers are warring over proposals on alternative fuels and clean-fueled cars. *(1989 Weekly Report p. 3145)*

● The acid-rain sections of both bills are aimed primarily at the big coal-

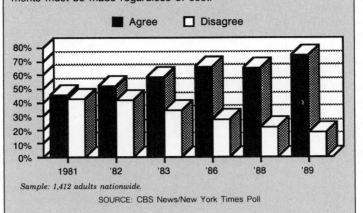

Willing to Pay

Question: "Do you agree or disagree with the following statement? Protecting the environment is so important that requirements and standards cannot be too high, and continuing environmental improvements must be made regardless of cost."

■ Agree   □ Disagree

Sample: 1,412 adults nationwide.

SOURCE: CBS News/New York Times Poll

BARBARA SASSA-DANIELS

burning utilities in the Midwest that produce the sulfur dioxide and nitrogen oxide emissions that are widely believed to kill lakes, streams and forests hundreds or thousands of miles downwind.

Some of the hottest regional disputes arise out of this section, whose proposal for a strict cap on emissions worries growth states that want to be able to build coal-fired plants. The bills' focus on Midwestern utilities has prompted angry calls for cost-sharing from the affected states. *(1989 Weekly Report p. 2934)*

● The bill's third element focuses on toxic air pollutants, and perhaps nowhere else in the legislation is the fundamental disagreement over clean-air policy more starkly drawn.

Toxic Air Disputes

At issue here are the carcinogenic or merely poisonous emissions of large sources such as chemical plants and steel mills and small ones such as neighborhood dry cleaners and gas stations.

Those toxic emissions come from a long list of noxious substances such as arsenic, benzene, trichloroethylene (a solvent), toluene (found in gasoline), perchloroethylene (dry cleaning fluid), ethylene oxide (a sterilizing agent used in hospitals) and methyl isocyanate (a pesticide feedstock — and the chemical released in the catastrophic accident in Bhopal, India). *(Chart, p. 8)*

Toxics can cause a wide range of severe health problems, including can-

cer, birth defects, genetic damage and instant death. Compared with other air pollutants, toxics are the truly bad actors of the clean-air debate.

When Congress set out to regulate them in 1970, it proposed standards so tough that they couldn't, as it turned out, be met.

The 1970 bill required the EPA to list all those toxics likely to increase deaths or serious illnesses and to set emissions standards for their sources that would provide "an ample margin of safety to protect public health."

The trouble was that there is virtually no safe level of emissions for carcinogens, because any exposure can pose some risk of cancer. In part because the EPA feared forcing industries to shut down for emitting minute quantities, the agency regulated toxics only excruciatingly slowly, if at all. Most congressional proposals contain lists of nearly 200 individual toxics; in the 19 years since Congress passed the 1970 law, the EPA listed only eight and established emissions standards for only seven.

What Comes Next?

All sides agree that the 1970 air-toxics law has been a failure, and all sides agree, at least in general terms, that the best way to begin overhauling it is to attack sources of toxics with technology-based restrictions, rather than health-based limits. All of the major proposals would require sources of the listed toxics to install the best available cost-effective technology to reduce emissions.

It is what to do next that causes industry and environmentalists to part company.

The bill, approved by the Environment and Public Works Committee and now headed to the Senate floor, would add a second round of restrictions to reduce remaining health risks.

It would require sources of carcinogenic emissions to seek to reduce risks to less than 1-in-1-million for the "most exposed individual" — generally interpreted as a hypothetical person who lives next to the plant or other source for a 70-year lifetime. Failing that, a source must keep the risk below 1-in-10,000 or be forced —

after a one-time five-year extension — to shut down.

This is a do-or-die issue for industry, which warns that compliance costs could be exorbitant, that the necessary technology in some cases simply does not exist and that enforcing the rule would very likely force some industrial operations to simply go out of business.

"This is the hardest for me to discuss, because we're talking about cancer — I don't want anybody to get cancer," says Bill Fay, administrator of the Clean Air Working Group, the major industry coalition in the clean-air wars. "Risk needs to be assessed, but it needs to be assessed from a rational standpoint. . . . I don't think just pulling a number out of the air is the right approach."

Fay and others find the language in Bush's bill much more appealing. It would create a second round of emissions restrictions but would leave it up to the EPA's discretion to set health-based limits only in the case of "unreasonable risk."

Environmentalists find that standard way too lax; in fact, many of them find even the tougher Senate version too loose.

"There should be nobody getting cancer as a result of breathing these pollutants," says David Doniger, a senior attorney for the Natural Resources Defense Council and an expert on air toxics. He maintains that industry's bid to factor cost into decisions about what sort of cancer risk to tolerate is "ethically and morally indefensible."

Doniger favors requiring industry to move gradually toward zero toxic emissions, with reasonable time to develop and adopt technology but with an inflexible goal at the end of the road.

"Ten years ago, I would have been lampooned as a 'zero-risker,' " he says, "but now [zero emissions] is corporate policy" for several of the nation's big chemical companies, which he says have announced plans to phase out toxic emissions altogether.

Doniger says industry's charges that the Senate standards will force companies out of business are vastly overblown. Even those industries that appear to face the greatest threat from the Senate bill — such as coke ovens, which emit toxics in heating coal to produce the coke used in steelmaking — have at least 16 years to meet the 1-in-10,000 risk standard, he says.

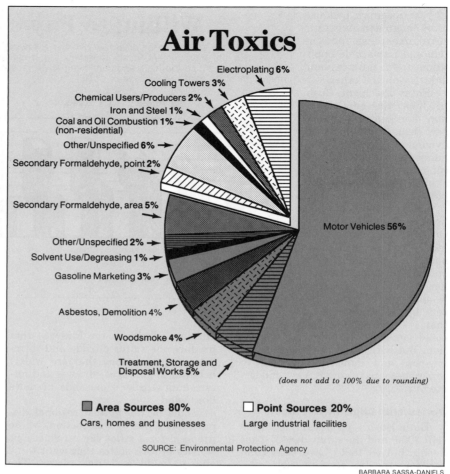

Air Toxics

- Electroplating 6%
- Cooling Towers 3%
- Chemical Users/Producers 2%
- Iron and Steel 1%
- Coal and Oil Combustion 1% (non-residential)
- Other/Unspecified 6%
- Secondary Formaldehyde, point 2%
- Secondary Formaldehyde, area 5%
- Other/Unspecified 2%
- Solvent Use/Degreasing 1%
- Gasoline Marketing 3%
- Asbestos, Demolition 4%
- Woodsmoke 4%
- Treatment, Storage and Disposal Works 5%
- Motor Vehicles 56%

(does not add to 100% due to rounding)

■ **Area Sources 80%**
Cars, homes and businesses

□ **Point Sources 20%**
Large industrial facilities

SOURCE: Environmental Protection Agency

BARBARA SASSA-DANIELS

"We'll never get any substantial progress from coke ovens or any of these other industries unless you set ambitious targets," Doniger says.

Fay and industry officials cite the EPA to buttress their claims that the Senate bill would mean severe hardship for particular areas of industry.

The EPA has produced a list of 17 industries that it says may have difficulty meeting the Senate bill's 1-in-10,000 risk standard. Included with coke ovens are makers of pharmaceuticals and pesticides, and copper and lead smelters.

The reason, Fay says, is that the technology to allow affected industries to reduce risks below 1-in-10,000 simply does not exist.

This question — whether to impose pollution reductions that industry cannot meet using current technology — is a familiar dispute that goes to the heart of clean-air legislation.

When the 1970 bill was written, it was the automobile industry that argued against more tailpipe restrictions on the ground that the technology did not exist. Environmentalists countered that mandating new restrictions would force development of the technology to meet them.

Twenty years later, the argument over whether to set "technology forcing" pollution limits continues to divide industry and environmentalists, not just over air toxics, but throughout the clean-air debate.

In 1970, Congress did impose tough restrictions on automakers, and technology eventually developed to meet them. But the results did not come quickly or painlessly enough to prevent Congress from having to revisit the issue in 1977, when in the face of overwhelming protest from the auto industry it watered down and stretched out the tailpipe restrictions it had written into the 1970 law.

'There's a New Dimension'

The 1990 clean-air bill will likely continue this three-steps-forward, two-steps-back approach to clean air. While Congress will almost certainly move forward for the first time to explicitly control such problems as acid rain, it will also likely back up and undo the unworkably ambitious 1970 toxics standards, setting something more practical in their place.

Advocates of tough new clean-air restrictions go into this incremental process with strong backing from the public, according to pollsters. For a while, environmental fears seemed to have been partly offset by cost worries or diminished by greater concerns about jobs or the economy. But now, polls have shown increasingly broad public concern about the environment and strong demand that something be done about it.

The paroxysm of environmental legislation in the 1970s convinced people that the problems were being taken care of, says Ethel Klein, a Columbia University political science professor and an expert on public opinion. "It became a latent issue," she says, until a succession of news stories about environmental problems in the 1980s convinced people that the problems had not been solved after all.

"It's come back, but not just the way it was in the 1970s — there's a new dimension to it," she says.

Increased Concern

The new dimension is global warming. There is concern that the whole planet may be at risk and that the problem could soon accelerate beyond mankind's capacity to correct it. The increased apprehension translates into a new urgency behind demands for action by the government.

"People are concerned about what we're doing to the stuff we breathe," says Breglio, the former Bush pollster.

Breglio, president of the polling firm Research/Strategy/Management Inc., recently conducted a poll that showed that Americans want industry to produce more environmentally benign products, even if that means consumers will have to pay more for them.

True, but only to a point, says Celinda Lake, a Dukakis pollster and vice president of Greenberg/Lake and

PHOTOS BY R. MICHAEL JENKINS

Dingell of Detroit and Waxman of Los Angeles cut a deal on auto emissions that caught everyone by surprise.

The Analysis Group. Lake says many polls, borne out by her recent work with focus groups around the country, show that Americans urgently want action on pollution problems and that they expect to have to pay something.

But "people want moderation," she says. "They know they've got to start paying a price here. They'd just as soon keep that price to a minimum."

Lake says people tend to view both industry and environmentalists as extremists, which leaves an opening in the center of the debate for some faction to portray itself as the sensibly moderate alternative.

Bush has already begun moving toward that moderate opening, warning during Congress' winter recess that he will veto any bill that drives the costs of attaining clean air too high. The

threat is clearly aimed at backers of the bill about to go to the Senate floor, and it will give GOP critics ammunition in trying to amend a measure they say is far too extreme and costly.

But is a veto threat credible? Would Bush really pull down a clean-air bill in an election year?

A White House official unhesitatingly says yes.

"You've got to know George Bush," he says. "The president is putting out a signal, and it's a signal that some people ought to pay attention to."

Some on the Hill will treat the warning with skepticism. There will be enormous pressure to generate a bill that both sides can tout to voters by this fall. The competition to take credit for it may eventually overshadow the struggle to keep it sensible, and, having done so much to get the process off the ground, Bush stands first in line when it comes time to take credit.

Added Incentive

This election-year pressure may give environmentalists who favor a tough bill one more advantage in the fight to shape the legislation.

Business and industry hope to make a compelling case for moderation, but as the debate heads for the floor, it sheds detail along the way. The careful arguments for compromise tend to give way to the raw question of whether a member is "for" or "against" the environment.

Environmentalists are riding the wave of public anxiety, which will force industry allies to be especially careful about how they craft their positions.

"If you were to take a clean-air bill to the floor today, environmentalists would probably win most key votes," says Rep. Terry L. Bruce, D-Ill., often an ally of Dingell. "Every vote seems to be 'the environmental vote of the century.' ... Guys are very sensitive to that. [So] how do we structure a vote so that we don't hang people out to dry?"

They are working on it, hoping to acquaint members with the political pain of potential job loss back home. "As this issue matures," Bruce says, "guys are going to hear the other side of it." ■

For Industry and Opponents, A Showdown Is in the Air

Sometime later this year, when the buzzers summon members to the Senate or the House floor to vote, the nearly impenetrable complexities of the Clean Air Act will be boiled down to a few hurried words from a colleague: "Great environmental vote," someone may say, or "this one'll cost you jobs back home."

All the patient lobbying on such arcane matters as the second-stage restrictions on non-methane hydrocarbon emissions will begin to fade, dimmed by a member's sense of where political danger lies. Which is worse: the outrage of industry or bad ratings in year-end environmentalist vote wrap-ups?

Lately, environmentalists like the odds.

For despite their carefully nurtured reputation as the underdogs of congressional lobbying, environmentalists wield enormous clout on Capitol Hill. Broad national support for their agenda has made them, in the words of a Hill aide, "the 500-pound gorilla" of congressional lobbying on such issues as clean air. And after a decade or more of having sand kicked in their faces over proposals to rewrite clean-air law, environmentalists appear to be driving the process as the issue heads toward the Senate and House floors.

"Members are deathly afraid of being labeled anti-environment," says a House staffer. And for a good reason: "The votes on the floor are tallied" by environmental watchdog groups, says Bill Richardson, D-N.M., a member of the House Energy Subcommittee on Health and the Environment, which marked up clean-air legislation (HR 3030) in the fall. Members "don't want to get a bad environmental reputation on floor votes," he says. (Story, p. 13)

Though they cannot begin to match industry political action committees in political cash, environmental groups' big membership rolls generate more than enough money to maintain a corps of experienced Washington lobbyists who can go hand to hand with industry heavy-

By George Hager

weights. And just as important, the groups back up their Washington operations with vocal, well-organized grass-roots organizations that are not shy about letting Congress know how they feel.

"They can dump 5,000 or 10,000 signatures on you in pretty short order," says Robert Meyers, legislative aide in charge of clean air for Rep. Michael Bilirakis, R-Fla., who like Richardson is a heavily lobbied member of the Health and the Environment Subcommittee.

Environmental groups in Bilirakis' district stage "neighborhood walks," going door to door to win support and raise voter consciousness on issues and on who votes how — precisely the sort of campaign members have to pay attention to.

"We're still answering the mail" from the last neighborhood walk, Meyers says. "These guys are very well organized.... They speak loudly with one voice, and that's what politics is about."

Credibility War

Industry has worked to match that kind of grass-roots organizing, trying to mobilize employees, plant managers, shareholders and retirees to offset the environmentalist masses, but it has not had the same impact at all. "There's no comparison," Richardson says.

Nor is industry much better off when it comes to the credibility war waged in the media and in public opinion polls. In the view of frustrated industry lobbyists, environmentalists play the media and the public like a piano. "They have instant credibility," says Robert A. Beck, a lobbyist for the Edison Electric Institute, which represents electric utility interests in the clean-air debate. "If they make an allegation, it's true."

Mark Dungan, clean-air aide for Rep. Edward Madigan, R-Ill., another Health and the Environment Subcommittee member, agrees. "There's a fear right now that environmentalists have the minds of the American public [and that] people are willing to believe just about anything they're told," he says. "Members realize that [the public] has gone over to the side where they think the environment is heading down the hill and getting worse and worse.... How do you fight that? A politician can't fight that. As soon as you have to start explaining, you're in trouble."

Public opinion polls back Dungan up, showing widespread, growing concern about the environment and broad support for more controls, even if that means paying more for such things as electricity and automobiles.

Crying Wolf?

But in the judgment of several members, staff and lobbyists on both sides of the issue, many of industry's problems stem not from the new environmentalism, but from industry's own intransigence. The consensus criticism is that big segments of industry have said no to so many proposals for so long that they have irreparably damaged their credibility and their ability to influence events now that there is momentum to pass a bill.

Delaying and stonewalling worked fine throughout the Reagan years, when the president was indifferent to or opposed rewriting clean-air laws. But with the advent of the Bush administration, which made a new clean-air bill one of its highest legislative priorities, those tactics have come back to haunt industry.

"I don't think we've exactly made our bed very well," says Bill Fay, administrator of the industry-funded Clean Air Working Group (CAWG). "It used to be our position that the only good clean-air bill was a dead clean-air bill.... The perception that we've always been 'against' clean air haunts us."

Now CAWG has its back to the wall, and it and its constituent industries are waging a campaign on Capitol Hill, in the media and in paid advertising to get across the new mes-

The 'Environmentalists'

National Audubon Society (founded 1905)

Members: 516,220
Budget: $32,852,672
Staff: 337
Offices: 16

Defenders of Wildlife (founded 1947)

Members: 80,000
Budget: $4.5 million
Staff: 30
Offices: 4

Environmental Action (founded 1970)

Members: 20,000
Budget: $1.2 million
Staff: 24
Offices: Washington only

Environmental Defense Fund (founded 1967)

Members: 125,000
Budget: $12.9 million
Staff: 100
Offices: 6

Friends of the Earth (founded 1969)

Members: 50,000
Budget: $2.5 million
Staff: 35
Offices: 2

Greenpeace (founded 1971)

Members: 1.4 million
Budget: $33.9 million
Staff: 1,200
Offices: 30

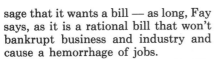

Izaak Walton League of America (founded 1922)

Members: 50,000
Budget: $1.8 million
Staff: 26
Offices: Washington and St. Paul, Minn.

League of Conservation Voters (founded 1970)

Members: 15,000
Budget: $500,000
Staff: 40
Offices: 3

National Clean Air Coalition (founded 1974)

(Coalition group, made up of 35 other groups)

National Parks and Conservation Association (founded 1919)

Members: 100,000
Budget: $3.8 million
Staff: 30
Offices: 4

National Wildlife Federation (founded 1936)

Members: 5.6 million members and supporters
Budget: $85 million
Staff: 700
Offices: 12

Natural Resources Defense Council (founded 1970)

Members: 125,000
Budget: $13 million
Staff: 125 (40 lawyers)
Offices: 5

Sierra Club (founded 1892)

Members: 553,246
Budget: $28 million
Staff: 185
Offices: 16, plus 57 chapters divided into 355 groups

The Wilderness Society (founded 1935)

Members: 330,000
Budget: $20 million
Staff: 130 staff
Offices: 15

—Robert Clayton

sage that it wants a bill — as long, Fay says, as it is a rational bill that won't bankrupt business and industry and cause a hemorrhage of jobs.

That strikes some critics as too little, too late — especially in the case of utilities and the auto industry, which get the lowest marks for non-cooperation over the years.

"I've got friends on the Hill who say they're going to screw the auto industry and the utilities no matter what," says an industry lobbyist, who asked not to be identified.

Utilities receive the most scorn, for having stonewalled acid-rain proposals even when some of their Hill allies were counseling compromise. Carmakers get mixed but mostly negative reviews for having howled about the impossibility of emissions limits they ultimately buckled down and met.

The auto lobbyists insist that they are getting a bad rap. "When we said we couldn't do it, we weren't kidding," says General Motors lobbyist Ron Sykes. "We're still recalling hundreds of thousands of cars per company."

But the message is not playing well in Congress so far, and even industry defenders stick up for the automakers with faint praise. "When they were to the wall, they bent and compromised," Rep. Terry L. Bruce, D-Ill., says of auto lobbyists' reaction to a House subcommittee move to compromise on motor vehicle emissions standards last fall.

Staying in the Game

The oil industry gets better marks for bowing to political reality and working to deal itself into the drafting process. But the lobbyists who get

near-universal praise are those from the chemical industry, who did an about-face after years of intransigence.

"They [the chemical industry] used to have the worst reputation of anybody," says Bill Becker, executive director of the State and Territorial Air Pollution Program Administrators. "They've actually been very, very smart in their lobbying." Becker and others give the chemical company lobby credit for abandoning its no-bill stance and suggesting ways to write new legislation.

"It's no secret that there are perception problems with our industry," says Mark Nelson, director of legislative affairs for Du Pont Corp. and chairman of the industry's Clean Air Working Group. Nelson said his industry's decision to moderate its stance provoked some "raised eyebrows" when it was floated at a CAWG meeting, "but they came around."

Living down its no-bill image is not CAWG's only problem. Just as tough is trying to reach consensus among industries with competing clean-air goals, or even within industries that are at war with themselves.

In the case of acid rain, for example, utilities themselves split over the need for a new law depending on whether they have cleaned up their sulfur dioxide emissions already (the "cleans") or have yet to do so (the "dirties"). And oil and auto companies split over whether gasoline refueling evaporation should be reduced by putting canisters in cars (which the oil companies would like) or bulky controls on gasoline pumps (which the car companies prefer).

Fay says CAWG's goal is to resolve disputes like that and avoid repeating the mistakes industry made the last time Congress revamped clean-air laws, when some industries cut separate deals to exempt themselves from tight new controls. That allowed legislators to form an environmental coalition that had the votes to pass the 1977 amendments to the Clean Air Act.

Never again, Fay says. With the CAWG rule, he says, "you've got to work your issues, but you have to stick with the group even after you may get your amendments."

Birds and Bunnies

The environmentalist lobbyists are arrayed against CAWG as the National Clean Air Coalition (NCAC), which came together when Congress was working on the 1977 clean-air amendments.

These organizations range in size, scope and longevity, from the 98-year-old Sierra Club to the 20-year-old group Environmental Action. The coalition ranges from wildlife preservationists to hunting groups and steelworkers, a diversity that belies its monolithic image but also broadens its appeal. *(Chart, p. 9)*

The steelworkers "can open doors in Pennsylvania that the birds and bunnies folks can't open — that's why we're a coalition," says Marchant Wentworth, a lobbyist for the Izaak Walton League of America, a hunting and fishing group.

R. MICHAEL JENKINS   R. MICHAEL JENKINS

Bill Fay, left, of the Clean Air Working Group, an industry coalition, and Richard Ayres of the environmentalist National Clean Air Coalition.

Wentworth puts his outfit in the "hook and bullet" category of environmental groups, as opposed to "birds and bunnies" organizations like the Sierra Club.

The coalition, which worked in vain for tighter clean-air legislation on acid rain and other air pollution problems in the decade-plus since the 1977 amendments, got a tremendous boost from Bush's pledge to back a strong clean-air bill.

Bush's decision led to what NCAC Executive Director Richard Ayres called one of the group's most significant successes — the Bush bill's tough acid-rain provisions that establish an emissions cap and an innovative emissions trading scheme.

Both were the result of lobbying by the Environmental Defense Fund (EDF), an NCAC member group, and they constitute one of the clearest examples of a direct, major impact on the clean-air bill by a lobbying group for either side.

Bush "couldn't introduce [a clean-air] bill without the endorsement of an environmental group," says Jim Cooper, D-Tenn., a House Energy Committee member. "That gave EDF tremendous bargaining power in negotiations."

CAWG has not been without its lobbying successes, the most celebrated of which came during markup in the House Health and the Environment Subcommittee. An oil- and auto-industry team combined to push a proposal that knocked out the Bush bill's mandate that the auto companies build up to a million alternative-fuel cars a year to run on superclean fuels.

The success of that amendment, sponsored by Texans Ralph M. Hall, D, and Jack Fields, R, was a classic case of aggressive, unified, smart lob-

bying, according to the winners and losers alike. Fay cites it as a CAWG success story, proof of the importance of forging industry groups into a united front so they multiply their efforts instead of undercutting one another.

New Mexico's Richardson, whose competing amendment was brushed aside in the process, has grudging respect for the muscular auto-oil team that did him in. "They had their act together," he says. "I've never seen them this effective."

Key to the success was dividing the administration, so that while Environmental Protection Agency Administrator William K. Reilly was lobbying to hold the Bush language, White House Chief of Staff John H. Sununu was in effect working against it by remaining neutral on Hall-Fields. What's more, Richardson adds, the lobbyists had clearly done their homework. "The drafting of the amendment was skillful, [and] the talking points were skillful."

No Love Lost

Though some lobbyists on opposite sides purport to be friends or at least friendly opponents, the stakes are high, and the relationship is often strained.

Industry lobbyists resent the ease with which the environmentalists seem to be able to set the terms of the debate and how their allegations come cloaked in an aura of credibility.

"Let me rave about the other side," CAWG's Fay says sarcastically. "They're way ahead of us in how they've couched the debate and scared the American public."

Environmentalists charge industry with a familiar litany of sins: indifference to health, distorting the facts, buying votes and so on. But underneath it all, there is a barely disguised sense of mission. "The bottom line is they're mercenaries and we're true believers," says Dan Weiss, a lobbyist for the Sierra Club. "And remember, Machiavelli said in 'The Prince,' don't hire mercenaries."

The record so far suggests that CAWG and NCAC are evenly matched. "They're certainly matched in zeal," says a House staff member who works with both groups. "They both feel very put upon by the other side." ∎

LCV to Congress: We're Watching

As House members filed into the chamber to vote on a federal oil-spill liability bill last November, they knew they were being watched.

"The biggest environmental vote in the Congress," said California Democrat George Miller as he worked the floor and the halls nearby.

Peter A. DeFazio, D-Ore., stood in a chamber doorway, handing colleagues an inelegant, photocopied flier. "As the League of Conservation Voters begins preparation of our 1989 National Environmental Scorecard," the flier said, "we will be watching carefully the upcoming votes on oil-spill liability legislation."

Although the presentation was crude, the message was as clear as the waters of Prince William Sound before the *Exxon Valdez* spilled its cargo. The League of Conservation Voters' (LCV) environmental report card provides the industry-standard ratings of House members' environmental records. Activists use the scores, news media report them and electoral challengers invoke them.

"They didn't spend a lot of time talking about it . . . on the floor, but that's what they were talking about in the back" of the chamber, said a Democratic leadership aide, referring to the LCV warning. "It dictated a lot of the oil-spill votes: Whether you would be seen voting pro-environment or not."

Members know their constituents will hear about their environmental voting records — and that is exactly what the LCV and like-minded groups want. "I'm not saying the environment as an issue is going to turn an election, especially against an incumbent," said Ruth Caplan, executive director of the advocacy group Environmental Action. "But in a close race, it really can come into play."

With issues including the oil-spill legislation and Nevada wilderness designation, the scorecard is designed to filter out empty rhetoric and "easy" votes. The LCV board of directors, composed mostly of leaders from other state and national environmental groups, decides which votes in each chamber will go into the scorecard ratings.

Neither House nor Senate final votes to pass oil-spill liability legislation will wind up on this year's scorecard, but votes on key amendments will. One amendment the LCV supported will even count double because the House voted on it twice. Miller's effort to extend unlimited liability to negligent parties passed 213-207 one day, but failed the next, 185-197. *(1989 Weekly Report p. 3043)*

A key environmental vote in the Senate, according to the league, was on a motion by John B. Breaux, D-La., to table (kill) an amendment by Brock Adams, D-Wash.,

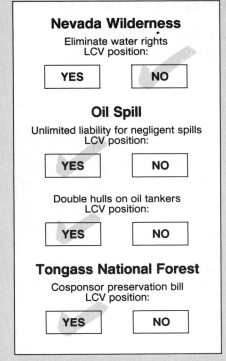

Nevada Wilderness
Eliminate water rights
LCV position:

| YES | NO ✓ |

Oil Spill
Unlimited liability for negligent spills
LCV position:

| YES ✓ | NO |

Double hulls on oil tankers
LCV position:

| YES ✓ | NO |

Tongass National Forest
Cosponsor preservation bill
LCV position:

| YES ✓ | NO |

to require large tankers to have double hulls. To earn points on the LCV scorecard, members had to vote "no" on Breaux.

"We look for close votes," said Ali Webb, LCV's director of communications and elections, "not [those] for final passage of 400 to 35, but votes where people had to make some tough choices."

The league occasionally — and judiciously, Webb maintains — warns members that a particular issue or particular vote will show up in its next scorecard.

In October, Executive Director Jim Maddy sent a letter to senators telegraphing LCV's interest in two pending issues: the confirmation of James E. Cason as assistant secretary of agriculture for natural resources and environment and a bill to curtail logging in Alaska's Tongass National Forest. Opposed by environmental groups, the Cason nomination never made it to the floor. The Tongass bill is pending. *(Tongass, 1990 Weekly Report p. 17; Cason, 1989 Weekly Report p. 3149)*

In a Nov. 16 letter to House members, LCV warned that it would watch their votes on an amendment by Barbara F. Vucanovich, R-Nev., to deny federal reserved water rights to wilderness areas of Nevada. "It would not only weaken wilderness protection for areas in Nevada, but also create a dangerous precedent for weakened wilderness protection in other states," Maddy wrote. The amendment failed, 118-285. *(1989 Weekly Report p. 3237)*

Does such overt advocacy taint the group's ratings? No, says Webb. "Our goal is to elect environmentally conscious members to the House and Senate and, once they are there, to make sure they stay conscious," she said. "Some members think we should telegraph more. . . ."

Beginning in 1988, the league's board chose to include in the scorecard actions other than recorded votes, such as whether House members put their names to a letter urging Energy and Commerce Committee leaders to mark up a clean-air bill, or whether senators signed up to cosponsor the bill to preserve Tongass National Forest, introduced by Tim Wirth, D-Colo.

LCV officials say they began the practice largely out of necessity. There have been few environmental votes on the chambers' floors in recent years and still fewer that were controversial or close enough to draw sharp lines.

"A lot of stuff languished this session," Webb lamented. "We can't give a grade to the 101st Congress yet, but if they don't pick up the [pace of] passage of legislation, they're going to flunk."

—Barry S. Surman

<u>KEY PLAYERS</u>

Their Spheres of Influence Go From Heavens to Earth

Parochial interests and institutional roles offer new opportunities for leadership

Asked in 1988 why he voted for George J. Mitchell as Senate majority leader, Democrat Joseph I. Lieberman of Connecticut cited their mutual concern for environmental issues.

A year later, Mitchell is about to deliver in spades for the likes of Lieberman.

The majority leader has vowed to make cleaning the air the first order of legislative business when the Senate reconvenes Jan. 23. It is a highly visible example of how Mitchell, the former chairman of the Environment and Public Works Subcommittee on Environmental Protection, has committed the power and prestige of his new office to his longstanding agenda, with far greater effect.

The Maine Democrat's decision to call up the clean-air bill (S 1630) is a shift in emphasis from his predecessor, Robert C. Byrd of West Virginia, who was an impenetrable obstacle to such efforts when he controlled the Senate schedule. And this turnabout shows how a particular cast of players can make the difference in how Congress disposes of environmental legislation.

Some of the major players are by now well-known. The clash of the clean-air titans, House Energy and Commerce Committee Chairman John D. Dingell of Michigan and his adversary on the Health and the Environment Subcommittee, Chairman Henry A. Waxman of California, has produced sparks for years. The two men most clearly personify the House's decade-long struggle over government efforts to regulate auto emissions. Dingell's Detroit district is home to the headquarters of the Ford Motor Co.; Waxman represents smog-choked Los Angeles. *(1989 Weekly Report p. 2622)*

The broad scope and technical complexity of environmental legislation allow many members to play equally significant if less-celebrated roles. Their spheres of influence range from the forests to the outer continental shelf,

By Chuck Alston

and their interests reflect not only their constituencies at home but also their various institutional duties.

These members can be prominent figures such as Mitchell or rising subcommittee chairmen now flexing their muscles in the shadows of aging committee barons. They can also be found among ranking minority

Mitchell

members whose statures are enhanced by the Republican White House and among appropriators who control the purse.

What follows is a sampler, with the members chosen for their positions or the parochial interests they represent.

Senate Leaders

Robert C. Byrd is a coal miner's senator, and few industries have so much at stake in air-pollution laws. To be sure, Byrd was majority leader when the 1977 amendments to the Clean Air Act became law. Since then, however, acid rain has become a major issue; President Bush has proposed legislation that could force major utilities in the Midwest to cut back on their use of high-sulfur coal, thus heightening the pressure on the coal-mining jobs Byrd must defend. *(Story, p. 3)*

As chairman of the Appropriations Committee, Byrd still wields considerable clout, but his priorities are no longer the Senate's. George Mitchell's are.

"All of a sudden you have someone who wants to bring environmental bills to the floor as opposed to someone who didn't care or actively opposed them," says David Gardiner, a Sierra Club lobbyist.

The shift in leadership cuts even deeper. For the first time in years, the oil and gas industry lacks a strong advocate in the highest echelons of leadership in either chamber. The Senate poses the least concern for the oil and gas industry because Texan Lloyd

Bentsen runs the Finance Committee and Louisianan J. Bennett Johnston runs the Energy and Natural Resources Committee.

But in the House, the resignations last summer of Speaker Jim Wright of Texas and House Majority Whip Tony Coelho of California deprived oil and gas interests of strong voices.

The sense of urgency Mitchell brings to environmental issues showed in November when he leaned on the Environment and Public Works Committee to produce an air-pollution bill. While Sen. Quentin N. Burdick, D-N.D., is nominally the panel's chairman, his age and infirmity have created a leadership vacuum that subcommittee chairmen must fill. Max Baucus, D-Mont., now heads Mitchell's old subcommittee, but the majority leader remains the driving force. Indeed, industry lobbyists complained about the stiff-arm tactics Mitchell used to force a bill through committee.

"The direction he's headed is one of discouraging debate, discouraging amendments and discouraging controversy," says Bill Fay, administrator of the Clean Air Working Group, an industry coalition.

Nonetheless, there are signs that Mitchell the majority leader has recognized the need to moderate the views of Mitchell the senator from Maine, if only to tend to his Senate constituency. "He considers opposing views more," says John H. Chafee, R-R.I., a longtime colleague of Mitchell on the Environment Committee.

For example, Mitchell last August used his clout to bring oil-spill liability and compensation legislation (S 686) to the floor despite objections that it transgressed certain budget laws. Once on the floor, however, he worked to limit the liability faced by oil companies, at one point confronting liberal Democrat Howard M. Metzenbaum of Ohio in a heated, off-microphone exchange visible from the gallery. And again, in the Environment Committee's deliberations on acid rain, Mitchell pressed the committee to soften language against giving cost-sharing breaks to coal-fired utilities for acid-rain controls, giving him the room needed to accommodate Midwesterners.

One of those Mitchell sought to accommodate on oil-spill legislation was John B. Breaux, D-La., a conservative Southerner with an energy industry constituency. "This was the art of compromise, and he was doing what is possible," Breaux said.

Minority Republican

Norman F. Lent, a New York Republican, followed one of the House's consummate insiders, former Rep. James T. Broyhill, R-N.C. (1963-86), as ranking GOP member on the Energy and Commerce Committee. The committee's broad jurisdiction and tendency to make environmental policy in the political center give Republicans wide berth to maneuver and assert influence at critical points. But where Broyhill accomplished this by playing his cards close to the vest, Long Island's blunt, combative Lent lays his on the table.

"Norm is pretty much up front," says Republican Michael G. Oxley of Ohio, a committee member. "He's taken on some tough issues, some of which have not been all that popular back home."

Lent's advocacy of nuclear power is one such issue. Local, state and federal politicians throughout the 1980s debated whether the Shoreham nuclear power plant on Long Island's North Shore should be switched

Lent

on. The island's narrow configuration and dense population led many, including New York Gov. Mario M. Cuomo, D, to question the adequacy of evacuation plans. Lent plunged ahead, arguing that nuclear power is essential for energy security. He not only cast the only pro-Shoreham vote among the island's five-member delegation during a 1987 showdown, he led the floor fight with vehemence.

Lent's district includes Levittown, where tract housing was invented after World War II. The island's dense population and dependence on wells for drinking water propel Lent into groundwater and toxic-waste issues. He was a key player in the battle fought in the mid-1980s over the reauthorization of "superfund" legislation governing the cleanup of hazardous-waste sites.

The bill he co-authored with Ohio Democrat Dennis E. Eckart gained Energy and Commerce Committee approval in typical fashion, with the support of 14 Democrats and 17 Republicans. Environmentalists considered it too weak, and the Reagan White House criticized its cost.

As the superfund measure illustrated, Democratic Chairman Dingell

is most comfortable working with the committee's center and right on environmental issues. The fight over clean-air legislation that has dominated the committee in the 101st Congress is no exception: Lent and Dingell are the chief House sponsors of Bush's clean-air bill (HR 3030).

Lent describes himself as "low-key, generally conservative though not doctrinaire." Committee members and staffers say he relies heavily on staffers and consults widely with other members. Like many Northeastern Republicans, he is sensitive to environmental issues, although not sensitive enough for some environmentalists: It is not unusual for Lent to trade testy letters with the Sierra Club in Long Island's *Newsday.*

Still, Lent can be a critical, bellwether vote. "Because he is not an anti-environment Republican, it is hard for us when he takes a position against us," says Sharon Newsome, a vice president at the National Wildlife Federation.

Regional Interest

Idaho Republican Sen. James A. McClure hails from a state where the federal government is more than Social Security, the post office, an Army base and the April 15 tax deadline. Uncle Sam owns and manages nearly two-thirds of Idaho's land — the resource that drives an economy built on forests, farms and mines. The "Sagebrush Rebellion" against federal control of lands within state borders caught fire in states such as Idaho, and it has shaped some conservative Western senators.

But unlike many laissez-faire Westerners, McClure is a crafty lawmaker, not a guerrilla legislator. He sees the government not only as an impediment but also as a tool for developing the West's vast resources.

Though he has decided to retire at the end of the year, McClure, 65, will wield considerable clout on environmental legislation this session.

The six years McClure spent in the majority put him in the powerful position of running both an authorizing committee, Energy and Natural Resources, and its appropriating counterpart, the Appropriations Subcommittee on Interior and Related Agencies. There, and in the years in the minority, he honed an attentiveness to detail and the craftiness to take advantage of it.

McClure is one of the Senate's strongest advocates of nuclear power,

and he is deeply suspicious of government environmental regulations that do not weigh economic costs against health benefits and consider the cost of unemployment on health. His latest concern is the standard for radionuclide emissions that could shut down a phosphorus plant in Pocatello, Idaho.

He is "slicker" than most Sagebrush rebels, says the Sierra Club's Gardiner. "He can make life very unpleasant for people. At the same time, he's very, very smart. He's effective at appearing to give you something."

McClure

On the other hand, Rep. Ron Marlenee, R-Mont., a strident development advocate, says McClure is "a shrewd guy, but he's playing on the other side of the fence from me." Translation: He's too willing to compromise.

McClure is a reliable advocate of timber companies that use government roads to log in national forests, and forest-road construction is a McClure specialty in the Interior spending bill. Conservationists often oppose heavy road-construction budgets because they promote development beyond logging. Last year, when the Senate, on an amendment by Georgia Democrat Wyche Fowler Jr., cut the road budget by $65 million to $140 million for fiscal 1990, McClure went to work. Playing the roads against other contentious issues before the House-Senate conference, he restored funding to the $164 million level approved by the House, and he arranged for $32 million elsewhere in the bill.

Conservationists remain suspicious of his motives.

When Defenders of Wildlife President M. Rupert Cutler met with McClure in his office in 1988 to talk about McClure's proposal to reintroduce wolves into Yellowstone National Park, Cutler asked, "What's your real motivation?" McClure fell easily into a discussion of land-management issues and the wolf's appropriate role in the ecosystem, and in doing so he described the role he sees for himself. "I'm doing what I attempt to do on most issues — attempt to produce a compromise that will allow us to move forward."

As he knows well, it is often the environmentalists who win when Western land decisions are stalemated

Environmental Turf

Environmental legislation takes many forms and, as a result, falls within the jurisdiction of many committees in Congress. House and Senate Agriculture committees, for example, have responsibility for forestry policy in general and private timberlands, but national forests and wilderness areas are the preserve of the House Interior and the Senate Energy and Natural Resources committees. In addition, the Appropriations subcommittees on the interior control the budgets of the U.S. Forest Service, Bureau of Land Management, and Fish and Wildlife Service.

Similarly, many committees can stake a claim to offshore oil-drilling issues by virtue of their overlapping jurisdictions over the outer continental shelf.

Here are the legislative areas assigned to each panel.

SENATE

Agriculture
Soil conservation, groundwater
Forestry, private forest
  reserves
Pesticides, food safety
Global change

Appropriations
International monetary
  and financial funds
Forest Service
Army Corps of Engineers
Nuclear Regulatory Commission
Tennessee Valley Authority
Occupational Safety and Health
  Administration (OSHA)
Mine Safety and Health
  Administration
Soil conservation programs
Food and Drug Administration
Environmental Protection Agency
Council on Environmental Policy
National Oceanic and Atmospheric
  Administration

Armed Services
Military weapons plants
Nuclear energy
Naval petroleum, oil shale reserves
Air Force jet emissions

Commerce, Science, Transportation
Coastal zone management
Inland waterways
Marine fisheries
Oceans, weather, science research
Outer continental shelf
Global change

Energy and Natural Resources
Energy policy, conservation
National parks, wilderness
Nuclear energy, public utilities
Public lands, forests
Global change

Environment and Public Works
Environmental policy, oversight
Air and water pollution
Outer continental shelf
Toxic substances

Fisheries and wildlife
Flood control, deep-water ports
Ocean dumping
Nuclear energy
Bridges, dams, inland waterways
Solid-waste disposal
Superfund, hazardous waste
Global change

Finance
Revenue measures, user fees

Foreign Relations
Nuclear energy, international
International Monetary Fund
International environmental affairs

Government Affairs
Nuclear export policy
Nuclear weapons plant cleanup

Judiciary
Environmental law, penalties

Labor and Human Resources
Occupational health and safety
Pesticides, food safety

HOUSE

Agriculture
Agricultural and industrial chemistry
Soil conservation, groundwater
Forestry and private forest reserves
Pesticides, food safety
Global change

Appropriations
International monetary funds
Forest Service
Army Corps of Engineers
Nuclear Regulatory Commission
Tennessee Valley Authority
Occupational Safety and Health
  Administration (OSHA)
Mine Safety and Health Administration
Soil conservation programs
Food and Drug Administration
Environmental Protection Agency
Council on Environmental Policy
National Oceanic and Atmospheric
  Administration

Armed Services
Military weapons plants
Naval petroleum, oil shale reserves
Nuclear energy

Banking, Finance and Urban Affairs
International financial and monetary
  organizations

Education and Labor
Occupational health and safety

Energy and Commerce
Energy policy, oversight
Energy conservation
Health and the environment
Interstate energy compacts
Public health and quarantine
Nuclear facilities
Transportation of hazardous materials
Solid-, hazardous-waste disposal

Foreign Affairs
Foreign loans, IMF
International environmental affairs
Global change

Government Operations
Environment, energy, natural
  resources oversight

Interior and Insular Affairs
Forest reserves (public domain)
Public lands
Irrigation and reclamation
Petroleum conservation
  (public lands)
Conservation of radium supply
Nuclear energy industry

Judiciary
Environmental law, penalties

Merchant Marine and Fisheries
Coastal zone management
Fisheries and wildlife
Oil-spill liability
Wetlands

Public Works and Transportation
Flood control, rivers
  and harbors
Pollution of navigable waters
Bridges and dams
Superfund, hazardous waste

Science, Space and Technology
Research and development
National Weather Service
Global change
Nuclear energy, facilities
Agriculture research
National Oceanic and Atmospheric
  Administration

Ways and Means
Revenue measures, user fees
Superfund

—*Philip Marwill*

in Congress because the land is locked up from use until decisions are made. Idaho wilderness issues nagged at McClure for more than a decade.

While his tenure as Energy and Natural Resources chairman produced a raft of wilderness measures for states, Idaho was not among them. McClure recently has joined Idaho Democratic Gov. Cecil D. Andrus to press a wilderness bill disliked by environmentalists and developers alike.

Power of the Purse

Within the "College of Cardinals," the 13 subcommittee chairmen who run the House Appropriations Committee, Sidney R. Yates is the vicar of the environment. A Democrat from Chicago's liberal North Side, Yates, 80, wields power over environmental issues through his control of the purse.

Yates has chaired the Subcommittee on the Interior and Related Agencies since 1975. The $10 billion it spends each year includes funds for agencies that manage the nation's public lands, parks, for-

Yates

ests, and fish and wildlife preserves. Their jurisdiction covers nearly one-third of the land mass of the United States.

The committee is in the thick of conservation and development issues that prove intractable in corresponding authorizing committees, generally House Interior and Insular Affairs and Senate Energy and Natural Resources. "If you want to get something done, you use the appropriations bill, because it's a train that's going all the way to the station," says Ralph Regula of Ohio, the ranking Republican on the Interior spending subcommittee.

In other cases, the Appropriations Committee doesn't actually write law and attach it to the spending bill — a technical violation of House rules. Instead, says Regula, "With the power of the purse, we set *de facto* policy." The amount of timber that private companies cut in the nation's forests, for example, is decided in part by how much the government spends to cut logging roads.

Yates is an old-school politician — an insider's insider, he has never called a news conference — who rarely comes unbuttoned. He does much of his own staff work, and after 15 years

as chairman, he has an intimate knowledge of each agency. He calls foresters and park superintendents by name and is unfailingly polite.

It took the Reagan administration's first interior secretary, James G. Watt, to establish the limits of Yates' self-control. When Watt went before Yates' panel for his budget, Yates dropped his gentlemanly demeanor. "That's really the only time I've ever really seen him combative," says Mary Anderson Bain, Yates' longtime administrative assistant.

The subcommittee approved measures to rein in Reagan administration policies on the leasing of federal lands offshore for oil and in wilderness areas for coal and oil. A Yates-led House consistently appropriated more than either the Senate or the administration for the acquisition of park, refuge and recreation lands.

By 1982, Yates had proved so instrumental to environmentalists that, when it appeared Yates might face a tough campaign in his new 1982 congressional district, the Sierra Club gave him its first endorsement ever.

On the Rise

Democrat George Miller of California is most visible as an advocate for children, thanks to his post as chairman of the House Select Committee on Children, Youth and Families. But it is on the Interior Committee where he will someday wield real power.

The best way to understand Interior's heir apparent is to look at a California map. It points the way to one of the state's long-running political struggles: the north and its precious snow-melt water vs. the south and its thirsty soil and cities. Miller earned his environmentalist's spurs riding shotgun over northern waters.

His congressional district is across San Pablo Bay from San Francisco. It includes the mouth of the river basin that drains most of northern and central California. State and federal aqueducts east of the area supply drinking water for half of California's residents and irrigate the San Joaquin Valley.

"He has the water hole, and we have a straw in it," says Tony Coelho, a former House majority whip from California who represented a San Joaquin Valley farming district.

Miller's grip on California's water is about to tighten. He is the ranking Democrat on Interior behind Chairman Morris K. Udall of Arizona, who has Parkinson's disease. Udall, 67, has begun to delegate committee respon-

sibility but plans to run for re-election.

Miller, 44, is a second-generation politician in his eighth term; he probably can hold his seat as long as he likes. He is well-positioned to fight his district's water battles as chairman of the Subcommittee on Water, Power and Offshore Energy. At Udall's request, he also handles Alaskan issues, which now dominate his Interior agenda. One day Miller will inherit a committee that holds sway over public lands, a battleground for timber, oil, mining and farming issues.

Interior is not the only committee with environmental jurisdiction where the leadership could soon change. Aging and infirm chairmen also run the House Merchant Marine and Fisheries and the Senate Environment and Public Works committees.

A preview of the future came in November, when Miller joined Gerry E. Studds of Massachusetts, the ranking Democrat and heir apparent at Merchant Marine, to toughen oil-spill liability legislation on the House floor. They succeeded by framing the issue as a response to the *Exxon Valdez* oil spill. *(1989 Weekly Report p. 3043)*

Miller

Miller offers a simple guide to the intellectual framework he brings to Interior: "Thou shall not rape or ruin." He continues, "We have encouraged exploitation, and I use the word exploitation, not development, with subsidies and pricing policies." He is praised by environmentalists, which concerns developers.

"There's a great pool of anger out here at him," says Jason Peltier, manager of the Central Valley Project Water Association, which represents beneficiaries of California water diversion.

Coelho says it took Miller years to "open up" to dissenting voices. Miller now "comes to issues as an environmentalist but realizes that people also come sincerely to opposing viewpoints." His negotiating style? "He likes to get every last drop he can," Coelho says.

One brake on Miller may be the jobs provided by the seven oil refineries in and near his district. "There again, because I have refineries it doesn't mean my constituents are knuckleheads," he says. "They don't want the offshore destroyed, and they want a fair return for their resources." ∎

A Quarter-Century of Activism Erected a Bulwark of Laws

Environmentalism became part of the political fabric, but the movement had to mature

Some years back, a freshman senator urged the president to get out in front of an issue that he believed Americans cared deeply about but that politicians had not yet recognized: preserving the Earth's resources.

"This is America's last chance," declared Wisconsin Democrat Gaylord Nelson. The year was 1963; the president was John F. Kennedy.

Kennedy eventually took Nelson's advice, touring several states to talk about conserving resources. Yet it would be 25 years before environmental issues became so prominent in political discourse that both parties' nominees would compete over who would make a stronger "environmental president."

The intervening 2½ decades brought a revolution in how Americans felt about their environment and how politicians and government responded to the threat of its destruction.

Like all revolutions, the times were marked by tumult — from the euphoria of "Earth Day" and the rush of environmental legislation in the 1970s to the almost violent clashes between environmentalists and free-market advocates in the early Reagan years.

Yet, over this period, the nation slowly built an array of laws and institutions that transformed environmental concerns from an issue that excited mainly college students to, in the words of Russell Train, a former administrator of the Environmental Protection Agency (EPA), "part of the way our society did things."

A naive environmental movement was also forced to mature and recognize that some of its solutions would need to be weighed against economic factors.

A Better Life

Setting the stage for this revolution was a shifting postwar society. Ameri-

By Pamela Fessler

THE ASSOCIATED PRESS

Earth Day 1970 raised the political profile of environmentalism.

cans were rapidly growing wealthier, but they had more free time and the knowledge to recognize the side effects of that growth.

"The most widespread source of emerging environmental interest was the search for a better life associated with home, community, and leisure," Samuel P. Hays, a history professor at the University of Pittsburgh, writes in his book on environmental politics "Beauty, Health and Permanence."

Suburbanization, desire for vacation homes in the country, automobile travel — each of these soared during the 1960s. "Millions of urban Americans desired to live on the fringe of the city where life was less congested, the air cleaner, noise reduced, and there was less concentrated waste from manifold human activities," Hays writes.

Gradually, the country's undeveloped regions stopped being viewed as "wastelands that could be made valuable only if developed," he adds. After World War II, "many such areas came to be thought of as valuable only if left in their natural condition."

These changing attitudes came at a time when the nation's expanding industrial and urban base put more strains on resources — most notably air and water. Simultaneous advances in science and the media made the danger-

ous health effects of pollution all too apparent. Rising cancer rates juxtaposed with pictures of smog-filled air and dead fish brought the issue home.

But for many, it was the 1962 publication of Rachel Carson's "Silent Spring," which told of the insidious effects of pesticides, that planted the first seeds of fear that growth was not free.

Turning Fear into Action

But it would take some time before this fear would germinate into political action.

Nelson says that one year after Carson's book was published he could find no Senate cosponsor for his legislation to ban the pesticide DDT or a single House member willing to introduce a companion bill.

"In 1963, I would say, there were two or three in the Senate and maybe half a dozen in the House who you could really identify as genuine environmentalists," he says. In fact, it was almost 10 years before DDT was banned.

But during those years, the nation slowly grew to realize the need for government action.

In 1963, Congress enacted the first Clean Air Act, authorizing $95 million for state, local and interstate agencies to control air pollution. In 1964, it acted to preserve 9.1 million acres of wilderness and to expand the National Wilderness System. *(Chart, p. 19)*

The next year, at the behest of President Lyndon B. Johnson and his wife, Lady Bird, Congress passed a law to "beautify" federal roadways.

Other laws followed, including measures to expand the federal role in controlling water and air pollution (1965 and 1967), to establish a National Wild and Scenic Rivers System (1968) and to protect endangered animals and plants (1969).

Despite these advances, environmental issues were not dominant in politics. They were rarely mentioned in a 1968 presidential campaign absorbed in the Vietnam War and urban poverty.

The horror stories continued, however — such as a 1969 oil-rig blowout in the Santa Barbara Channel that leaked thousands of gallons of oil off Southern California's popular beaches.

The event quickly illustrated for the nation just how fragile the relationship was between man and the environment — and how ill-equipped government and business were to handle such a disaster. *(California, p. 54)*

Major Environmental Laws

1963
Clean Air Act

1964
Wilderness Act

1965
Highway Beautification Act
Water Quality Act

1967
Air Quality Act

1968
Wild and Scenic Rivers Act

1969
National Environmental Policy Act
Endangered Species Conservation Act

1970
Clean Air Amendments
Water Quality Improvement Act

1972
Federal Water Pollution Control Act
Marine Mammal Protection Act
Marine Protection, Research and Sanctuaries Act
Coastal Zone Management Act
Federal Environmental Pesticide Control Act
Noise Control Act

1973
Endangered Species Act

1974
Safe Drinking Water Act

1976
Federal Land Policy and Management Act
National Forest Management Act
Resource Conservation and Recovery Act
Toxic Substances Control Act

1977
Clean Air Act Amendments
Clean Water Act
Surface Mining Control and Reclamation Act

1978
Outer Continental Shelf Lands Act Amendments

1980
Comprehensive Environmental Response, Compensation and Liability Act ("Superfund")
Alaska National Interest Lands Conservation Act

1984
Hazardous and Solid Waste Amendments

1986
Safe Drinking Water Amendments
Superfund Amendments and Reauthorization Act

1987
Water Quality Act

1988
Endangered Species Act Reauthorization
Federal Insecticide, Fungicide and Rodenticide Act Amendments

Shortly after the spill, Sen. Nelson was flying to speak at the University of California at Berkeley when he picked up a copy of the now-defunct radical magazine *Ramparts*. Articles about "teach-ins" and protests against the Vietnam War caught his attention.

"I thought, hell, why not have a nationwide teach-in on the environment?" says Nelson, who is now counselor for The Wilderness Society. He proposed the idea to his Berkeley audience and got a hearty endorsement.

Before long, the idea sparked interest at campuses across the country, and Nelson formed a non-profit group to organize the event for the next April 22. It was to consist largely of educational and other activities to celebrate the environment, but Nelson said he also hoped that the event would do what his letter to Kennedy in 1963 did not.

"For years, my view was that the public was way ahead of the politicians in their concern with the environment, but I wasn't sure how to force the issue into the public dialogue of the country," he says. "I wanted a demonstration so big that Congress and the president couldn't ignore it."

Earth Day 1970 hit the right nerve in the psyche of a nation that had been torn by inner-city riots and violent anti-war protests. Celebration of the Earth was an event almost anyone could support, from conservative Republican Sens. Barry Goldwater and James L. Buckley to liberal Democrats Edward M. Kennedy and Edmund S. Muskie.

An estimated 20 million Americans participated in Earth Day events. New York's Fifth Avenue was closed to vehicles, governors rode bicycles to work and students cleaned up parks and rivers across the country. Nelson said he

19

had requests from 75 to 80 of his congressional colleagues for copies of his past speeches to help write their Earth Day talks. For many, it was the first time they had ever spoken on the issue.

As Nelson and other organizers had hoped, the outpouring of public sentiment on Earth Day was too great for almost any politician to ignore.

The Nixon administration quickly grasped the significance of an issue that would divert attention from other national woes. Although President Richard M. Nixon did not directly participate in the celebration, and Earth Day organizers turned down an invitation to meet with presidential adviser John D. Ehrlichman, Interior Secretary Walter J. Hickel called the event an important "first step."

In July, Nixon sent Congress a proposal to establish an Environmental Protection Agency to consolidate all federal pollution-control programs. Earlier that year, he had signed legislation that established the Council on Environmental Quality (CEQ) and required environmental impact statements for large federal projects.

Train, who was the first head of the CEQ and later took over at the EPA, acknowledges that Nixon's enthusiasm for the environment sprang largely from pragmatic concerns.

"There was a sense that this was an important political issue," says Train, who is now chairman of the World Wildlife Fund and The Conservation Foundation. "But whatever the motivation, the Nixon administration had a very positive outlook on the environment, at least in its initial years."

The Environmental Decade

With the White House and Congress generally agreeing on the need for action, he says, the early '70s saw "the greatest outpouring of legislative initiatives ever" on a single issue.

Besides establishing the EPA and the CEQ, Congress cleared two far-reaching pollution-control measures, the Clean Air Amendments of 1970, which set national air-quality standards, and the Water Quality Improvement Act, which established liability for oil-spill cleanup costs.

In 1971, legislators began work on a series of bills that would make the 92nd Congress the most productive in history for environmental protection. The legislation, much of which was not enacted until the next year, included bills setting up federal controls over water pollution, ocean dumping, coastal zones, noise, pesticides and sea mammals.

R. MICHAEL JENKINS

Gaylord Nelson found that his old speeches were in demand for Earth Day.

During the next few years, other significant legislation passed, including measures to toughen endangered-species laws, to protect the nation's drinking water supply, to regulate the disposal of hazardous waste, to control toxic substances and to manage federal lands and the national forest system. At the same time, hundreds of regulatory and legal decisions throughout the country tightened environmental controls.

Signs of Opposition

But as government involvement grew, so did the opposition.

Some in fact had been heard on Earth Day, when representatives of inner-city residents expressed annoyance with the public's new preoccupation.

Said Richard G. Hatcher, mayor of Gary, Ind.: "The nation's concern with the environment has done what George Wallace was unable to do: distract the nation from the human problems of the black and brown American, living in just as much misery as ever."

Others began to question whether environmentalists were adequately weighing economic and other costs. "Perhaps with all good intentions we are moving too fast," said a 1972 House Appropriations Committee report.

But these views were largely in the minority — until the nation confronted a worldwide energy crisis in 1973. The Arab oil embargo that year set off a sequence of events that would seriously slow the environmental movement. Suddenly, the need for energy was paramount. With the economic slump that followed, these two issues had a sobering impact on environmental activism.

(Energy policy, p. 22)
"I pursue the goal of clean air and pure water, but I must also pursue the objective of maximum jobs and continued economic progress," President Gerald R. Ford said in 1975. "Unemployment is as real and sickening a blight as any pollutant that threatens the nation."

Industry leaders received more sympathy from politicians for their complaints about the financial burdens of environmental regulations. They joined labor leaders, in some instances, to prevent stringent regulations proposed by environmentalists. For example, the United Auto Workers union, an early supporter of environmental protection, sided with the auto industry in 1976 to block a pollution cleanup timetable environmentalists favored.

Environmental activists found that they had to spend much of the last half of the decade preventing the changes of the first half from unraveling.

Carter's Environmental Roots

They were buoyed, however, by the coming of the Carter administration in 1977. President Jimmy Carter campaigned on a strong pro-environment platform, and his record as governor of Georgia showed that he felt strongly about conserving resources. He pulled many of his early appointees from the environmental movement.

Several important bills were passed in the early Carter years, including amendments to the Clean Air Act and clean-water laws, and legislation to establish environmental protection standards for surface mining.

But by the last half of that administration, economics and energy once again came to the fore. The nation was confronted with rising energy prices, inflation and unemployment. While the energy shortage led to some moves environmentalists favored — including energy conservation and incentives to develop alternative power sources, such as solar energy — it also meant that the movement had to take a back seat to other national concerns.

The honeymoon between Carter and environmentalists came to a quick end in 1979, when the president announced plans to help wean the nation from its dependence on foreign oil, in part by developing synthetic fuels and giving energy production precedence over protecting the environment.

During the late '70s, new fears of catastrophe arose after chemical waste was discovered near Love Canal in New York and polychlorinated biphenyls (PCBs) were found in the Hudson River.

A more sophisticated environmental movement and a more cautious electorate were beginning to realize that solutions to the nation's environmental problems, while needed more than ever, would be far more complex than originally thought. As a result, the 10th-year celebration of Earth Day — although it involved about 1,000 communities — was a far more modest and sobering affair than the first.

'Sagebrush Rebellion'

But nothing was quite so sobering to the environmental movement as the Reagan administration.

Jokes about the new president's belief that trees caused pollution quickly turned grim when activists realized how serious a threat his administration posed to their cause.

President Ronald Reagan did not seek legislative changes but instead attacked the heart of environmentalism through deregulation. He filled key posts with appointees who shared his free-market ideas and a desire to reduce government involvement, and he slashed budget requests for the EPA and other environmental programs.

The two most notorious appointees were James G. Watt as interior secretary and Anne M. Gorsuch as EPA administrator.

Watt, especially, saw the Reagan landslide over Carter as a mandate to dismantle much of the environmental regulatory structure that had been put in place over the previous decade. He saw his constituents as Western miners, ranchers, state legislators and others who had formed a so-called "Sagebrush Rebellion" against public land ownership and the conservation policies of the Carter administration.

Historian Hays writes that after an early 1981 meeting with environmentalists, Watt told them there would be no more such meetings, "because there was nothing further to discuss."

One of Watt's first announced goals was to shift federal lands policy from preservation toward developing coal, oil, gas, timber and other natural resources. And he announced that, when in doubt, he would "err on the side of public use vs. preservation."

At the same time, Gorsuch's EPA undertook to develop more cooperation with the industries it was supposed to regulate and to negotiate with them on the agency's enforcement of pollution-control standards.

But these new policies and Watt's abrasive ways soon caused a backlash, both in Congress and among the public.

Earth Day? Still Spinning

Former Democratic Sen. Gaylord Nelson of Wisconsin says last year was the first since the early 1970s that some reporter didn't call to ask, "Whatever happened to Earth Day?"

The reason, he believes, is that environmental issues have finally returned to the top of the political agenda, where they were shortly after the first Earth Day celebration, on April 22, 1970, when 20 million Americans showed their support for protecting the environment.

Now Nelson (1963-81), recognized by many as the founder of Earth Day, and numerous national organizations are working hard to put together a 20th-anniversary celebration that they hope will dwarf the first.

Unlike Earth Day 1970, the April 22, 1990, event is expected to extend around the world in recognition of the worldwide impact of most environmental problems. Educational activities, mass demonstrations, television presentations and political events are envisioned.

Also, unlike in the first celebration, politicians and businesses are getting in on the action early. Several companies, for example, are already planning an exhibit in Washington on new cleanup technologies. Congress, the administration and state and local governments also are readying activities.

On Jan. 3, President Bush held a White House ceremony to declare April 22 as Earth Day. Nelson predicts that the event will lead to "the largest grass-roots demonstration in history. . . . I think the pressure is building now so that political leaders can't blink at it."

Through well-publicized oversight hearings and legislative riders on Interior appropriations bills, Congress slowed many of Watt's initiatives. At first, Democrats led most of the opposition, but after large GOP losses in the 1982 congressional elections, Republicans also became concerned about Watt's impact on the party's image.

In 1983, Watt and Gorsuch resigned in the face of congressional investigations. Reagan replaced them with more moderate appointees, Interior Secretary William P. Clark and EPA Administrator William D. Ruckelshaus, who worked to mend fences with environmental groups and congressional committees while keeping administration ties with business and industry.

Hays notes that the backlash against the early Reagan policies led to a dramatic increase in membership and funding of environmental groups.

"With larger staffs they could lobby more effectively in Congress on more issues, undertake more litigation, and mobilize members more fully," he writes.

"For in challenging the environmental movement, Reagan tested its strength and vitality and thereby demonstrated the degree to which it had become a broad and fundamental aspect of American public life."

Although Congress tightened federal controls over toxic wastes in 1984, 10 important environmental laws had expired or were in need of renewal by the end of Reagan's first term.

Partly as a result of this backlog and a less combative administration, Congress was almost as active on environmental legislation over the next four years as it had been during the 1970s.

One of its big accomplishments came in 1986, when it renewed and strengthening the "superfund" hazardous-waste cleanup fund. That year, it also reauthorized the Safe Drinking Water Act. In 1987, Congress amended clean-water laws, and in 1988, it toughened pesticide safety and endangered-species laws.

As the decade neared the end, much had changed. Another Republican president, George Bush, took office after his political advisers found that one of the best ways he could win public backing was to distance himself from his predecessor's environmental policies.

New environmental concerns were also emerging — about planetary warming, about diminishing landfill sites, about pollution of the oceans, about nuclear waste at defense plants.

Environmental activists and businesses, although still in conflict over the details of how to balance jobs and protection of the Earth's resources, at least had begun to acknowledge each other as players on the same field.

Sen. Nelson and others were also planning for a 20th-anniversary celebration of Earth Day, an event organizers hoped would far outstrip the first. ∎

ENERGY

Using Environmental Goals In Name of Independence

But factions in Congress continue to pose obstacles in the search for a lasting national policy

Ever since OPEC turned off the spigot on America's oil pipeline in 1973, government efforts to ensure the nation a steady supply of energy have required environmental trade-offs. The use of virtually every natural resource exacts a toll on the air, water and land.

In the list of national priorities, energy always came first.

Each administration since Richard M. Nixon's has shared a tenet first enunciated in his televised address shortly after the embargo began: The environment is merely a shared interest; energy is an indispensable requirement. Clean air and clean water are important, but inexpensive, reliable, domestic sources of fuel are more important.

Nevertheless, forces in the marketplace and various parochial and ideological interest groups, including environmentalists, combined to doom every attempt to craft a long-term policy aimed at guaranteeing an affordable supply of fuel for homes, cars and industry. Today the United States is as dependent as ever on foreign oil.

Now, with environmentalism re-emerging as a political force for the first time since the heady days of the early 1970s, policy makers are wondering whether they had it backward: Perhaps the goal of increased energy independence can be achieved through environmental protection, not in spite of it. Maybe concern about acid rain, global warming, smog and oil spills can be an impetus for energy policy instead of a roadblock.

Leading the way is the Bush administration. Though allied with industry interests during the Reagan administration's hands-off approach to environmental protection and the energy marketplace, President Bush is embarking on an ambitious campaign to reassert a federal role in both. He has ordered his top advisers to craft a

By Phil Kuntz

CHECKLIST

Issue: Energy policy.

Need for action: No immediate deadlines.

Main venues: House: Energy and Commerce Committee, Interior Committee; Senate: Energy and Natural Resources Committee, Environment and Public Works Committee

Outlook: Energy Secretary James D. Watkins is conducting hearings across the country and plans to have a National Energy Strategy ready for President Bush's 1991 State of the Union address.

"National Energy Strategy" to devise ways to wean the nation from its dependence on foreign sources.

Key members of Congress are receptive and hope that Bush can succeed where his predecessors have failed. They agree with Bush that increasing foreign dependence is dangerous, more so in the face of complacency bred during the 1980s by low and stable fuel prices.

Some energy leaders are banking on hopes that the environment is the one *national* interest that might overcome the many conflicting interests that have stymied previous efforts to craft a federal energy policy.

"Most of our energy policy is going to be made as a byproduct of environmental policy," says John A. Riggs, a top aide to the House Energy subcommittee for power issues. "In the '70s, it was the other way around."

For years, says Philip R. Sharp, D-Ind., now chairman of the House Energy and Power Subcommittee, energy

security was his panel's primary goal. Now the environment is "a higher priority," he says, so he has "switched the emphasis." His goals — increased conservation efforts and greater use of alternative and renewable sources of energy — are the same, but they have been made "much more salable because of the environment," if only because voters seem more conscious of the damaging effects of fossil fuels.

The Bush administration has picked up from there. While expressing concern for what Energy Secretary James D. Watkins called an addiction to foreign oil, officials are crafting the National Energy Strategy largely around environmental concerns.

"It's become clear that unless conservation and efficiency are at the focal point of our attention, then we're not going to get anywhere," Watkins says, dropping key buzzwords of the environmental movement. His deputy secretary, W. Henson Moore, says: "The American people today want a clean environment. We can use that. It gives us the needed momentum."

But the Bush administration's emphasis on their cause makes some environmentalists suspicious. They have only partly supported Bush's rewrite of the Clean Air Act and, while giving Watkins generally neutral marks, some still do not trust Moore, a former adversary in Congress. *(Moore, this page)*

So while environmentalism may be the driving force behind a new energy policy, it could just as easily stand in the way. Jim Middaugh, a spokesman for the Environmental Defense Fund, says, "Yeah, we're going to be a roadblock if they're going to do it wrong."

Administration Initiative

Since Watkins in July announced plans to draft an energy strategy, the environment has received high billing in the effort.

Two of the top three objectives for the Energy Department would help protect the environment. Watkins has held 12 hearings in cities across the country and heard testimony from several environmentalists. A session in Atlanta on Dec. 14 addressed environment issues specifically and was jointly presided over by Watkins and William K. Reilly, director of the Environmental Protection Agency (EPA).

In November, Moore surprised many environmentalists and energy-policy watchers by telling reporters that the administration was strongly committed to conservation and the use of renewable fuels, an about-face from Reagan administration policy.

Watkins plans to release a draft report by April 1, solicit public comment on it through the summer and, after refining the document in the fall, place it on Bush's desk by the end of the year. That would allow the National Energy Strategy to be a major component of Bush's State of the Union message in January 1991. Some aspects of the strategy may be officially proposed before then; Bush's pending fiscal 1991 budget proposal is expected to include a call for increased research and development funding to encourage conservation and the use of renewable energy sources.

Scare Tactics

Few experts or politicians doubt that the nation needs some sort of energy policy, that the federal government needs to assert a role — perhaps the leading role — in steering the country's energy marketplace from

Bush's Mr. Conservation

SUE KLEMENS

W. Henson Moore

ATLANTA — Washington's best measure of the shifting political winds on the environment may be W. Henson Moore, the Bush administration's point man for developing the National Energy Strategy.

Now deputy energy secretary, Moore was a Republican House member from Louisiana in 1975-87, the years during which the nation unsuccessfully attempted to forge a lasting energy policy.

Back then, Moore consistently received dismal "environmentalist" ratings from the League of Conservation Voters (LCV). Moore never voted with its pro-environmental stances more than half the time, and some years his LCV ratings dipped into the single digits and were lower than those of members from fuel-producing districts.

Now Moore is Mr. Conservation and Renewable Fuels, professing support for environmentalists' favorite "soft energy" policies. He says he has been "converted" and he is trying to persuade environmentalists that he is sincere.

Last month in Atlanta, at a Department of Energy hearing on energy and the environment, Moore was praised by William K. Reilly, President Bush's activist director of the Environmental Protection Agency.

But many environmentalists are suspicious of Moore's change of heart. Jim Maddy, executive director of the LCV, called Moore's pro-conservation statements "not credible" given his record in Congress.

When questioned closely, Moore seems to lean toward the existing order, much like members of Congress from energy-producing states whose constituents would be hurt by environment-protection policies that cut the use of oil and coal.

In an interview here, Moore said he is still "very much a supporter" of the use of fossil fuels and predicted that the nation will continue using the same mix of fuels, perhaps with some pie-chart shifting far down the road. Soft energy alone "isn't going to solve your energy problem," he says. "But you have to do that first" to establish needed "credibility."

"We believe that all the fuels are necessary in the short run and the medium run," he says. "There's no way to divert the use of coal and meet the country's energy needs.

"I'm willing to bet," Moore adds, "that we'll find there's room for all these at their current level of production and maybe even increased levels."

Moore insists that environmentalists will be happy with the Energy Department strategy and denies that he is just "throwing them a bone" by stressing conservation and renewables.

But he also said environmentalists may have to give a little: "If they hold to the position that they want an immediate reduction by 15 to 20 percent in fossil fuels, we don't know how you can do that. That's not a real national energy strategy. That's not going to get a consensus behind it."

And a consensus policy that offends as few geographical interests as possible is clearly what Energy Secretary James D. Watkins wants. "We have to be regionally oriented," Watkins told reporters here.

That kind of agreement has never been possible before, even during energy crises.

"I wish him well," said Louisiana Democrat J. Bennett Johnston, chairman of the Senate Energy Committee. "You always get back to the same old choices, the same trade-offs."

—Phil Kuntz

production to end use.

Although some free-marketeers, including Reagan administration hard-liners, have argued that the United States' energy "vulnerability" is not as great as its "dependence" suggests, most consider the situation increasingly grave. Shortly after taking office, Bush declared increasing oil imports an unacceptable threat to national security.

That scare line, however, is wearing thin.

With widely varying approaches and degrees of urgency, every president since 1973 has emphasized that danger and tried unsuccessfully to spur the nation into accepting their prescriptions for a cure. Nixon said that "we are running out of energy." Gerald R. Ford spoke of "a future of shortages," and Jimmy Carter declared "the moral equivalent of war" on a potential "national catastrophe." Even Ronald Reagan announced that "petroleum imports threaten to impair our national security."

The situation is now potentially worse, yet the level of concern is considerably lower. This winter's low temperatures and jumping heating oil prices are stirring some jitters in the chilly Northeast, but that is to be expected and likely will pass.

U.S. oil production continued to plummet last year to its lowest point in 26 years. Imports took up the slack, accounting for 46 percent of consumption. The nation was more dependent on imports only once, in 1977, when imports accounted for 48 percent of consumption, precipitating the energy crisis of 1979.

Some experts say U.S. dependence may hit 70 percent by 2000. Nevertheless, says House Energy's Riggs, "Energy doesn't have any political muscle anymore. Nobody cares about energy security except producers. Consumers are happy because prices are low and relatively stable."

Before 1973, America's dependence on foreign energy was an issue for just a handful of experts and politicians. Meanwhile, America's environmental movement was celebrating numerous successes in the aftermath of 1970's massive Earth Day demonstrations. *(History, p. 18)*

Many provisions of those laws neg-

Energy vs. Environment

Question: If it came to a choice between developing new energy resources and preserving publicly owned wilderness . . .

- - -□- - - Preserve Wilderness   ——□—— Develop Energy

Sample: 1,500 adults nationwide.

SOURCE: Cambridge Reports

BARBARA SASSA-DANIELS

atively affected the nation's ability to be energy independent — increasing the cost, difficulty and risk of producing energy in the United States.

The National Environmental Policy Act of 1969 required arduous environmental impact statements on all major government decisions, including those that allowed private firms to dig for coal, oil and gas on public property. The Clean Air Act opened the door for limits on pollution from stationary sources, including power plants that use coal, an abundant and messy domestic fuel source; it also placed strict emissions standards on cars. Water quality laws required oil spillers to reimburse the government for cleaning up accidents.

The Earth Turns

Everything changed Oct. 17-18, 1973, when the Arab-dominated Organization of Petroleum Exporting Countries (OPEC) began cutting off the oil supply, protesting the United States' pro-Israel stance in the Yom Kippur War. Thus was the modern-day energy issue born.

More than any other political issue of the time, the energy crisis directly affected Americans. They paid sharply increased fuel prices, costing each consumer $500 extra a year by one estimate. They waited hours in lines for gas and sometimes had to go without. They shivered through the winter at decreased room temperatures.

Voters demanded action; they got a stalemate. Congress would kill or gut

remedial policies proposed by various administrations, or adopt them and throw them out a few years later.

Some examples:

● In 1973-74, Nixon's proposed Project Independence, a multifaceted package designed to wean America off foreign fuel by 1980, bogged down when the House insisted on capping crisis-related windfall profits of fuel companies, but oil-state senators refused to go along. When the two chambers finally agreed on an alternative — oil-price ceilings — Nixon successfully vetoed the bill on ideological grounds, killing much of his energy package with it.

● In 1975-76, Ford got much of his package approved, but its major focus — higher prices through decontrol and import fees — was rejected by a Congress loath to stick it to consumers, especially those in cold states. Instead, Ford was forced to sign a measure extending and expanding oil-price controls.

● In 1979-80, in the wake of the second oil crisis, Carter proposed a new federal research program aimed at creating a new generation of synthetic fuels. At more than $80 billion over five years, it was the largest peacetime non-defense authorization in history. Congress, initially cool to the idea, approved a version of the bill, but only after turning it into a massive energy pork bill, spreading money for all sorts of pet projects throughout the country.

Much of what did survive from policies created during the Nixon, Ford and Carter administrations was dismantled during the Reagan years as a free-market philosophy prevailed during a time of falling energy prices. Reagan's energy policy was no policy, and with the 1970s fading into memory, Congress went along with many of his anti-big government proposals.

Most notably, Congress abolished the so-called synfuels program in one of Reagan's biggest budget-cutting successes. Also repealed were tax breaks for installing energy-saving devices, programs designed to force power plants to use domestic coal and the windfall tax on oil profits, which had been enacted in 1980. Reagan also killed remaining oil price controls and successfully proposed dramatic cuts in federal support for conservation and renewables.

In the end, even the best-known and seemingly most enduring holdover from the energy crisis was thrown out, as Congress in 1988 decided to raise the 55-mph speed limit on interstate highways.

Within the span of four presidencies, observes Walter A. Rosenbaum of the University of Florida in his 1987 book, "Energy Politics and Public Policy," the federal government's approach to the nation's energy economy "changed drastically, from growing regulation to increased deregulation, from market intervention to market nonintervention, from more long-term planning to less."

Role of Environment

Throughout the formative years of energy policy, the environment played an important but secondary role. Each administration proposed limiting the scope of environmental laws when they interfered with the U.S. quest for energy independence.

Nixon tried first. Among other things, he asked Congress to loosen some environment-protection laws, "thus permitting an appropriate balancing of our environmental interests, which all of us share, with our energy requirements, which, of course, are indispensable."

Congress went along with some of the proposals and killed others.

Sometimes, however, the environment's protectors managed to gum up the works. Carter's synfuels program ran into trouble because, among other things, it would have given a proposed Energy Mobilization Board power to override environment-protection laws that otherwise would block the exploitation of existing fuel sources and their conversion into synfuels.

A coalition that included environmentalists and local and state officials worried about the federal government's overriding their often-tougher laws scotched that idea. Joining them were oil interests and Westerners who feared that the board would impose restrictions on water rights, and conservatives worried about expanding bureaucracy.

The death of the board saved the synfuels program from defeat, but the environmentalists were not done. They worked against the program from its inception and found an odd bedfellow in the Reagan administration, usually no friend of theirs.

Reagan's free-market advocates joined environmentalists, who were worried about synfuel plants' strip

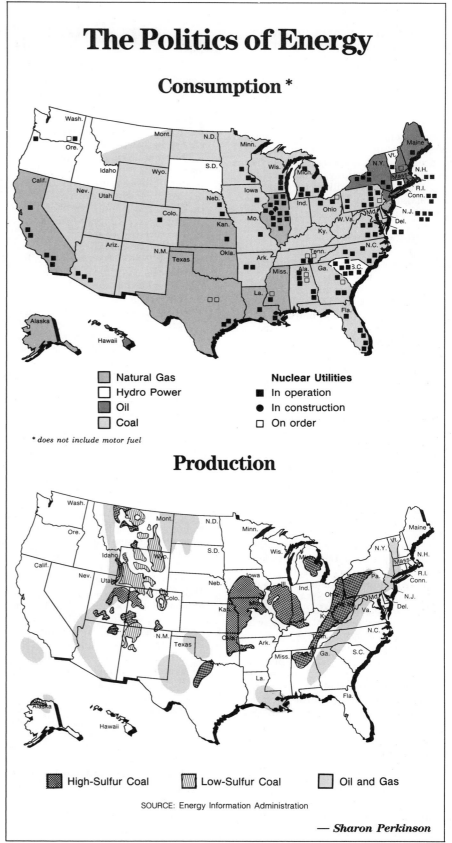

The Politics of Energy

Consumption *

Natural Gas
Hydro Power
Oil
Coal

Nuclear Utilities
■ In operation
● In construction
□ On order

* does not include motor fuel

Production

High-Sulfur Coal   Low-Sulfur Coal   Oil and Gas

SOURCE: Energy Information Administration

— *Sharon Perkinson*

mining, water exploitation and pollution production, with budget-cutters ready to cut the deficit at all costs and with others outraged over alleged ethical abuses by those running the program.

But a mainstay of Reagan's energy policy — increased exploitation of U.S. energy reserves, especially those on public lands — did not sit well with environmentalists either. Their loud protests resulted in a tenfold expansion of the annual congressional ban on offshore oil drilling, which prohibited leasing on 84 million acres in fiscal 1990, up from 736,000 acres in fiscal 1982. *(Oil drilling, this page)*

Bush in the Middle

Now comes the Bush administration, apparently ready to re-establish a federal role in the energy marketplace.

Some experts say his proposal to rewrite the Clean Air Act would have a dramatic impact on the markets, discouraging the use of certain coals to combat acid rain. In addition, research into renewable energy sources, conservation and alternative fuels is again getting administration support (although White House antipathy for conservation grant programs for the poor and for state and local governments appears likely to remain).

Deputy Energy Secretary Moore says that Bush's policy will be "somewhere between the obtrusiveness of the Carter administration and the laissez faire of the Reagan years."

Toward that end, Bush's advisers want to join the same environmentalists who spent years fighting his allies in the Reagan administration — in large part because they are the ones with today's biggest new claim to power.

Some administration officials, such as Bush's aggressive EPA director, Reilly, are optimistic that the resurgence of the environmental cause will carry a new energy strategy into the coming decades.

"That's going to help us put together a much better, much more useful energy policy," Reilly says.

As Moore sees it, once the environmentalists are enticed on board by the administration's commitment to their causes, they will be willing to deal on other energy policies they may not have supported before — presumably those aimed at increasing domestic production. "Then, if you have shortages, you have the credibility [with environmentalists], and you can fill in the gap," he says.

But the environmentalists intend

Drilling Fight Continues

On the frozen tundra of Alaska and along the country's most scenic coasts, balance and compromise seem impossible. Oil and gas interests want to drill; environmentalists want to preserve. Congress must choose between the two but can't.

Nowhere are the nation's energy needs and environmental responsibilities more diametrically opposed. Nowhere are the forces in Washington more stubborn.

For nearly 10 years, the question of whether to permit oil drilling in Alaska's massive Arctic National Wildlife Refuge (ANWR) and on the coastline's outer continental shelf has been left open. ANWR has never reached the floor of either chamber, and each year Congress has used an appropriations bill to impose temporary moratoriums on offshore explorations. Every effort to resolve the central

AMERICAN PETROLEUM INSTITUTE

questions of whether, where and how to search for oil has ended in stalemate.

Rep. Leon E. Panetta, D-Calif., a leader in the fight to prevent exploration off parts of his state's coast, says: "I don't think fighting this guerrilla war on a year-to-year basis is in anybody's interest.... What we need is a permanent solution."

But resolutions seem as distant now as they did both in 1980, when Congress quit trying to settle the ANWR issue by ordering the Interior Department to study it, and in 1981, when then-Interior Secretary James G. Watt tried to allow drilling on a billion offshore acres.

The Reagan administration's final ANWR study in 1987 called for opening up the entire 1.5 million-acre coastal plain to immediate development. But after more than 25 hearings in four committees, drilling bills died on their way to both floors in the 100th Congress. Last year, action quickly stalled again after the *Exxon Valdez* oil spill in Alaska's Prince William Sound.

Watt's proposal prompted Congress to approve bigger and bigger one-year bans. Each was aimed at protecting sensitive areas from pro-drilling forces at Interior, which oversees leasing rights on public lands. In fiscal 1982, 736,000 acres off California were covered. This year the ban was expanded to include 84 million acres, off California as well as off New England, the Middle Atlantic region, Florida and Alaska.

President Bush attempted to defuse the issue by commissioning an interagency study, which reportedly called for delays in drilling in the two most controversial areas — off California and off Florida, where, unlike in Alaska, most residents oppose drilling.

Bush appears to be well-suited for the task of conciliator. He comes from a decidedly pro-business, pro-oil background, but he is also trying to become an "environmental president." But the task force recommendation, if accepted by Bush, may only delay the fight again. It is only a matter of time before those favoring drilling in Alaska try to move their bills again.

Both sides realize that the environmentalists have the upper hand for now, by virtue of the public's increasing outrage over oil spills and other environmental problems. Both sides also know, however, that the advantage is good only until the next energy shortage.

Oil-state Sen. J. Bennett Johnston, D-La., says, "There will be a time when we will be terribly short [of oil], and people will say, 'Why didn't you do something when you could have?' "

—*Phil Kuntz*

to use their new strength to pursue their own ends, the same policies they have chased for years: those that would reduce the use of "dirty" fuels. Encouraging conservation, efficiency, renewables and other alternative energy sources, they say, will foster a cleaner environment, increased energy independence and, therefore, a stronger economy.

"It's a triple win," says Tim Wirth, D-Colo., of the Senate Energy and Natural Resources Committee.

All Politics Is Local

The other forces that contributed to the 16-year stalemate also may not be willing to fold under Bush's new environmental banner. Chief among these forces in Congress are those based on regional alliances.

As then-Speaker Thomas P. "Tip" O'Neill, D-Mass. (1954-88), said in 1975, after Congress rejected both Ford's and the Democratic leadership's energy packages: "This, perhaps, has been the most parochial issue that could ever hit the floor."

No wonder.

The Northeast, where it is cold and few energy sources are produced, wants a constant supply of cheap energy, so it wants nothing to do with any increases aimed at curbing consumption. Voters there are the first to cry for government controls when prices jump.

The oil states, mainly in the South and the Southwest, want domestic prices to remain "fair," meaning profitable and without controls. But they want Congress to put fees on imports to give them an edge in the market. They also would like to expand the ability of energy producers to exploit public lands. But wildlife advocates and even some NIMBYs (not-in-my-back-yarders) — especially those fearing more big coastline oil spills — will have nothing to do with that idea.

Natural-gas regions, generally the same as oil states, want to see their resource promoted as the "cleanest fuel," in response to stiffening regulations on auto exhaust. Michigan and other car-producing states disdain such fuel-economy standards, but smog-choked California embraces them.

The high-sulfur coal states along the Appalachian corridor and the Ohio Valley want to remain big producers. So they will resist any policy that threatens their livelihood, as the current debate over the acid-rain provisions of Bush's clean-air bill has shown. Meanwhile, the Western, low-sulfur coal states are doing back flips

because the Bush proposals would increase their share of the market unless clean-coal technology catches up.

A plan to use "alternative fuels" policies to wean the nation off foreign-oil imports sounds like a nice compromise, but even that causes regional conflicts. The Farm Belt favors an emphasis on ethanol, which relies on corn, while the natural-gas industry prefers methanol, which uses its product.

As Senate Energy Committee Chairman J. Bennett Johnston, D-La., says, "When people think of an energy policy, they usually have in mind their pet components."

The Nuclear Question

These regional conflicts are complicated by other interest-group concerns.

Consider the nuclear-power industry, which has been stalled since the late 1970s. Nuclear proponents say the next generation of "safe" plants is coming soon, and they maintain that environmentalists are beginning to come

around to the idea that nuclear energy may not be so evil after all — especially in comparison with dirty fossil fuels.

Some anti-nuclear activists say they may be willing to reconsider their opposition if the waste, safety and high-cost problems can be solved — three big ifs. A leading environmentalist in the Senate, John H. Chafee, R-R.I., has softened his previous position: "I can't help but believe that, if we are really serious about looking at the energy problems, people are going to have to look at nuclear energy."

Chafee says, however, "This is heresy for environmentalists."

Middaugh of the Environmental Defense Fund has relaxed his opposition to nuclear power but only slightly, and he says the industry and the media have blown such statements out of proportion. "All I said was I'm no longer willing to categorically rule nukes out," Middaugh says.

"I'm not sure how much that says," he says. "I would definitely question

any policy that would say we have to build more nukes."

Other self-proclaimed solutions to the energy-environment dilemma have obstacles of their own.

Although methanol is "clean" and can be produced domestically, it eventually may increase imports because the next inexpensive sources of natural gas are foreign. Low-sulfur coal is also considered to be cleaner fuel, but strip-mining concerns are ever-present. And if global warming theories are accepted, all carbon dioxide-producing fossil fuels are in trouble. Even hydroelectric power has negative effects on rivers and lakes.

"Each of these results in its own problems, all of which are environmental," Chafee says.

The environmental resurgence gives alternative fuels and conservation — so-called soft-energy sources — the most cachet these days.

Funding for such research will increase this year, but the members of Congress who control the purse strings on some federal energy research harbor doubts about such energy-saving panaceas, and they have their own regional interests to protect.

Both chairmen of the Appropriations subcommittees on Energy and Water are from fuel-producing states. Johnston watches out for oil; Rep. Tom Bevill, D-Ala., protects his district's coal interests.

"To do without coal would be a luxury we can't afford," Bevill says. Added Johnston: "Oil is not the problem right now, except that we're not producing enough of it."

Thus, it appears that the competing forces that created and perpetuated the energy stalemate — what political scientist Eric M. Uslaner has called the "destructive coalitions of minorities" — may pose as strong an obstacle in the 1990s as they were in the '70s and '80s.

The real question is whether environmentalists can use their newfound influence in national politics to transform their movement from yet another destructive minority into a constructive one that could help forge a permanent energy policy.

"If anything, it might make it more complex," says Uslaner, a University of Maryland professor and author of "Shale Barrel Politics."

"The greater the concern for the environment, the more difficult it's going to be to come up with a consensus on what to do when the next energy crisis hits." ∎

Tough Talk Is Heating Up; Specific Action Unlikely

Action to combat the warming of the planet, experts say, must be global, sweeping, coordinated — and probably expensive. But Congress tends to find solutions that are parochial, piecemeal, ad hoc and (nowadays) free of federal expenditures.

So while individual members have become increasingly alarmed that manmade gases seem to be gradually warming the Earth's atmosphere — many scientists predict an increase of between 4 degrees and 9 degrees Fahrenheit by the middle of the next century — legislative action against the "greenhouse effect" does not seem imminent.

Sens. Tim Wirth, D-Colo., and Al Gore, D-Tenn., each have omnibus bills offering solutions such as curbing the world's birthrate, discouraging deforestation, encouraging development of alternative fuels and imposing fuel taxes designed to cut carbon dioxide emissions 20 percent by 2000.

But the senators, along with Rep. Claudine Schneider, R-R.I., who has introduced similarly broad legislation in the House, say their initiatives are more like policy papers than viable bills. Pushing broad bills through the committee system would be nearly impossible.

"We would be here until the glaciers melted," Schneider says, referring to the multiple jurisdictions involved in the 12 titles of her bill.

With this in mind, Wirth plans to tear off part of his omnibus bill this year and deal separately with such issues as energy efficiency, conservation and clean-coal technologies, thus keeping jurisdiction within the Energy and Natural Resources Committee on which he sits.

Still, Congress will find it difficult to take the reins on global warming, even though the Reagan and Bush administrations have been reluctant to assume a leading role.

There are signs, however, that the Bush administration may be re-evaluating its stance toward the greenhouse effect. And a flurry of upcoming international conferences, plus continued scientific debate in the media, will raise the issue's profile.

Other opportunities for more fo-

cused legislative action will present themselves in the 101st Congress.

The first comes when Congress debates a bill to raise automobile emissions standards as part of its renewal of the Clean Air Act. *(Stories, pp. 5, 29)*

Two other efforts, by Sen. Ernest F. Hollings, D-S.C., to coordinate federal research efforts, and by Sen. Patrick J. Leahy, D-Vt., to study the relationship between agriculture and the greenhouse effect, are relatively non-controversial and could become law this year.

On the Vanguard

Wirth and Gore have long been town criers of the global warming threat. Gore has made such environmental issues a theme of his quest for the presidency, maintaining that the public is ahead of most politicians on this issue. *(Gore, p. 53)*

Indeed, 72 percent of respondents to a recent poll want the United States to lead in fighting global warming. Vince Breglio, chief pollster for the Bush-Quayle campaign, conducted the poll in November for the Union of Concerned Scientists. About 80 percent of respondents were aware of the problem, compared with 58 percent in 1988.

Wirth, for his part, allows that having a high profile on the issue has drawbacks. He says his stance repels some corporate campaign contributors and makes enemies of utilities and oil, auto, timber and publishing companies.

"I'm taking on industry. It's not an easy thing to do," says Wirth.

As concern about global warming increases, doubts that scientists raise

about their data have heightened meaning in policy debates. Raising fuel taxes to dissuade U.S. automobile and utility use, for instance, might be too high a price to pay if the warming trend takes hundreds of years instead of decades.

"We have about 10 years before we have to make some very hard decisions," says Michael Schlesinger, a climatologist at the University of Illinois. "But do we have to bite the bullet [now], making these changes . . . that have the potential of changing people's lives?"

Wirth questions whether absolute certainty should be expected. "We spend $300 billion a year on defense, yet we don't know exactly when the Russians are going to attack," he says. Cutting carbon dioxide emissions and searching for alternative energy sources are "all things we ought to be doing anyway. It's prudent. It's an insurance policy."

Bush Shift Possible

Mounting public attention is pressing the Bush administration to take the lead on global warming. But the president's advisers remain divided on how to proceed in a year when nearly a dozen major worldwide environment-related events are scheduled.

The U.N. Intergovernmental Panel on Climate Change will meet in Washington in February and again in the fall. Another multinational conference begins April 29, sponsored by Gore and other members of Congress.

The White House took a drubbing from Capitol Hill critics in 1989 for censoring the May congressional testimony of James E. Hansen, director of NASA's Goddard Institute for Space Studies, before Gore's Commerce Subcommittee on Science, Technology and Space. *(1989 Weekly Report p. 1112)*

The testimony followed reports that administration officials opposed efforts by EPA Administrator William K. Reilly to have the United States host an international global warming conference. Chief of Staff John H. Sununu, White House Science Adviser D. Allan Bromley and Richard G. Darman, director of the Office of Management and Budget, were reported to oppose Reilly's proposal.

Environmentalists predict a shift in administration policy. Bush's proposal at the Malta summit for a U.S.-Soviet-sponsored meeting on global warming this summer reportedly came at Reilly's insistence. Gore says Bromley also may be a catalyst. Bromley "has been getting up to speed on the whole issue," Gore says. "There's a chance he may stop parroting the Sununu line." ∎

By Mike Mills

Japanese Drive a Hard Bargain On Emissions Standards

The Big Three U.S. automakers are running up against more efficient lobbying competition

For nearly 20 years, U.S. automakers have been eating the dust of their Japanese competitors in a high-stakes race for American consumer loyalty.

This year, as Congress considers new standards for automobile gas mileage, the biggest wheels of Japan are parked on Capitol Hill, engines gunning. They are worried that tougher fuel-economy proposals would shut them out of the U.S. luxury-car market and are threatening to turn the old energy and environment issue into a miniature trade war.

The issue — whether to require all automakers to meet the same fleetwide miles-per-gallon (mpg) targets or to require proportional increases based on each manufacturer's 1988 fuel economy — has thrown the Japanese against Detroit's "Big Three": Ford Motor Co., General Motors Corp. and Chrysler Corp.

The Japanese and their dealers in this country want to keep the current mpg formula because they specialize in small cars that have already made sizable advances in fuel economy.

U.S. carmakers would rather go to a percentage measure of fuel economy that would raise standards for Asian manufacturers, discouraging them from moving into the larger-car markets.

Japan's break with Detroit's Big Three has set up a confrontation of big-money powers in Congress, although some observers predict that, like the battle for U.S. car sales, it will be no contest for the Japanese.

"They can beat the Big Three with one hand tied behind their back," says Pat Choate, a vice president of TRW Inc., who is writing a book about Japanese lobbying. "They are better organized. They have the full support of their government and more influence in the White House."

Japanese Fighting for Themselves

One thing is clear: Japanese automakers and dealers are no longer letting Detroit fight their battles for

By Alyson Pytte

CHECKLIST

Issue: Automobile gas mileage.

Legislation: To revise Corporate Average Fuel Economy (CAFE) standards.

Impetus for action: Proposed new tailpipe standards in clean-air bill (S 1630).

Main venues: House: Energy and Commerce Committee; Senate: Environment and Public Works Committee.

Outlook: Action as a separate bill or as a floor amendment to S 1630.

them. That leaves the domestic industry competing for congressional attention with a well-organized Washington lobby of import automakers, as well as import dealers across the nation.

According to the Federal Election Commission, the import Auto Dealers and Drivers for Free Trade (AUTOPAC), a political action committee, far outspends domestic manufacturers in Congress, contributing $3.8 million in the 1988 elections, compared with combined contributions of $1.2 million by the Big Three.

What has import automakers and dealers worried now is proposed legislation (S 1224) by Sen. Richard H. Bryan, D-Nev., to revise Corporate Average Fuel Economy (CAFE) laws, which were first mandated in the 1975 Energy Policy and Conservation Act (PL 94-163). Language to cut back on carbon dioxide emissions — which could be achieved only by increases in CAFE standards — has also been added to the Senate version of pending

omnibus legislation (S 1630) to rewrite the nation's clean-air laws. *(Clean air, p. 5)*

Bryan's CAFE bill would push all auto companies to make substantial improvements in their gas-mileage rates — by 20 percent in 1995 and by 40 percent in 2001 — over their 1988 fleetwide average. "It requires everyone to put their shoulder to the wheel to do better," he says.

Asian automakers say Bryan's legislation is unfair to companies that have made the most progress in increasing fuel economy. "Punishing people for good works just seems to be bad public policy," says Charles E. Ing, a lobbyist for Toyota Motor Sales U.S.A. Inc. "It certainly doesn't provide any incentive to better government mandates."

Foreign automakers and their U.S. dealers are ready to test their substantial lobbying muscle to make sure Bryan's plan does not go forward. Kathleen Mordini, vice president of public affairs for the American International Auto Dealers Association, which represents about 9,200 import car franchises, says U.S. dealers began visiting members of Congress in May to fight the bill.

Japanese corporate officials have also gotten involved, making an unusual appearance at congressional hearings in September to testify against the CAFE legislation. Toni Harrington, manager of industry and government relations for Honda North America, says Honda "strongly, strongly, strongly" opposes Bryan's bill.

Suzuki Motor Co. Ltd. has taken a more aggressive and politically charged stance — circulating a legal analysis prepared by Petit & Martin, a Los Angeles-based law firm, arguing that Bryan's bill would discriminate against imports and violate U.S. obligations under the General Agreement on Tariffs and Trade, the international treaty that governs nearly all world trade.

An Uneasy Alliance

But for the time being, Japanese and U.S. industry officials are largely united against new CAFE legislation, particularly as an amendment to the clean-air bill. Their strength could make it difficult to pass higher CAFE standards.

Bryan has already experienced the double-barreled attack. AUTOPAC poured money into television advertisements that came close to defeating him in his 1988 race against Republican Sen. Chic Hecht (1983-89).

The Big Three joined the fight in September by hiring FMR Group Inc., a Washington political consulting firm, to begin a grass-roots campaign in Nevada and other states against the CAFE bills.

Industry lobbyists say consumers should know of the safety and comfort problems of the smaller cars that would be built to new CAFE standards. "The effort is essentially a public information campaign to get folks to understand that there are two sides to the issue," says FMR President Les Francis.

Parrying for the auto industry in the Senate are Carl Levin, D-Mich., and Don Nickles, R-Okla. They plan to offer an amendment to strike language in the Senate's clean-air bill to place strict limits on carbon dioxide emissions, which the industry has dubbed "back-door CAFE" because the limits could be met only through severe increases in motor vehicle fuel-economy targets — about 40 mpg by 2000.

In the House, any fuel-economy initiative must face the bulwark of Energy and Commerce Chairman John D. Dingell, D-Mich., the Big Three's strongest political ally.

Dingell backs industry efforts to keep rising concern about air pollutants from translating into gas-mileage standards they call impossible to achieve.

From the industry's perspective, any standard above about 30 mpg is not possible without dramatic changes in U.S. consumers' car-buying behavior. "Sales of Festivas and Escorts would have to go up dramatically," says David Kulp, manager of fuel economy, planning and compliance at Ford's automotive emissions office.

But the auto companies' warnings are viewed with increasing skepticism on Capitol Hill. Bryan and others, including Sen. Howard M. Metzenbaum, D-Ohio, the sponsor of another CAFE bill (S 984), have reminded automakers of the industry's 1974 prediction that new gas-mileage standards would force them to produce only Pinto-sized subcompacts by 1985. "The automakers, obviously, were dead wrong," Metzenbaum says.

Bryan adds: "Their testimony now is almost a carbon copy of their testimony in 1974, the thrust of which is: It can't be done."

This draws sighs from auto indus-

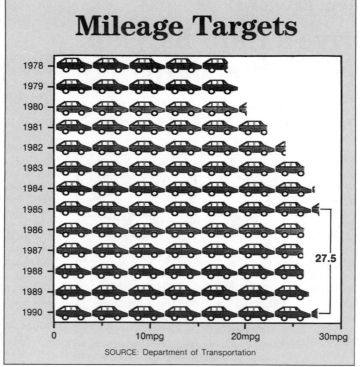

Mileage Targets

SOURCE: Department of Transportation

BARBARA SASSA-DANIELS

try officials. Kulp says, "Some things we said in the mid-1970s we would have preferred that we didn't say."

Still, industry officials say, no one predicted that the Arab oil embargo and rising fuel costs would so radically change what kind of automobiles consumers were willing to buy.

With fuel costs down, U.S. consumers are now looking for faster and more commodious cars. Current law allows automakers to petition the administration to roll back the CAFE standards when they are unable to meet them because of consumer preference or other factors. But bills pending in Congress this year would limit or abolish such discretion. That, too, indicates to Big Three officials that their arguments fall on deaf ears.

"When . . . you're trying to develop credible information and people are saying to you, 'We don't believe what you're saying' and 'We're going to take away discretion from the agencies that have oversight' — yeah, you get very worried about how you're perceived on the Hill," Kulp says.

CAFE Cooks Up Divisions

If CAFE legislation becomes inevitable, Chrysler and Ford (along with the United Auto Workers union) will part company with the Japanese and support Bryan's percentage approach. General Motors opposes any change in

CAFE standards.

Chrysler and Ford officials argue that the percentage formula in Bryan's bill is better than current law, which they say gives Asian manufacturers the competitive edge because the standards are easy to satisfy with their small-car fleets.

"The current standard is targeted to the capability of U.S. manufacturers," says Ford's Kulp. "Asians basically have no requirement."

As an alternative, import manufacturers are pushing to raise CAFE standards based on vehicle size or class. This would mean different overall fuel-economy standards for companies based on their mix of vehicle sizes — companies that made more small cars would have to meet higher standards, which would fall if the company began producing larger vehicles.

But environmentalists are working hard to keep this size-class option on the shelf. They argue that it would encourage U.S. automakers to stick with what they make best: larger, more profitable, less efficient vehicles.

For environmentalists, any incentives for larger cars would defeat the purpose of CAFE legislation — reducing carbon dioxide emissions, which some scientists say are adding to dangerous changes in the temperature of the atmosphere. It is largely concern about such global warming — as well as about rising U.S. dependence on foreign oil — that has given political impetus to the long-dormant CAFE issue.

Environmentalists are pushing hard for as high standards as possible: perhaps 45 mpg by the year 2000.

"The technology that will be required to achieve a 45-miles-per-gallon fuel economy standard is already on the shelf and is just not being put on the cars by most of the manufacturers," says the Sierra Club's Daniel Becker. "These are not exotic technologies."

Supporters of new CAFE standards say domestic automakers may have to be forced to stake a claim to a U.S. technological edge in fuel-efficient cars.

"Our industry has not been looking toward the future and investing in [research and development] for lighter materials," says Rep. Claudine Schneider, R-R.I. "As a result, once again the foreign competition has beat us." ∎

AGRICULTURE

Farmers Reap a Crop of Scorn From Anti-Chemical Forces

Environmentalists have spent a quarter-century repudiating the notion that tillers of the soil are the best stewards of the land, water and food supply. They finally have the public nodding its head — and farmers shaking theirs, bewildered by their sudden unpopularity.

No theme of farm-state politics is more prevalent as Congress begins to retool federal agriculture and nutrition programs, most of which must be renewed before the year's end.

Since World War II, U.S. farmers have led a worldwide expansion of agricultural production by steadily increasing their use of synthetic pesticides and fertilizers. Until recently, the environmental sacrifice was mostly ignored or poorly understood. Now it is becoming clear that farming causes long-term water and soil pollution. From 2.7 billion tons to 3.1 billion tons of soil erodes from U.S. cropland each year.

Even so, when the farm bill is completed, those decrying farming's ill effects on the environment may find themselves all but ignored and their powerful critique mostly discarded.

The simple truth is that the traditional partnership between farmers and the members of Congress who represent them still constitutes one of the most formidable picket lines against the environmental movement.

"Nobody gets on the Agriculture committees because they want to be seen as a strong environmentalist," says a top-level Senate aide.

That fact, in the end, will probably scotch tough new controls on farming practices that may be polluting the water and denuding the soil. Indeed, some weakening of current prohibitions — on the draining of wetlands, for example — is a good possibility.

The Bush administration hopes to streamline procedures to remove dangerous pesticides from the market. But it proposes to do so only in return for looser standards on assessing the health risks of the chemicals. That issue may be resolved in the farm bill.

Why, then, are environmentalists, farmers and policy makers insisting

By David S. Cloud

CHECKLIST

Issue: Soil and water conservation; pesticides control.

Legislation: Farm bill reauthorization.

Need for action: Current farm law expires in 1990.

Main venues: House: Agriculture Committee; Senate: Agriculture Committee.

Outlook: House and Senate committee action imminent.

that this will be the long-awaited "environmental farm bill"? It is partly because, 28 years after Rachel Carson's lyrical book "Silent Spring" hatched the environmental indictment of modern farming, there is now widespread agreement on two counts: First, U.S. agriculture is among the worst abusers of the environment, and second, federal farm programs encourage the abuse.

That is a powerful development — all the more so because the Farm Belt, wrung by depression in the mid-1980s, is relatively tranquil now. Once, the Agriculture committees could simply ignore the environmental crowd when they wrote the farm bill. Not anymore.

No longer is there a farm crisis to deflect attention from the environment. Unlike the last time Congress wrote an omnibus farm bill (PL 99-198), in 1985, commodity prices are mostly healthy, and government-controlled surplus stocks are low. After several years of record expenditures for agriculture, farm income hit a record $57 billion in 1988.

Even the budget is no longer the

driving policy force it was. Most agricultural concerns recognize that government support will probably keep falling.

Chemical Use Decried

Even as the age-old "farm question" has waned, public concern about agricultural chemical use is shriller than ever. And the environmentalists, after a smattering of success in the 1985 farm bill, will no longer sit by while farm-state lawmakers craft policies that encourage soil erosion, heavy use of chemicals and planting on fragile land.

To be sure, there is plenty of gamesmanship at work. The threat of an environmental clampdown provides many of the players with a useful weapon.

For example, Agriculture Secretary Clayton Yeutter proudly calls himself an environmentalist. He often borrows the movement's rhetoric, as when he calls for the next farm bill to enshrine an agricultural system that is "environmentally sustainable."

But Yeutter really means something entirely different. His instincts, like those of many in agriculture, are old-fashioned: Conservation is a tool to help farmers expand production. In Yeutter's vision, the farm economy will remain robust by working off the surplus abroad, in widening export markets.

To environmentalists, this is misguided policy — production for its own sake or for the dubious goal of carving out small, undependable markets abroad, without regard for the environmental consequences.

Like most farmers, Yeutter does not want new environmental controls to turn U.S. agriculture inward, gumming up production and threatening its dominance of world agricultural trade. Unlike most farmers, however, Yeutter wants to see farm programs gradually dismantled and U.S. producers turned loose in a liberalized world market.

And the environment clearly gives Yeutter a wedge to drive into the farm bill debate over reducing the expense of government farm programs. The problem is not that farmers are predisposed to pollute, Yeutter argues. It is that government support programs give them incentives to pollute.

Are 'Sodbusters' Failing?

Federal farm programs would never be the same. Or so environmentalists thought after Congress in 1985 passed an omnibus farm bill putting the first conservation controls on farmers' crop practices.

Under the most revolutionary provision of the bill, environmentalists secured the first hard promise that farmers who did not comply with the new guidelines on soil and wetlands erosion would lose their cherished government subsidies.

A new "sodbuster" law required farmers to adopt government-approved soil conservation plans on erodible land. A companion "swampbuster" placed similar restrictions on farmers' use of wetlands. And a new "conservation reserve" offered payments to farmers to remove a total of 45 million acres of highly erodible land from production for 10-year stretches. Farmers also had to adopt conservation plans for their remaining cropland or risk losing government benefits.

Conservation and farm groups hailed the provisions as landmark advances in responsible farm policy. No small factor in the Farm Belt's support was the almost desperate need for the surplus-laden Agriculture Department to cut back on U.S. grain production.

But as ambitious as these programs sounded, they have not worked out as environmentalists had hoped. The failure suggests that, even if they are able to build on their 1985 legislative successes, environmental advocates face even stiffer resistance among farmers in the agricultural establishment.

According to the National Wildlife Federation, only 26 producers nationwide have been denied farm program benefits since swampbuster was enacted. During that time, more than 1 million acres of wetlands have been drained, mostly because of agricultural production, according to the Environmental Protection Agency.

Slightly more than 30 million acres of cropland have been idled, far short of the 45 million goal Congress set

DEPARTMENT OF AGRICULTURE

for the Conservation Reserve Program (CRP). The reduction in soil erosion will indeed be substantial — roughly 574 million tons a year — and lower amounts of harmful farm chemicals will wash into streams and rivers.

But much of the land being idled is not the fragile land that Congress intended to put into the CRP. In fact, according to the General Accounting Office, only about 30 percent of the most highly erodible land is now in the program, largely because the Agriculture Department relaxed eligibility standards to boost yearly enrollment. Instead of conserving delicate soil, many farmers are putting their unproductive property into the conservation reserve.

Then there is the requirement that, by 1995, farmers participating in federal support programs manage their erodible fields in accordance with an approved soil conservation plan. In setting the standards for sodbuster plans, the department has substantially loosened the tolerable erosion rates.

Environmentalists are increasingly critical of the programs. "These provisions have real teeth. They would do a lot. They just have not been enforced effectively in many cases," says Justin Ward, an agricultural policy analyst with the Natural Resources Defense Council.

But one of those who crafted these programs defends the Agriculture Department's conservation efforts. "On balance, they're doing a good job," said Peter C. Myers, who was head of the Soil Conservation Service when the 1985 law was drafted and who later served as deputy secretary of agriculture. "We have not gone as far as some people would like. But it's a balancing of interests."

Myers contends that lowering the erosion rates in the conservation plans was "a reasonable compromise," adding that the plans have brought conservation "much further than it would have been."

—David S. Cloud

As Yeutter told the American Farm Bureau convention Jan. 8, "I suspect there's not a farmer in this room who would not reduce his level of agricultural chemicals . . . if he could do so."

Thus Yeutter's answer is not for Congress to remove pesticides from the market or to withhold payments unless farmers comply with strict conservation standards. His answer is to reform the farm program, preferably by removing some of the artificial incentives — such as inducements for growing the same

crops year after year — that prompt farmers to produce as much as possible.

In the process, Yeutter hopes to reduce the massive potential outlays inherent in farm programs. Inject market discipline into farming, the theory goes, and fertilizer and pesticide use would drop, leading to clean water. Erosion would drop, too, as farmers aimed for greater efficiency.

Many environmentalists agree with Yeutter's critique of the farm program, but not with his proposed cure. Even

farm-state lawmakers and many trade associations that represent farmers are willing to concede that farm programs do not reward — and even retard — sound environmental practices.

The National Research Council (NRC), an arm of the National Academy of Sciences, recently concluded that "federal programs often tolerate and sometimes encourage unrealistically high yield goals, inefficient fertilizer and pesticide use, and unsustainable use of land and water."

Some of the worst offenders are in the Corn Belt. Once farmers provided most of the nitrogen their crops needed by rotating corn and small grains with leguminous crops, such as soybeans.

Since the end of World War II, dramatic increases in chemical use have enabled farmers to produce such major crops as corn or wheat continuously, thus decreasing their dependence on animal manure and natural nitrogen sources and greatly lowering their production costs. Between 450 million and 500 million pounds of pesticides, mostly herbicides, are applied to row crops every year, according to the NRC.

Many farmers have begun growing corn continuously or in short rotation with soybeans. Corn farmers apply 44 percent of fertilizers, 55 percent of herbicides and 44 percent of insecticides used on field crops. These chemicals have fueled the biggest production increases ever. (Chart, this page)

The environmental cost has been largely ignored, until lately. Agriculture is generally considered the largest contributor among industries to groundwater pollution. Seventy percent of the nutrients and 33 percent of the sediment reaching waterways comes from farmland. In California alone, 22 pesticides have been found in the groundwater because of farming, the NRC says. Major aquifers in California and the Great Plains have been depleted.

Sediment, fertilizers and pesticides are carried into the water supply, polluting wells and aquifers, killing animals and plants and contaminating estuaries. Wildlife habitat and wetlands are often injudiciously converted to cropland. And fragile ecosystems are disrupted by intensive cultivation.

Dismantling the farm program is not a particularly popular answer to these problems — from the point of view of farmers or environmentalists. Farmers do not want to lose the federal government as an automatic market for their surpluses. And environmentalists do not want to lose the leverage that federal farm programs give them over production practices.

Yeutter's suggestions sound much like the free-market approach to agricultural reform that the Reagan administration tried. When "decoupling" surfaced then, it was not billed as an environmental panacea. Instead, it was simply a conservative administration's pragmatic plan to dismantle federal farm programs. And it fell flat.

Yeutter's proposals to reform farm programs are expected to be much more modest this year. His quixotic effort to

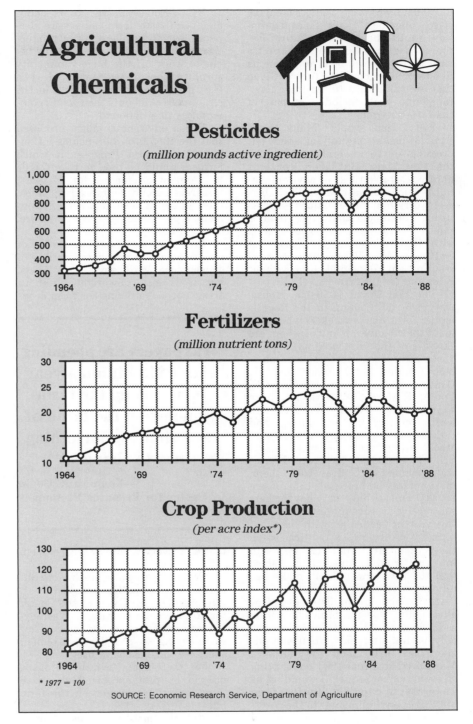

Agricultural Chemicals

Pesticides
(million pounds active ingredient)

Fertilizers
(million nutrient tons)

Crop Production
(per acre index*)

* 1977 = 100

SOURCE: Economic Research Service, Department of Agriculture

negotiate away what he calls trade-distorting subsidies at international trade talks has been all but squelched, hampered by a visceral reluctance on the part of U.S. competitors — particularly the European Community (EC) — to end subsidies. What the EC fears most is the U.S. farmers' vast production capacity, spurred by the government's munificent farm program.

To unlock the negotiations over a new General Agreement on Tariffs and Trade (GATT), the Bush administration needs a way to show that it has the clout to scale back U.S. farm subsidies if the EC and others will do the same. Many U.S. observers think that is too tall an order, mainly because of the entrenched support the existing farm program has in Congress.

"That's why what Yeutter is saying is so ridiculous," says Janet Hathaway, an attorney for the Natural Resources Defense Council. "It's pretty clear that there will be farm payments tied to production in the future. Given that, we would like to see more environmental goals included as part of the farm program."

Few others would. Many farm-state lawmakers are talking about addressing "environmental concerns" for the first time. But their concerns hardly resemble those of environmentalists such as Hathaway. Their biggest worry is public relations — reassuring consumers that their food is safe. Their toughest task is not dealing with the environmental lobby, but crafting a farm bill that projects a reassuring environmental aura without going too far for farmers.

The real threat is in the House. Any farm bill coming to the floor is fodder for urban lawmakers who dominate the chamber, many of whom are skeptics of the farm program.

In past years, Northeastern members Charles E. Schumer, D-N.Y., Barney Frank, D-Mass., and Silvio O. Conte, R-Mass., in particular, have waged war on federal farm subsidies with a mixture of moral outrage and ridicule. Though generally unable to crack agriculture's political armor, Schumer and Conte have forced farm-state members to deal with them, most notably on proposals to impose a $50,000 annual limit on what farmers can receive in subsidy payments. But this year in particular, with the environment cresting as a political issue, the Agriculture Committee may run into real trouble, unless it can show that the new farm bill will make significant environmental strides.

Still, environmentalists are not at all sanguine that the farm bill will be as tough as they hoped. Optimism was only natural after 1985, when environmentalists made their first inroads. Many predicted that 1990 would bring an even tougher sequel. It would be, as a lobbyist put it in 1988, "the first farm bill that is environmental to the core."

Now that prediction seems wildly optimistic. Few of the conditions that provided environmentalists with their initial successes in 1985 still prevail.

Five years ago, there was one major issue on Congress' agenda: soil erosion. And there was fairly broad agreement that not only would the environment benefit if millions of acres of highly erodible soil were taken from production, but farmers would profit too.

The farm crisis was at its nadir, and farm-state lawmakers were desperate to get farmland out of production. Only then could the economy begin to work off the huge commodity surpluses that had accumulated when U.S. export markets collapsed in the early 1980s. And only then would commodity prices rebound.

When environmentalists proposed that the 1985 farm bill include a Conservation Reserve Program, in which farmers would be paid to take fragile land out of production for 10 years, Congress quickly embraced the idea, then threw in several other environmental provisions for good measure. (Box, p. 32)

Five years later, agriculture is not only reluctant to renew its marriage of convenience with environmentalists, but it is also downright stubborn about not jeopardizing the farm econ-

---

"Taxpayers are spending about $13 billion a year just to keep the farm economy on the brink of recession.... Something has to change."

—Kenneth A. Cook, Center for Resource Economics

---

omy's recovery with new environmental controls.

"We're looking at a much more difficult task," says Kenneth A. Cook, vice president for policy at the Center for Resource Economics, a Washington environmental think tank. "Now we're trying to change management practices, not just land use."

For their part, environmentalists, buoyed by past success, have much more ambitious designs on the farm bill.

Still, the goals are vaguer than in 1985. Environmentalists have a theme, making the farm program more environmentally sound, but they do not have a program. An idea gaining support is to give farmers incentives to move to what was once called organic or alternative farming and is now called low-input sustainable agriculture.

The basic proposition is that farmers who reduce or eliminate their use

of agricultural chemicals while conserving natural resources can compete economically with those who ignore the environmental effects of their farming. Of course, that proposition has not been widely tested, and some experts think the potential of alternative agriculture is overstated.

The NRC recently concluded that "farmers who adopt alternative farming systems often have productive and profitable operations, even though these farms usually function with relatively little help from commodity income and price-support programs."

Of course, farmers are not averse to new programs that pay them to be environmentally conscientious. And voluntary alternative agriculture programs — such as that proposed in a Senate bill (S 970), sponsored by Georgia Democrat Wyche Fowler Jr., to promote crop rotation and reduced use of agricultural chemicals — appear certain to become part of the farm bill in one form or another.

Agriculture leaders, particularly in the Senate, which is more protective of farm-state interests than the House, recognize the political currents. They seem eager to head off mandatory environmental controls by passing voluntary legislation before something more drastic is forced upon them.

But, for wheat farmers, even voluntary forms of alternative agriculture hold little promise. They generally plant in arid regions of the Great Plains, which can support few of the suggested alternative crops, such as soybeans. "From our point of view, alternative agriculture is not the solution to environmental problems," said Margie Williams, a spokeswoman for the National Association of Wheat Growers.

In a sense, the debate about alternative agriculture is academic. Any changes in agricultural chemical use will occur gradually.

However, it seems increasingly probable that the 1990 farm bill will try to break down some of the policy barriers to protecting the environment.

The most basic of these barriers is what is known to farmers as their "base acreage," the portion of a farmer's land eligible for program payments.

Base acreage is calculated as a five-year rolling average of the acreage enrolled in a particular crop-subsidy program. It is supposed to ensure that farmers will not be unfairly penalized for abnormally low-producing seasons, nor unfairly aggrandized in boom years. But because federal income payments are collected against the base acreage, the program has effectively forced corn farmers to keep planting corn, wheat farmers planting wheat and so on, to assure those farmers (and their bankers) of a predictable income at harvest.

So any practice, such as crop rotation, that would reduce the acreage planted in a particular program crop would probably reduce a farmer's base acreage — and thus his support check.

Corn farmers recently demonstrated the problem. Despite a domestic shortage of soybeans and a high price for the taking, many corn farmers in 1989 declined to plant significant soybean acreage, even though it is an excellent natural source of nitrogen. Instead, they stuck with corn to "protect their base" — and their support checks.

Many farmers of major crops want the new farm bill to inject flexibility into the farm program. They want to be able to shift their cropping patterns without losing their payment base.

Farm groups are trying to sell "flexibility" as environmental reform, but the environmentalists are not buying. Crop diversification alone will not solve the agricultural chemical problem, the environmentalists say. To them, flexibility seems like just another way for agriculture to get a better price for its goods, while avoiding basic environmental controls.

Even if environmentalists succeed in overhauling food safety laws governing what pesticides may be sold, it will not solve the groundwater pollution problem, they maintain. To do that, Congress must set tolerance levels that actually restrict the amount of chemicals that can be used.

However, splits within the environmental community about how to proceed may dilute its ability to press its agenda during farm-bill debate. Some environmental groups are implacable in their opposition to existing farm programs and favor complex schemes to impose tougher environmental requirements on farmers who want to receive income-support payments.

But there are other groups, such as the Center for Resource Economics, who see part of their job as protecting agriculture, and they view such anti-farm program schemes as politically unrealistic. What is needed, they argue, is a combination of carrots and sticks, which would primarily pay farmers who reduce their chemical use

The Not So Silent Whitten

In 1962, when Rachel Carson's best-selling book "Silent Spring" gave an early, forceful voice to environmental concerns about pesticide use, Rep. Jamie L. Whitten was there with modern agriculture's rebuttal.

Mississippi's New Deal Democrat wrote his own book, this one defending the benefits of pesticides, and titled it "That We May Live." "Both sides of the story must be told," he wrote.

That We May Live

Here are the facts about the effects of pesticides on our national health—their use, dangers, and contribution to our welfare—based on a scientific report made in behalf of Congress.

No one personifies better than Whitten the reason the environmental movement has had such difficulty pressing its agenda for restructuring agriculture. He has been in Congress nearly half a century. He has been chairman of the Appropriations Subcommittee on Agriculture since 1948 — chairman of the full committee since 1978 — and always an implacable fixture in the environmental debate.

In 1971, when a power shuffle gave Whitten jurisdiction over the Environmental Protection Agency (EPA) and the Food and Drug Administration, he did not mince his words. He called environmentalists a "small, vocal group of extremists" and said "those people at EPA have been given more money than they can possibly use."

Whitten was soon stripped of his power over environmental and consumer agencies, but his views have not noticeably changed.

In 1989, when environmentalists were arguing in favor of a program that helps farmers reduce their use of chemicals without diminishing crop yields, the redoubtable Whitten was still around to debunk the idea.

He blocked a $1.1 million appropriation for the Agriculture Department to continue the project. "I wrote a book about it," Whitten told reporters.

Whitten views it as his special mission to defend New Deal-era agriculture programs from the budget ax and from environmentalists. Like many in agriculture, he thinks the nation's physical resources ought to be exploited for the nation's benefit, not just preserved for the future.

Irrigation projects, soil conservation, rural electrification, agricultural chemicals and crop subsidies are farmers' tools to expand their production. And over the years, Whitten has insisted on billions of dollars for such aid.

Environmentalists insist the money would be better spent teaching farmers how to be careful stewards of the land. But Whitten's views were shaped by the ravages of the Depression. He thinks the environmentalists' call for reducing chemical use and taking farmland out of production is a prescription for food shortages, pestilence and economic disaster.

And it is a measure of Whitten's success how little the debate has changed. "The overwhelming number of Americans living in the towns and cities . . . must become aware of the fact that they are heavily dependent on the latest and best chemical pesticides," he said in 1966.

He is still saying it.

—David S. Cloud

and better protect their land.

The problem is that there is not a lot of spare money in the agriculture budget to underwrite that approach.

"Now, at the end of the 1980s, taxpayers are spending about $13 billion a year just to keep the farm economy on the brink of recession, and the environment is suffering," said Cook

of the Center for Resource Economics. "Something has to change."

Environmentalists are fond of saying the chemical era of U.S. agriculture is drawing to a close. And it may be. But if farmers and their representatives continue to get their way in Congress, the 1990 farm bill will not be the reason. ∎

TIMBER

In Battle Over Forest Land, Ecologists Gaining Ground

When Georgia Democrat Wyche Fowler Jr. stood up on the Senate floor last summer and announced that timber interests had "gone from the position of strength to a position of weakness," it seemed like a manifesto for a revolution.

After all, here was an energetic senator, the chairman of a subcommittee with jurisdiction over forestry, saying the timber industry could no longer take for granted its access to timber on public lands.

"Time is running out on this waste of the taxpayers' money," he said, adding that national forests "are not private tree farms for the few."

Reality did not square with Fowler's bravado, however.

The first-term senator had just gone after one of the timber industry's cherished federal subsidies — the forest road-building program that unlocks public lands for tree harvesting. But he had been rolled like a log. Not only had the industry's defenders in Congress restored the $65 million that Fowler tried to cut from the Senate's $205 million appropriation for road-building, they made available another $56 million at the last moment.

It was an impressive display of political muscle for an industry supposedly declining into a "position of weakness." It was also a reminder of how inconsistent federal timber policy has become. Congress has yet to resolve the underlying conflict between environmentalists, who want forests better protected for their ecological value, and logging companies and local communities (mainly in the Northwest), which depend on a steady supply of wood.

For years, Congress has ignored this contradiction. Its approach has been simple: Pump millions of dollars a year into timber-cutting on one hand; protect millions more acres of wilderness on the other. And let the courts and the U.S. Forest Service resolve — or, at the very least, mull over — most of the recurring disputes between the two.

Suddenly, though, timber is a cutting issue again, and Congress' strategy may no longer work.

By David S. Cloud

CHECKLIST

Issue: Logging in national forests.

Legislation: Interior appropriations, Tongass Forest preservation (S 346).

Need for action: Current law expires in fiscal 1991.

Main venues: House: Agriculture, Interior, Appropriations Subcommittee on Interior; Senate: Agriculture, Energy and Natural Resources, Appropriations.

Outlook: Possible Senate action on S 346.

A rare breed of bird called the spotted owl, threatened by old-growth timber-cutting in the Pacific Northwest, received temporary protection from Congress last year. Meanwhile, new restrictions on logging in Alaska's Tongass National Forest, one of the world's last temperate rain forests, have passed the House and have a real chance in the Senate this year.

Not since the mid-1970s has the environmental critique of logging carried more cachet. "There's been a resurgence of concern from members across the country," said Jim Blomquist, a timber policy analyst with the Sierra Club.

Yet the flowering of the timber debate is not due only to environmental consciousness. Congress is also besieged by the logging industry, which is frustrated at being blocked from thousands of acres of public land by court-ordered injunctions against tim-ber sales. It wants legislative relief to break the logjam.

Cheap Timber

Only 13 percent of the U.S. timber cut each year comes from national forests, and only 56 million acres of the 191 million-acre National Forest System is economically suitable for logging. The real battle is over an even smaller area: those potential timber regions that are still road-free — and thus could either be opened for logging or be preserved as wilderness. Most of this coveted timberland is in mature forests of the Oregon and Washington Cascades and in the central and northern Rockies.

The Forest Service is positively Roman about road-building. There are nearly 360,000 miles of roads winding through the national forests, a network eight times as long as the interstate highway system. And the Forest Service is planning to cut 700 to 900 miles more every year for the remainder of the century.

After paving the way to the virgin timber, the Forest Service frequently sells logs at rock-bottom prices, sometimes so low that the government does not recover its own costs.

According to Randal O'Toole, author of "Reforming the Forest Service," the agency received $85 for every thousand board feet of lumber cut in 1985. However, the Forest Service spent close to $89 per thousand board feet preparing and administering sales, building timber access roads, and reforesting and managing new stands of timber, he concluded.

Many of these "below-cost" sales are made on timber cut in Alaska, the Rockies and the Northeast. Profitable sales in the Pacific Northwest enable the Forest Service to claim that the timber program as a whole turns a profit. However, environmental groups such as The Wilderness Society contend that even that claim is misleading because continued logging does uncounted damage to fragile ecosystems.

"It is the agency's overwhelming emphasis on cutting trees in the national forests, and building roads to get to them, that is the cause for the severe permanent damage," said Brock Evans, vice president of the National Audubon Society.

Conflicting Priorities

The Forest Service concedes that some of its priorities are out of step with those of the public and claims to be trying to improve.

As Forest Service Associate Chief George M. Leonard told the House Agriculture Committee, "The American people have spoken out, and the message is loud and clear — fish, wildlife, wilderness, recreation . . . are important." He promised that the agency would lessen its emphasis on timber-cutting.

It may not be that easy, thanks to Congress. The Forest Service has a built-in incentive to cut a lot of trees because timber sales generate about $1.5 billion in receipts every year, and about $300 million of that gets pumped back directly into the agency's $2 billion-plus budget.

Congress designed the system in the early 1950s, when the housing boom was fueling a rising demand for timber.

Over the years, logging in national forests has supplied jobs for many of the surrounding communities. And county governments have come to rely on their 25 percent cut of the gross federal timber receipts. It has been a bountiful harvest for all.

O'Toole concludes, "Unlike a private company, whose job it is to keep stockholders happy by producing profits, the Forest Service must keep Congress happy by creating jobs and income for local constituents."

Like the national forests themselves, the timber sales program has proven both enduring and fragile. It has survived largely intact for decades, yet it has bred a debilitating dependence in areas where log supply has shrunk. And the scars left behind — notably from "clear-cutting" large tracts of forest land — have helped energize the environmental opposition.

Neglected Congressional Mandate

How has Congress responded to the problem?

Controversy over national forest management has surfaced repeatedly in the past 30 years, and Congress has repeatedly passed legislation encouraging the Forest Service to stop thinking of itself as a custodian for the timber industry. The agency is required to balance timber production and what the Forest Service calls "non-commodity values" — things such as protecting wildlife and wilderness and promoting recreational use of the national forests.

Even so, environmental organiza-

DEPARTMENT OF AGRICULTURE
Congress has mandated that timber cut from national forests be replaced, so that the overall supply is not depleted.

tions often accuse the Forest Service of neglecting its broader mandate. To a large extent, the agency is only following orders. Annual appropriations bills over the past 30 years have frequently called for increasing timber-sale levels on national forests. The timber-sale level in recent years has remained steady at about 11 billion board feet annually.

According to environmental organizations, that level is too high. Congress has mandated that the amount of timber cut from national forests should be "sustainable" — in other words, replaced so the overall supply is not depleted over time. But the Audubon Society and other organizations maintain that, in setting timber-sale levels every year, Congress is ignoring its own requirement.

"A way must be found to make certain that allowable sales-quantity levels are truly set on the basis of what the land can sustain, not what the political demands of the industry might happen to be in any one year," said Evans.

Of course, the industry sees it differently. It points out that a large amount — more than 33.2 million acres — of wilderness has been newly protected in recent years, while 32.4 million acres of national forest land has been opened for economic development, including logging.

In some areas, particularly in the Northwest, access to timberland is being blocked by court-ordered injunctions as a result of lawsuits filed by environmental organizations. Moreover, some industry officials maintain that the Forest Service's ongoing forest-planning process is proceeding too slowly — and emphasizing environmental protection too strongly.

"Forest Service planners . . . have essentially 'zoned' the national forests," Bruce Beckett, regional manager of the Northwest Forestry Association, said at a House Agriculture Committee hearing last year. "They have created areas where timber production is either prohibited entirely or severely limited in its intensity."

Federal timber policy is becoming so controversial that Congress is finding itself drawn into the fray. Yet there is little prospect for a fundamental change of course.

Partly that is because timber policy making is fractured. The Appropriations subcommittees on Interior control the service's purse strings. The Agriculture committees chart its policies, and the House Interior and Senate Energy committees oversee use of public lands.

Environmental and industry camps agree on little regarding the reform of Forest Service practices, and each has enough political power to block the other's agenda.

So Congress will likely end up tinkering with it or crafting temporary fixes. Its reaction to the timber dispute in Oregon and Washington is a good example of its likely course in the future. There, environmental organizations are demanding preservation of large areas of old-growth forests, in part because logging those areas may account for declines in populations of the spotted owl.

Forest Service plans call for a significant decrease in Northwest timber sales over the next four decades. Many mills in the region are already strapped for logs. Further logging limits would greatly harm the industry, industry officials argue.

All Congress did last year was broker a temporary settlement that gave both sides a little of what they wanted. In return for lifting existing injunctions and promising not to wage broad court challenges to old-growth timber sales in the future, environmentalists won a reduction in the level of timber sales in 1989 and 1990.

As a model for reforming federal timber policy, the deal does not go far. It does suggest that the days when the timber industry could override the environmental agenda are over. Conversely, pronouncements from Sen. Fowler that the industry is destined for political impotence still seem like wishful thinking. ∎

SOLID WASTE

Congress May Have To Intervene As Garbage Wars Intensify

States, industry looking for Hill's help with waste disposal as 'not in my back yard' protests gather steam

When waste-management companies proposed building seven regional landfills in Alabama, local residents told the garbage industry to take its trash and dump it.

"You are leaving Zip City" was no longer a polite road-sign salute when one small farming community in northwest Alabama found out it was slated for up to 1,500 tons of garbage a day — the bulk of it, town residents believed, to be shipped in from Mississippi and Tennessee.

It was also no idle threat from the likes of Bo Hunter, a Zip City homemaker. She helped organize a five-county coalition to take on the multinational Waste Management Inc. — and Alabama's business community — to oppose the landfill plan.

"Our state was under siege," she says.

In much the same way, grass-roots groups across the country are standing in the way of new dump and incinerator plans. Local officials and the waste-disposal industry are being stymied by a well-known and still powerful phenomenon in environmental politics: the NIMBY, or "not in my back yard," syndrome.

Hunter's group, for instance, pushed a bill through the Alabama Legislature last year imposing a two-year moratorium on regional landfills. Other states are following suit. Suddenly, waste managers' grand plans for regional solutions to the nation's garbage problem are grinding to a halt.

Corporate officials are as perplexed as they are frustrated. State moratoriums are "going to mean difficult times some years hence," says James T. Banks, director of government affairs for Waste Management. "The pressure to site new landfills will be enormous and politically difficult — much more so than today."

Facing a garbage capacity crisis, waste-disposal and transport compa-

By Alyson Pytte

R. MICHAEL JENKINS

CHECKLIST

Issue: Solid- and hazardous-waste disposal.

Legislation: Resource Conservation and Recovery Act (RCRA) reauthorization.

Need for action: Previous RCRA law expired in 1988.

Main venues: House: Energy and Commerce Committee; Senate: Environment and Public Works Committee.

Outlook: House committee action in February; Senate committee action after conference action begins on clean-air bill.

nies are coming to Congress in search of a federal solution.

Local officials, too, want help with the problem of mounting garbage. But some of them are worried that environmentalists and landfill-shy constituents will lead Congress to take a broad brush to issues that cities and counties have traditionally handled. "There is something upside down about the lowest level of government having to respond to the highest level of government that has no experience" in garbage issues, says Carol Kocheisen, legislative counsel for the National League of Cities.

Yet as landfill space declines and dumping costs soar, waste is becoming much less a local problem. Garbage is increasingly being shipped across state lines, confronting public resistance and a patchwork of state disposal regulations.

And because localities have difficulty finding sites for new dumps, garbage is ending up in old landfills that leak poisons into the groundwater and threaten to add to the nation's tally of "superfund" sites — dumps that pose the greatest threat to public health and are the most costly to clean up.

RCRA Reauthorization

In Congress, municipal solid-waste disposal tops the list of issues to be dealt with as part of a major reauthorization of the 1976 Resource Conservation and Recovery Act (RCRA). That law was initially passed to encourage the recovery and safe disposal of waste, including common trash, but over the past decade virtually all federal efforts have been focused on hazardous-waste dumps.

"Up until a few years ago we thought that if we buried things we could forget about them," says Thomas A. Luken, D-Ohio, chairman of the House Energy and Commerce Subcommittee on Transportation and Hazardous Materials. "But there's just as much volume of toxics and industrial poisons in garbage that is going into the environment through the ground and drinking water as into the air."

Authorization for RCRA expired in 1988, and the program was funded last year without a reauthorization bill.

The House is set to begin markup of RCRA legislation in early February. Senate sponsors say serious work on revamping the solid-waste portions of the law will begin as soon as a conference on clean-air legislation is under way.

However, Senate sources acknowledge that snags in the clean-air bill could delay a Senate RCRA bill until

1991. (*Story, p. 5*)

If that happens, separate legislation is possible on a number of RCRA-related issues, including a House-passed bill (HR 1056) to give the Environmental Protection Agency (EPA) and the states clearer authority to enforce hazardous-waste laws at federal sites. Some of the most dangerous waste dumps are located in facilities run by the Departments of Energy and Defense. (*Story, p. 43*)

But Luken, author of the House RCRA bill (HR 3735), says he wants to keep the umbrella legislation intact and force the Senate to move quickly, regardless of progress on the clean-air bill.

Congressional inaction will leave the states in a quandary, Luken says. "They're not getting any help," he says. "If they go to the EPA they might get a brochure dated 1976. They don't have any guidelines and they certainly don't have any standards."

Focus on Solid Waste

The bulk of the reauthorization legislation drafted so far deals with solid-waste source reduction and recycling — that is, with cutting the volume of items piling up in landfills, and with reducing their toxicity.

The idea behind many of these bills is not just to protect the environment, but to counteract the NIMBY phenomenon by improving public confidence in landfill safety.

Although the public is concerned about far more than city garbage — waste from industry, mining and nuclear bomb production is also at issue — it has become an explosive political issue because of the difficulty of finding new dump sites.

Most industrial waste, by contrast, is disposed of where it is generated, which means that public opposition is dulled by the appeal of new jobs and the other benefits of industry.

The task of easing public concern will be formidable. Even if new, state-of-the-art landfills and incinerators are built, older dumps promise to continue leaking hazards for at least another decade. "The expression of concern at the local level will be felt in Washington," warns Jacqueline Warren, senior counsel for the Natural Resources Defense Council (NRDC).

The NRDC and other major environmental organizations are pushing for a federal role in recycling and reduction of waste. But in the meantime, they want safer landfills and incinerators to keep garbage from being dumped in older, more hazardous pits that con-

TERESA ZABALA

"Up until a few years ago we thought that if we buried things we could forget about them."
—Rep. Thomas A. Luken, D-Ohio

taminate the nation's drinking water.

Local Residents Resist

Although some environmentalists call for new facilities, guerrilla garbage warfare from Zip City and other towns is sending Congress a different message.

The Citizens Clearinghouse for Hazardous Wastes, which is affiliated with about 6,300 community groups that have sprung up around proposed dump sites, steadfastly opposes new landfills and garbage incinerators.

The strategy is to prevent waste facilities from being built, thereby forcing cutbacks in the amount of waste that is generated and dumped, says Clay Carter, the Southern regional organizer for the clearinghouse.

"Why should people investigate ways to reduce waste if they already have an accessible source of disposal?" Carter says.

Indeed, the states that face the greatest landfill shortages — such as New Jersey and Massachusetts — are in the vanguard of recycling and other waste-reduction efforts.

But the issue has caused a rift in the environmental community. Some major groups say efforts to block new

sites at the local level are understandable but unworkable. The fundamental problem, says A. Blakeman Early, Washington representative of the Sierra Club, is that waste is still being dumped despite states' inability to build safer facilities.

"What I believe happens to the waste is, it goes somewhere worse," Early says. Without new sites, he adds, local officials and the EPA must find ways to extend the life of facilities built before current regulations were in place.

RCRA bills in Congress focus on encouraging states to come up with a mix of solutions that ultimately would rely on landfills and incinerators. "There are some utopians out there who think we can handle all waste through source reduction and recycling," says John G. Arlington, senior counsel for Luken's Subcommittee on Hazardous Materials. "State and local officials who have to deal with the real problems think that's pie in the sky."

Landfill Crisis

As more and more residents take their cases to city councils and state legislatures, local officials are facing real-world shortages of waste capacity.

The number of landfills in operation has dropped from about 20,000 in 1979 to about 6,000 today, and the congressional Office of Technology Assessment says eight states — Connecticut, Kentucky, Massachusetts, New Jersey, Ohio, Pennsylvania, Virginia and West Virginia — have fewer than five years of remaining capacity.

Opposition to new sites stems from a growing public record of contamination by city dumps. As national attention has focused on superfund cleanups of military and industrial hazards, the municipal garbage problem has festered.

EPA first began issuing regulations in 1979 to improve the safety of new city landfills and to ban open dumps. But the agency estimates that 70 percent of existing municipal landfills began operation before 1980. Many were not lined to protect drinking water from the dangers of items in common trash, such as lead-acid batteries, household cleaners, used motor oil and pesticides.

And although Congress banned industrial hazardous waste from city dumps 10 years ago, industrial poisons continue to find their way into landfills through loopholes in RCRA regulation. Nationwide, about 22 percent of municipal dump sites have made the superfund "national priority list,"

RCRA Bills

Legislation is pending in both the House and the Senate to reauthorize the Resource Conservation and Recovery Act (PL 94-580), the 1976 law governing solid and hazardous waste, which expired in 1988. Efforts in past years have focused on a "cradle to grave" monitoring system for hazardous waste. New legislation primarily deals with solid waste.

The House bills (HR 3735, HR 3736, HR 3737), introduced by Thomas A. Luken, D-Ohio, and the Senate bill (S 1113), introduced by Max Baucus, D-Mont.,

would set minimum federal standards and state permit requirements for solid waste and require the Environmental Protection Agency (EPA) to issue new regulations for municipal solid-waste landfills and incinerators.

Another Senate bill (S 1112), by John H. Chafee, R-R.I., would largely complement Baucus' bill by expanding waste reduction and recycling activities.

Here are examples of the scope of the House and Senate bills and their key differences. The bills would:

HOUSE

HR 3735
- Require the EPA to issue guidelines within nine months for state waste-management plans, consistent with the RCRA's waste reduction and recycling goals.
- Require state plans, including 20-year plans for waste capacity, to be submitted within two years and be approved or disapproved by the EPA within one year. States must recycle 25 percent of solid waste generated four years after the plan's approval.
- Give the EPA authority to develop a plan for the state if one is not submitted within three years. States also would face the loss of federal financial assistance for waste management.
- Allow states with approved plans and certifications of compliance to prohibit transportation of solid waste from out of state and to levy higher fees on out-of-state waste.
- Prohibit the export of waste without an approved plan for disposal.

HR 3736
- Prohibit export of hazardous waste to any country that has not signed a bilateral agreement with the United States providing that waste will be handled in a manner no less strict than in this country. This would apply also to solid waste, except for non-hazardous, separated items destined for recycling.

HR 3735
- Require the EPA, during each of five years following bill's enactment, to identify five of the most toxic and common constituents of municipal waste and to consider imposing one of the following: a ban on use, a ban on landfilling or incineration, special management standards, or use of a substitute.
- Require that used lead-acid and mercury batteries be recycled, and require the EPA to study the potential for recycling of household dry-cell batteries and methods for their disposal.
- Encourage recycling of oil.

HR 3735
- Authorize $250 million a year through 1993 for grants to states, for model recycling programs and for other programs.

HR 3737
- Set $7.50-per-ton fee, phased in over three years, on the use of virgin materials in a variety of products, including plastic, paper, batteries and packaging material. An estimated $300 million in annual revenues would be put in a trust fund to assist states in hazardous- and solid-waste management activities.

State Waste-Management Plans

Solid Waste Export

Hazardous Constituents

Financing

SENATE

S 1113
- Require the EPA to issue guidelines within six months.
- Require state plans to be submitted within two years.
- Provide that if no plan is submitted a state will lose certain federal financial assistance.
- Prohibit a state from accepting waste from out of state that is not accounted for in the state plan.

S 1112
- Build on S 1113 by requiring state plans to include additional incentives for recycling, including a policy to buy recycled products if they do not cost more than 10 percent more than virgin materials, and programs to encourage separation of recyclable materials before waste is deposited in landfills or incinerators.
- Bar federal financing for waste-to-energy incinerators if the state does not have an approved plan and if it or another entity building the unit cannot certify that the incinerator will be used to dispose of no more than 50 percent of the waste generated in the service area.

S 1113
- Bar solid-waste export for disposal, incineration or recycling unless the United States and the receiving country have agreed on enforcement procedures and standards. Solid-waste export to Canada would be prohibited after two years unless the United States and Canada enter into such an agreement.

S 1113
- Direct the EPA to publish within a year a list of at least 10 products that may release hazards when incinerated or disposed of, to be updated with at least 10 new products each year. The EPA could issue disposal regulations as necessary.
- Ban land disposal and incineration of lead-acid and mercury batteries.
- Prohibit certain industries within 10 years after enactment from releasing into the environment more than 5 percent of hazardous substances used in production.

S 1113
- Authorize $80 million in fiscal 1990 and $140 million a year for fiscal years 1991-94.

S 1112
- Set up a Source Reduction and Recycling Trust Fund for grants to states to encourage source reduction and recycling. No mechanism for raising the funds.

—Alyson Pytte

the nation's most dangerous waste sites, by the EPA's reckoning.

Many of these older city dumps will likely be shut down as more stringent landfill regulations are imposed. The EPA's new proposed standards are expected to go into effect in 1991. In some states, city and county dumps have already begun shutting down to avoid costly revamping.

That trend is bound to continue, leading to more reliance on private dumps that are run for profit, says Ron Farley, associate general counsel of Alabama's Department of Environmental Management. That raises a whole new set of problems, as waste-management officials grapple with ensuring access to private facilities at a reasonable cost.

Many state officials are pushing to keep local flexibility in RCRA landfill standards so that the problem of declining capacity — and rising landfill costs — is not worsened unnecessarily.

"We're manufacturing our own landfill capacity problem to a certain extent," says R. Steven Brown, director of the Center for the Environment and Natural Resources in the Council of State Governments.

It makes little sense, Brown says, to impose the same standards on landfills in wet areas in Florida and in Nevada's desert. "One-third of the landfills in rural states are going to shut down simply because of the new federal rules — not because we have a lot of leakage data that these landfills are hazardous," he says.

Danger in Status Quo

But state officials agree that the worst scenario would be for things to stay the way they are. The absence of up-to-date federal regulations for city dumps and incinerators — and the anticipation of new standards — has hampered local efforts to develop waste-management plans.

States are still waiting, for example, for the federal government to determine whether the ash left by

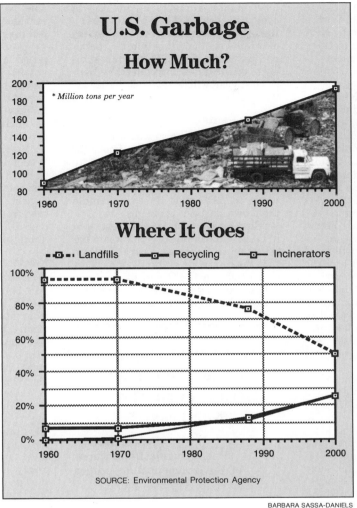

U.S. Garbage
How Much?

* Million tons per year

Where It Goes

- - □ - - Landfills   — □ — Recycling   — □ — Incinerators

SOURCE: Environmental Protection Agency

BARBARA SASSA-DANIELS

municipal incinerators can be disposed of as non-hazardous waste, or whether it must be dumped in more costly hazardous-waste landfills.

Many areas, particularly on the East Coast, have opted for "waste-to-energy" incinerators as a solution to their dump shortages. These incinerators leave behind ash residue that takes up much less space in a landfill than does raw garbage. The incinerators also create steam or electricity, which is then sold to industry or the local utility to recoup some construction costs.

But this option has also run into public resistance. Incinerators emit air pollutants and leave behind ash that is often laced with toxic substances. In 1988, public outcry about these dangers led Massachusetts to impose a one-year moratorium on all "mass-burn" plants.

The EPA on Nov. 30 released the first set of proposed new rules for incinerators that would require anti-pol-

lution devices to cut back on air emissions of hazardous substances, such as dioxin. The rules would also require incinerator operators to remove from garbage recyclable materials, such as plastics and lead-acid batteries, that emit poisons when burned. Similar provisions are included in the House and Senate RCRA bills.

But the EPA decided to let Congress decide how to treat the ash these incinerators produce, leaving some states' incinerator plans stranded. Michael Gagliardo, executive director of the Northeast Maryland Waste Disposal Authority, says such "moving regulatory targets" make it difficult for local governments to finance their waste-management plans.

Kocheisen, of the National League of Cities, says a federal resolution to the ash issue would make it easier to convince residents that new-style incinerators are safe. "It would give local officials an additional hook to hang their hats on," she says.

Both Luken's bill and a measure (S 1113) introduced in the Senate by Max Baucus, D-Mont., chairman of the Senate Environment and Public Works Subcommittee on Environmental Protection, would resolve the issue of municipal incinerator ash by declaring it non-hazardous. Both would also lay out disposal criteria that are stricter than those for regular municipal waste. State and industry officials have been pushing for the ash issue to be dealt with separately so incinerator plans can move ahead even if action on the RCRA reauthorization bill is delayed.

The Senate attached language on incinerator ash and emission standards to its clean-air bill (S 1630), but similar House action is unlikely. Luken wants to keep this side issue in RCRA reauthorization legislation to give the larger bill extra steam.

Recycling Plans

The core of Luken's RCRA bill is a requirement that states develop comprehensive waste-management plans to ensure adequate in-state garbage capacity for the next 20 years. Within four years of a plan's approval by EPA — which itself could take up to three years after the bill's enactment — states would have to recycle 25 percent of their waste.

Baucus' bill and complementary legislation (S 1112) introduced by John H. Chafee, R.I., ranking Republican on the Environmental Protection Subcommittee, would not mandate recycling as part of state plans, but would set up federal programs to spur states to recycle 25 percent of their waste within four years and 50 percent within 10 years.

The recycling drive has limits, however. Local and state officials argue that recycling mandates will be of little use if no one wants to buy the new products. Gluts in markets for recycled products, particularly newspapers, have forced many communities that go to the trouble of recycling to dump the unwanted goods in landfills. All three bills would require the federal government to buy more recycled products.

The RCRA bills also encourage cuts in the production of waste. One way to force such reductions, Chafee says, would be to impose a disposal tax to give companies incentives to cut back on wasteful products. "If people are going to make these plastic [disposable] diapers, they ought to help pay for some way to get rid of them," Chafee says.

But such a tax would go beyond the jurisdiction of the Environment Committee, he says, and would likely run into considerable Senate opposition.

Baucus' bill also takes the controversial step of mandating that industry, within 10 years, reduce the amount of toxic waste emitted to 5 percent of that used annually in the manufacturing process. In other words, if a company used 100 gallons of a chemical, it would have to use, recycle or reclaim all but five gallons.

The EPA has lauded such "pollution prevention" — as opposed to pollution control — as the new wave of environmental protection. But EPA officials still prefer market incentives to industry mandates.

Financing for Congress' ambitious solid-waste proposals remains a sticking point. All three bills would rely on trust funds to help states handle their garbage problems, but Senate sponsors have not yet addressed where the money would come from.

In the House, a separate Luken bill (HR 3737) would raise an estimated

$300 million annually by phasing in over three years a $7.50-per-ton fee on the use of virgin materials in a variety of products, including plastic, paper and batteries. That bill, which is similar to one (S 2774) introduced by Baucus last year, will be referred to the tax-writing Ways and Means Committee.

Border Patrol

The House bill also would respond to a rising din among state officials for authority to close their borders to waste imports. Luken's legislation would let states ban imports once they prove to EPA that they can handle their own garbage problems.

States have been largely frustrated in efforts to ban out-of-state waste because of a Supreme Court decision that the interstate shipping of garbage is protected by the Constitution. Some states have attempted to discourage imports by imposing moratoriums on

---

"We are not going to become some giant garbage dump for the Northeast."

—Susan Woods, Pennsylvania Department of Environmental Resources

---

new landfills, taxing waste disposal or allowing counties to prohibit outside garbage.

In Ohio, the Legislature has passed a law requiring counties to group into garbage districts, which must accommodate their own waste and which can choose to ban shipments from the outside. Like other state efforts to limit garbage imports, it is being challenged in the courts by the National Solid Waste Management Association.

Ohio officials defend the policy as their only way out of a potentially messier situation. "There is a need for Congress to push states to solve their own problems," says E. Dennis Muchnicki, chief of the environmental enforcement section of the Ohio attorney general's office. "If we were to do nothing, in five years we would be stuck doing what New York and New Jersey are doing now" — that is, loading up trucks and railroad cars with garbage destined for another region's dump.

Instead, Muchnicki says, "we were

able to take 'anti-out-of-state-trash' sentiment and turn it into a whole reform movement."

In Pennsylvania, which has imposed a moratorium on new or expanded landfills to discourage outside waste, roadside inspections of waste imports over a two-month period found 40 trucks hauling illegal garbage — such as hazardous or infectious waste labeled as city trash.

Before the moratorium, says Susan Woods of Pennsylvania's Department of Environmental Resources, the state was getting 2.5 million tons of garbage a year from New Jersey and 700,000 tons from New York. "We are not going to become some giant garbage dump for the Northeast," Woods says.

Haves and Have-Nots

But Luken's provision for an import ban could create tensions during the RCRA debate between members from states that export garbage — mostly New York and New Jersey — and those that have been inundated with out-of-state trash, including Alabama, New Mexico, Ohio, Pennsylvania, West Virginia and Michigan.

Luken says he does not expect much public opposition, however. "I can't imagine that any of the exporting states are going to publicly clamor for the right to export their waste," he says. "I think they are going to look pretty silly if they try to do that."

The strongest opposition to an import ban heard in the courts and in Congress is from the waste-disposal industry. Allen Moore, president of the National Solid Waste Management Association, a trade group representing private waste-service companies, warns that losing the "escape hatch" of sending waste across state lines could lead to "major public health and environmental problems."

"You're going to leave it on the borders, dump it in the road or reopen facilities that aren't safe," Moore says. "I think we still need breathing time."

But members from garbage-receiving states say they cannot handle an uncontrolled supply of waste. "It's impossible to do long-term planning if you have no control over what enters your state," says Rep. Ben Erdreich, D-Ala., sponsor of a bill (HR 3395) to expand state authority over imports.

With the backing of such potent political forces as the residents of Zip City and other communities, Alabama officials have been among the most active in trying to limit imports of waste destined for landfills. ∎

Need for a Massive Cleanup May Slow Weapon-Building

For nearly 50 years, the sprawling industrial complex that builds U.S. nuclear weapons has been operating in almost total secrecy, with little public or government scrutiny. But as the Cold War thaws and environmental wars heat up, the bombs fortress is crumbling.

The cracks start from within. The four reactors that produced nuclear warheads and the materials going into them in 1986 have since been closed because of environmental, health or safety problems — one was shut down permanently. Other plants that manufacture key nuclear weapons components have been closed at intervals for the same reasons. *(Chart, p. 44)*

As a result, the Energy Department's management of the complex has come under siege from all quarters. In Congress, the war cries are loudest among budget makers who must figure out how to pay for a weapons plant cleanup that, by some estimates, could cost $155 billion over 25 years. The mess could make last year's bailout of the savings and loan industry look easy.

Meanwhile, state governments, which the Reagan administration made mostly responsible for setting environmental standards, have begun to take a hard line on environmental, health and safety standards at weapons plants once welcomed for their payrolls. Governors are challenging the longstanding "sovereign immunity" of the federal government against states' efforts to enforce their environmental regulations. Legislation to revoke such immunity has passed the House and is pending in the Senate.

At the same time, liberal activists, who have opposed many weapons-production plants for arms control reasons, have seized on the environmental issue as a lever to slow the government's weapons-making capability.

Liberals are planning early attacks on the pending nomination of Victor Stello Jr. to be assistant energy secretary in charge of the nuclear weapons complex in hopes of scoring larger points later in the year when Congress

By Pat Towell

CHECKLIST

Issue: Nuclear weapons plant cleanup.

Legislation: Defense authorization, and energy and water appropriations.

Need for action: Requires annual funding.

Main venues: House: Armed Services, Appropriations committees; Senate: Armed Services, Appropriations, Energy and Natural Resources committees.

Outlook: Early Senate confirmation action on Victor Stello Jr. nomination.

must decide whether to build more weapons facilities.

The lessening of U.S.-Soviet tensions has made it politically easier for these critics to challenge Cold War practices and priorities and to raise the fundamental question of how large a bomb factory is needed, a key element in deciding how extensively to modernize the aging physical plant.

"We realized that the cleanup was something we could talk to members about," says Michelle Robinson of the Council for a Livable World. "It was a home issue."

'New Culture' Promised

None of the weapons complex's critics has been more scathing than retired Adm. James D. Watkins, President Bush's energy secretary. Blasting the agency last June for "years of inattention to changing standards and demands regarding the environment, safety and health," Watkins vowed to foster "a new culture" that would regard environmental protection and weapons-making as concurrent goals.

Last August, Watkins announced a 10-point reform program. One important change, he said, would hinge at least 51 percent of the annual fees earned by the companies running the weapons plants on compliance with federal and state environmental, safety and health requirements. Previously, most of the fees had depended on meeting production goals.

In another break with the secrecy of the past, Watkins announced Jan. 12 that his department would prepare formal environmental impact statements on the five-year cleanup program he unveiled last summer and on the so-called "2010 Report," which is a 20-year program for consolidating and rebuilding the complex, completed last January by the Reagan administration.

According to several arms-control and environmental activists who have targeted the weapons complex, Watkins' repudiation of past practices and his promise of a new regime took some political steam out of the issue last year. "He's politically astute," says David Lewis of Physicians for Social Responsibility. "He was able to say, 'That was then; this is now.'"

Still, even some of the Energy Department's staunchest allies, such as Sen. James A. McClure, R-Idaho, concede that the old ways have to change.

"When we initially built the defense production complex, and for many years of its operation, this nation collectively deferred or ignored its responsibility to fully deal with the related issues of health, safety and waste management," McClure said last October. "Now that bill has come due."

Indeed, the only question about the Energy Department's budget for cleaning up the weapons complex is how much larger it will get and how fast.

In fiscal 1989, the appropriation for defense-related waste treatment and environmental restoration was more than $1 billion. In fiscal 1990, Congress boosted it to nearly $1.7 billion. Under the five-year plan unveiled by Watkins last August, the environment-related

Status, Problems and Cleanup Costs...

Facility and Location	Functions, Problems, Status	Cleanup Cost FY 1990-95* (in millions of dollars)
Research Facilities		
Los Alamos National Laboratory, Los Alamos, N.M.	Designs nuclear weapons; blends plutonium. Radioactive materials and other poisons have been found on plant site.	$ 168.9
Lawrence Livermore National Laboratory, Livermore, Calif.	Designs nuclear weapons. Poisons have leaked into groundwater. Residents are in danger of having their drinking water contaminated.	n.a.
Nevada Test Site, Mercury, Nev.	Tests nuclear weapons. Approximately 75 square miles are contaminated with plutonium, cesium and strontium.	230.8
Sandia National Laboratories, Albuquerque, N.M.; Livermore, Calif.	Nuclear weapons research, development. Coordinates transportation among facilities. Provides engineering support. Waste-storage tanks have leaked. Area around the plant is contaminated by several poisons.	195.0
Production Facilities		
Bendix Plant, Kansas City, Mo.	Manufactures fuzes, electrical systems and telemetry units and other non-nuclear components. More than 200 tons of poisons have leaked into the air and sewer system.	30.5
Mound Laboratories, Miamisburg, Ohio	Manufactures detonators and other non-nuclear components; recycles tritium. There is concern that plutonium may leak into local groundwater. Tritium facilities being phased out.	193.9
Oak Ridge Reservation National Laboratory (Y-12 plant), Oak Ridge, Tenn.	Produces nuclear weapons components; assembles second stage of bombs. In the 1980s, a civic center near Oak Ridge was built using mercury-contaminated soil released by the plant. Arsenic, boron and sulfate have leaked into nearby streams. Uranium facilities are to be upgraded beginning early in this decade, to be completed by 2000. Uranium-enrichment plant has been shut down because of lack of demand and environmental problems. The lithium refining process was shut down because of use from other stockpiles.	1,300.0
Pantex Plant, Amarillo, Texas	Assembles final stage of bomb; maintains and disposes of nuclear weapons. Chemicals from the waste pit are believed to be leaking into the Ogallala aquifer, the major water source for area residents.	56.1
Pinellas Plant, Largo, Fla.	Manufactures neutron generators used in bomb triggers. Toxic storage tanks may be leaking.	22.3
Rocky Flats, Golden, Colo.	Assembles nuclear triggers for warheads. A key plutonium-processing building has been shut down because of safety problems. Soil around the site is contaminated with high levels of plutonium. Beginning this year, with completion due by 1997, the plutonium recovery is to be upgraded. Starting in 1995, activities at the plant are to be moved, dependent on funding.	219.0
Production of Nuclear Materials		
Ashtabula Extrusion Plant, Ashtabula, Ohio	Machines uranium metal ingots from Fernald facility (below) into fuel elements for reactors at Hanford plant and Savannah River and "targets" for tritium production at Savannah River.	n.a.
Feed Materials Production Center, Fernald, Ohio	Produces uranium ingots for nuclear fuel. Radon gas has leaked from storage silos. More than 300,000 pounds of uranium oxide has filtered into water supplies. Uranium production facilities are shut down. DOE plans to shut down the plant permanently.	700.6

...Of U.S. Nuclear Weapons Plants

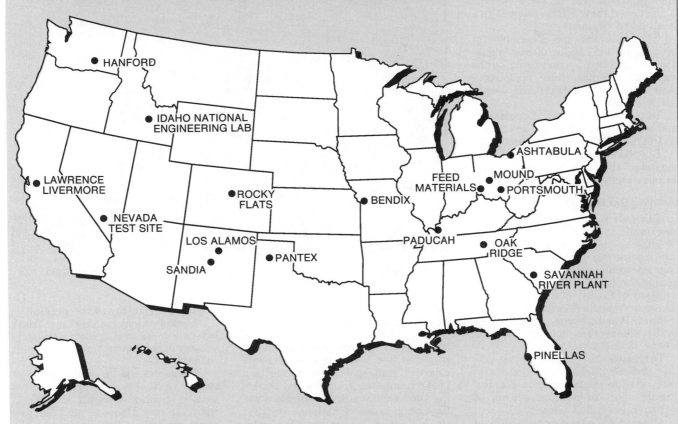

- HANFORD
- IDAHO NATIONAL ENGINEERING LAB
- ASHTABULA
- FEED MATERIALS
- MOUND
- PORTSMOUTH
- LAWRENCE LIVERMORE
- BENDIX
- ROCKY FLATS
- NEVADA TEST SITE
- PADUCAH
- OAK RIDGE
- LOS ALAMOS
- PANTEX
- SANDIA
- SAVANNAH RIVER PLANT
- PINELLAS

Facility and Location	Functions, Problems, Status	Cleanup Cost FY 1990-95 (in millions of dollars)
Hanford Reservation, Richland, Wash.	Closed in January 1989. Used to recycle uranium and extract plutonium. Billions of gallons of radioactive waste contaminate more than 100 square miles of groundwater. The weapons program at the plant is to be phased out from 1995 to 2000.	$ 1,000.0
Idaho National Engineering Laboratory, Arco, Idaho	Recycles irradiated fuel from existing reactors. Wastes from plant have polluted the Snake River aquifer. Plutonium waste is migrating toward the reservoir.	484.1
Paducah Gaseous Diffusion Plant, Paducah, Ky.	Enriches uranium. Production has been halted because of lack of demand and environmental toxicity problems.	n.a.
Portsmouth Uranium Enrichment, Piketon, Ohio	Enriches uranium. From 1974 to 1984, Energy Department roto-tilled radioactive waste into the soil.	99.7
Savannah River Plant, Aiken, S.C.	Produces tritium and plutonium; recycles uranium. The plant has released poisons into the Tuscaloosa aquifer. Accidents have caused tritium gas to be released into the atmosphere. Starting in the late 1990s, the plant's equipment used to make virgin plutonium is to be upgraded. In 1988 all three reactors were shut down. The tritium facility is operational. The chemical separations plant is operational, but not in use. DOE says the reactors are to become operational again later this year.	417.9

—*Kenneth E. Jaques*

* Department of Energy

budget would rise to $2.4 billion in fiscal 1991 and $3.7 billion in fiscal 1992. There will be concerted efforts on Capitol Hill to boost the final appropriations even higher.

But even these efforts amount to a small down payment.

The price tag and timetable for cleaning up the residue of past waste-disposal practices — and bringing the weapons complex into compliance with contemporary standards — are still not known.

In July the Energy Department said it would cost between $66 billion and $110 billion over 25 years.

But the General Accounting Office suggested that Energy had seriously underestimated the real cost.

Building the Bombs

The federal nuclear weapons complex employs about 90,000 workers at 17 sites to design nuclear weapons, produce nuclear fuel and mechanical and electronic components, and assemble the parts.

Many of the key plants in the complex date from the Manhattan Project of World War II. Nearly all of the rest of the plants were built in the first decade after the war.

Originally, the complex processed four critical nuclear materials: uranium, used to produce plutonium, and lithium, used to produce a form of hydrogen gas called tritium.

There has been no production of refined lithium or weapons-grade uranium since the early 1960s. Lithium and uranium for new weapons have been drawn from stockpiled material or reclaimed from older weapons headed for the scrap heap.

Plutonium and tritium plants continued operating into the 1980s. But in recent years, most plants involved in processing those materials have been closed periodically because of hazards resulting from the age of the plants, the lethality of the toxic and radioactive materials they handle, and the plants' operating practices.

In December 1988, an Energy Department report listed 155 instances of environmental contamination at weapons plants and laboratories, many of which resulted from disposing of nonradioactive toxic waste with techniques that had been banned in private industry for more than a decade.

The Breaking Point

Given the plants' age and the government's low investment in modernization, the complex was bound to fall

DEPARTMENT OF ENERGY

A key plutonium processing building at the Rocky Flats facility in Golden, Colo., has been shut down because of safety problems.

on hard times. But the problems inherent in obsolescence were exacerbated — at least politically — because the complex was run under a philosophy that also was a relic of wartime exigency: putting weapons production above competing priorities and shielding the operations from outside scrutiny, on grounds of national security.

Cold War tensions allowed the complex to stay free of such scrutiny for a generation. But the defense buildup begun by President Jimmy Carter and accelerated by President Ronald Reagan imposed considerable strains on the aging weapons plants.

Between fiscal 1978 and fiscal 1982, appropriations for nuclear weapons development and manufacture (including waste disposal) more than doubled to $3.85 billion from $1.67 billion. By fiscal 1986, the amount nearly doubled again, reaching $6.44 billion.

That same year, however, the Soviet nuclear reactor disaster at Chernobyl began drawing attention to the Energy Department's production reactors because, unlike any large civilian U.S. reactors, the N Reactor at Hanford, Wash., had some superficial similarities to the Soviet installation.

A blue-ribbon panel of technical experts discounted the risk of a Chernobyl-type accident at any Energy Department reactor. But in its October 1987 report, the commission branded the current arrangements for safety oversight as "ingrown and largely

outside the scrutiny of the public."

Weaknesses in management "have led to a loose-knit system of largely self-regulated contractors," the report concluded.

The report was "a significant milestone" in the weapons-complex debate, says John M. Spratt Jr., D-S.C., chairman of a House Armed Services panel created in 1989 to oversee the weapons complex. The group's technical credentials gave "an imprimatur to criticism that some had been making from the outside," Spratt says.

Time for Decision

By the end of 1988, the weapons complex was an industrial and political disaster. Of four reactors that had been in service two years earlier, one at the Hanford site had been shut down permanently while the three operating reactors at the Savannah River Plant near Aiken, S.C., had been shut down for safety modifications.

Moreover, the cutoff of tritium supplies from Savannah River and the accumulation of radioactive wastes at several plants made it harder to keep deferring choices about the complex.

Because tritium decays at the rate of 5.5 percent annually, the tritium supplies in warheads must be replenished regularly. For a time, the Pentagon could keep most of its warheads charged with tritium by scavenging gas from less important weapons. But at some point, a significant number of U.S. warheads will begin losing their punch.

Because engineering problems delayed opening of the Waste Isolation Pilot Plant — a massive underground depository for radioactive waste near Carlsbad, N.M. — the waste from the operating plants piled up in ostensibly temporary storage sites. But temporary sites in Colorado and Idaho are now at or near capacity.

The governors of Colorado and Idaho have threatened to enforce limits on amounts of toxic waste that could be stored, even at the risk of closing the weapons-production network. This is the most dramatic illustration of a tendency that has been under way since early in Reagan's second term: the willingness of states to put pressure on the Energy Department to clean up weapons-plant operations and to commit to clean up decades' worth of toxic and radioactive waste.

Ohio and Washington state, homes of two of the most severely polluted sites, have negotiated with the Energy Department for binding timetables for cleaning up radioactive and toxic-waste dumps.

Robert Alvarez, a longtime policy analyst for the Environmental Policy Institute and now an aide to Sen. John Glenn, D-Ohio, said the new state activism is a consequence of President Reagan's "new federalism," which spawned laws delegating to the states responsibility for enforcement.

"The states have taken on the role and are now pushing for tougher-than-federal regulations," Alvarez says.

The U.S. House, urged on by a coalition of state legal officials, labor unions and environmentalists, overwhelmingly approved a bill (HR 1056) last July that would waive the "sovereign immunity" of the federal government against states' efforts to enforce their environmental regulations. *(1989 Weekly Report p. 1856)*

Passed on a 380-39 vote, the bill would reaffirm the power of the Environmental Protection Agency (EPA) and state governments to enforce compliance with the Resource Conservation and Recovery Act (RCRA) at federal facilities. *(Story, this page)*

Majority Leader George J. Mitchell, D-Maine, has introduced the House-passed bill in the Senate, but it faces competition from other bills that would limit the states' ability to impose standards. One such measure (S 1802), sponsored by McClure and J. Bennett Johnston, D-La., would require the Energy Department, the

The Other Cleanups

BARBARA SASSA-DANIELS

Nuclear weapons plants are not the only costly, environmental hot spots for the U.S. military complex. Routine industrial and maintenance activities at more than 1,000 military installations across the country generate about 400,000 tons of hazardous waste annually, according to the General Accounting Office.

Proper disposal of effluents such as crankcase oil, cleaning solvents and lead-based paints will cost as much as $15 billion over 25 years, by the Pentagon's own estimate. That does not include the cost of cleaning installations the Pentagon has sold or abandoned.

The Pentagon's Defense Environmental Restoration Account program (DERA) was established in 1984 to coordinate the cleanup of hazardous and contaminated military installations. In 1986, the defense secretary was given the lead role in carrying out the program in conjunction with the Environmental Protection Agency (EPA).

By the end of fiscal 1988, the Pentagon had identified 8,139 potentially hazardous waste sites on 897 bases and had begun or completed inspections of more than 7,900 of those sites. At least some remedial action has been scheduled at nearly 2,500 sites, although only 216 of those projects have been completed (most are interim steps in more comprehensive, multiyear programs).

There are 29 sites listed on the Defense Department's national priority list. The cleanup process, which involves the Pentagon, the EPA and individual state environmental control agencies, takes several months to negotiate.

Of all federal facilities regulated by existing environmental laws, 70 percent to 90 percent belong to the Pentagon, according to a House Armed Services Committee panel reviewing the cleanup.

Between fiscal 1984 and fiscal 1989, funding for the DERA jumped from $150 million to $500 million a year.

In July 1989, the House panel criticized the Bush administration for recommending a five-year DERA budget for fiscal 1990-95 that fell $1.6 billion short of the Pentagon's own earlier projection.

As a result, in the fiscal 1990 defense appropriations bill (PL 101-165), Congress appropriated $601 million for DERA — $83 million more than President Bush had requested.

Defense Environmental Restoration Account

(as of fiscal 1988)

Region	Potential Sites	Preliminary Assessments[1]	Detailed Investigation[2]	Remedial Action[3]
Midwest	1,188	1,147	458	328
East	1,328	1,282	644	322
South	2,501	2,457	1,220	492
West	2,981	2,909	2,005	1,311
Territories	141	137	108	33
TOTAL	**8,139**	**7,932**	**4,435**	**2,486**

[1] *An installation-wide study to determine whether there are sites on the installation that may pose hazards to the public health or environment.*
[2] *Comprehensive studies of individual sites deemed as potential environmental threats.*
[3] *Includes the design and implementation of the chosen alternatives to address problems at the site.*

SOURCE: Department of Defense

—Pat Towell and Kenneth E. Jaques

Resources Protected, Abusers Punished . . .

One bill would impose long prison terms on polluters. Another would seek to protect groundwater from contamination. A third would promote research into global climate change.

In 1989, members of Congress introduced hundreds of environmental bills — more than 450, according to the Congressional Research Service. And while clean air and oil-spill liability received most of the media attention, dozens of other measures are riding the environmental bandwagon. What follows is a rundown of some of the legislation with the best chance of success.

● **Transporting Food and Hazardous Materials.** The House may soon consider legislation to ban "backhauling" — shipping food in trucks that have carried garbage or toxic chemicals. As landfill space is declining in the East, more trucks are taking garbage to the West and returning with apple juice and strawberries.

The Public Works and Transportation and the Energy and Commerce committees, which engaged in a turf battle over the issue last year, have begun meeting to resolve their differences over competing bills.

The bill (HR 3386) approved by the Public Works Committee would bar refrigerated trucks that have been used to carry solid wastes from transporting foods. It also would prohibit cargo tank trucks, which are often used to carry chemicals, from switching between loads of food and non-food products. *(1989 Weekly Report p. 3147)*

A broader bill (HR 3634) was approved by the Energy and Commerce Subcommittee on Transportation, which also has jurisdiction over railroads. HR 3634 would establish two categories of hazardous materials. Those in the more dangerous category could never be carried in vehicles used to transport food and other commodities intended for human consumption. Less hazardous materials could be shipped in the same vehicle if specific disposal and decontamination procedures were followed.

In the Senate, at least two backhauling bills (S 1751, S 1904) have been introduced, but no hearings have been scheduled.

● **Indoor Air Pollution.** Growing evidence that several indoor pollutants, including radon and asbestos, pose health threats comparable to, if not greater than, most outdoor air pollutants prompted Senate Majority Leader George J. Mitchell, D-Maine, and Rep. Joseph P. Kennedy II, D-Mass., to introduce companion measures (S 657, HR 1530) last year to combat air pollution in public buildings, schools, workplaces and homes.

The legislation would establish a federal program to study the health effects of indoor air pollutants and to develop methods for reducing exposure to such contaminants. It would require the Environmental Protection Agency (EPA) to list indoor contaminants and to issue health advisories on each, indicating the risks at various concentrations. The legislation also would authorize grants to help states develop indoor-air-quality programs. The Senate Environment Subcommittee on Superfund, Ocean and Water Protection approved S 657 on Nov. 14.

The House Science Committee plans to take up Kennedy's bill early, but the House Committee on Energy and Commerce, which also has jurisdiction, has not scheduled action.

● **Coastal Pollution.** Industries that pollute coastal waters would have to pay a discharge fee to help control pollution under a bill (HR 2647) sponsored by Rep. Gerry E. Studds, D-Mass., the chairman of the Merchant Marine Fisheries and Wildlife Subcommittee. Studds says the fee system would raise at least $100 million.

HR 2647 would require the EPA to set minimum federal water-quality standards, refocus state coastal zone management programs to consider the impact of land use on water quality, create a national coastal monitoring program and provide increased technical help to local officials. The subcommittee plans to mark up the bill very early in the session.

The Public Works Committee will be holding hearings as well, leading to a markup this session. The committee plans to draft its own bill.

No such fee system is included in Senate bills (S 1178, S 1179) that also aim to manage coastal pollution. Legislation (probably a combination of several bills) is expected to reach the floor this year.

There may also be an administration proposal later this year. The EPA has been investigating ways to get more money for states to implement coastal water management and other water programs. An EPA official said that investigation may result in a bill from the administration.

● **Worldwide Climate Change.** Bills that seek to advance scientific understanding of why and how the global climate is changing could become law. The big question is whether Congress can agree on who to put in charge of such research.

In the House, staffers have begun negotiations to reach a compromise between a bill (HR 3332) approved by the Merchant Marine Committee and legislation (HR 2984) approved by two Science subcommittees. An aide said a compromise could reach the floor as early as March. *(1989 Weekly Report p. 3153)*

Under both bills, the Committee on Earth Sciences (CES) — an arm of the Executive Office of the President's Federal Coordinating Council for Science, Engineering and Technology (FCCSET) — would coordinate federal agencies' research into global change, such as global warming. The administration also would be required to begin discussions leading to international research agreements.

The Science Committee bill would place CES solely in charge of the program. Under the Merchant Marine bill, however, the Council on Environmental Quality, which advises the president on environmental issues, would advise CES on which research efforts would best help decision making.

A new body created by the White House also could be given a role in a compromise bill, an aide said. It is the

... In Measures Most Likely to Succeed

Working Group on Global Climate Change, created within the Cabinet-level Domestic Policy Council (DPC), whose current role is to coordinate policy consideration and provide input for the DPC to create policy options for the president.

A Senate bill (S 169) on global climate research would place the FCCSET in charge of a similar program. The Senate Commerce Committee approved the bill April 18. But a turf battle between the Commerce and Environment committees has left it in limbo.

The Environment Committee has tried to assert its jurisdiction over the bill, but so far to no avail. An Environment Committee aide said introducing a new bill is possible. But he said the panel is now tied up with clean-air legislation.

● **Groundwater Research.** Bills that seek to coordinate groundwater research conducted by federal agencies could finally reach the president's desk this session.

The House has passed legislation to that effect in the past two Congresses. In the waning days of the 100th Congress, the Senate passed its own bill, but no agreement could be reached before adjournment.

As groundwater is the source of drinking water for one in two U.S. residents, its growing contamination could have devastating impacts. There are more than 200 contaminants in the nation's groundwater, according to the Office of Technology Assessment.

The Environment and Public Works Committee plans to approve a bill (S 203) and take it to the floor this year, according to a spokesman for panel Chairman Quentin N. Burdick, D-N.D.

S 203, which is identical to a bill the Senate passed in the 100th Congress, would create an interagency task force to coordinate groundwater research and would authorize several groundwater initiatives. It would require the EPA to conduct demonstration programs and groundwater studies, including risk assessments of contaminants. It also would provide matching grants for states' groundwater protection efforts.

It is similar to legislation (HR 2734) approved Nov. 16 by the House Science Subcommittee on Natural Resources, Agriculture Research and Environment. That bill also would create an interagency body to coordinate agencies' activities.

The initiatives the bill would create include a re-

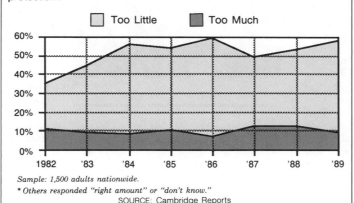

Government Regulation

Question: In general do you think there is too much, too little ... government regulation and involvement in the area of environmental protection? *

Legend: Too Little / Too Much

Y-axis: 60%, 50%, 40%, 30%, 20%, 10%, 0%
X-axis: 1982, '83, '84, '85, '86, '87, '88, '89

Sample: 1,500 adults nationwide.
* *Others responded "right amount" or "don't know."*
SOURCE: Cambridge Reports

search, development and demonstration program for groundwater protection and management, which the EPA would guide. EPA also would be required to assess the risks posed by contaminants.

Like the Senate bill, it would provide matching grants for groundwater protection efforts by the states, but would authorize less money for that purpose than would the Senate version.

● **Environmental Crimes.** "Those who might wreak havoc on our environment should be scared," said Rep. Charles E. Schumer, D-N.Y., who introduced legislation (HR 3641) that would stiffen penalties against those responsible for environmental disasters that cause death, serious injuries or grave damage to the environment. "Large gaps exist in our ability to deter" such crimes, he said. Schumer, who chairs the Judiciary Subcommittee on Criminal Justice, plans to take up the bill early in the session.

The measure would define three types of environmental crimes carrying penalties of up to $2 million in fines for corporations — or $500,000 for individuals — and jail terms of up to 30 years for repeat offenders.

It also would require the sentencing court to place guilty companies on probation. They would be subject to an environmental audit to identify pollutants and to recommend measures to reduce emissions levels; the court could then require the defendant to implement those measures.

At a Dec. 12 subcommittee hearing, G. William Frick, vice president of the American Petroleum Institute, called the legislation unnecessary. He said existing environmental statutes "have broad criminal enforcement provisions tailored to each particular regulatory scheme."

At the same hearing, George Van Cleve, deputy assistant attorney general for land and natural resources, said the administration supports "stiffening punishments for violations of federal anti-pollution laws," but he expressed reservations about the Schumer bill. He suggested integrating the bill's concepts into the existing body of environmental laws rather than separately inserting them in the U.S. Code. No similar legislation has been introduced in the Senate.

—*Karine Roesch*

EPA and the states to negotiate court-enforceable timetables for cleaning up any weapons plant not in compliance with state or federal laws.

Environmentalists strongly oppose the Johnston-McClure bill because it would allow those compliance agreements to supersede more stringent state and federal laws.

Fight Over Stello

The first congressional battle of 1990 will come over President Bush's nomination of Stello for assistant energy secretary. Watkins has invested extraordinary political capital in the nomination, insisting that Stello is just the technically knowledgeable hard-charger he needs to get the weapons complex back on track.

But Senate critics such as Tim Wirth, D-Colo., backed by Greenpeace and many other environmental lobby groups, contend that Stello was too "cozy" with the commercial nuclear power companies he oversaw as executive director of the Nuclear Regulatory Commission (NRC), thus belying Watkins' pledge of a new culture at Energy.

Specifically, former NRC members have testified that Stello had short-circuited several NRC inquiries into alleged violations of regulations.

Stello's numerous supporters, including former NRC Chairman Joseph M. Hendrie, said Stello simply had been willing to do whatever was necessary to fix significant environmental, health and safety problems in reactors, which in some cases meant relying on negotiation rather than strict regulatory enforcement.

"The people that do not like Vic Stello or do not like the nuclear industry say every time you talk to a utility fellow, that is cozy," Hendrie told the Armed Services Committee last year. "They seem to expect the regulators to act as some sort of prison guards."

The committee likely will approve the nomination, with a minority of five or six members voting against him. But Stello's critics promise stiff opposition on the floor. And even if Stello is confirmed, his critics think an open challenge will serve their purposes.

"He'll be on a short leash," says David Culp of the Plutonium Challenge, predicting that Stello's conduct would be closely scrutinized by Congress and the news media.

New Production Facilities

A more far-reaching confrontation should take place this year over how

R. MICHAEL JENKINS

Energy Secretary James D. Watkins vowed to foster a "new culture" in weapons production.

---

much to spend on new production facilities for nuclear material.

In 1988, the Energy Department announced plans to build two production reactors — one at Savannah River and another in Idaho. But even some staunch backers of the weapons complex have doubts about the cost of a two-reactor plan — projected to be $6.8 billion. "It's quite obvious that we're not going to have enough money," Sen. Jim Exon, D-Neb., says.

Most liberal critics of the weapons complex seem reconciled to the likelihood that Congress will allow the Energy Department eventually to restart tritium production in the existing reactors at Savannah River and will fund a new production reactor at that site.

Weapons-plant critic David Albright of the Federation for American Scientists predicts that the projected second reactor, in Idaho, will "never be killed; it'll be postponed, further and further."

The Energy Department also has plans for a third production facility — a controversial new plant, also in Idaho, that would use lasers to refine plutonium. The process is called Special Isotope Separation (SIS).

Last year Congress approved only $40 million of the $115 million requested for work on the SIS plant. And

it barred work at the construction site until Watkins certified that the plant was essential for national security.

There has been speculation, even before the announced retirement of McClure, ranking Republican on the Senate Energy Committee, that the Energy Department would drop SIS because of budgetary limits. In December, the National Academy of Sciences found the $1.35 billion project to be superfluous.

Effects of Radiation

Bills introduced in both houses would transfer to the Department of Health and Human Services (HHS) the Energy Department's research program on the medical effects of radiation. Sponsors say Energy's responsibility to keep the weapons plants operating raises questions about the scientific integrity of its research.

Wirth has introduced one such bill (S 972) in the Senate. Ron Wyden, D-Ore., has introduced essentially the same bill in the House, with the added provision that HHS also study the medical effects of non-radioactive toxic materials in the weapons complex.

Two Senate bills touching on several aspects of the weapons complex — one (S 1304) sponsored by Glenn and a competing measure (S 1802) co-sponsored by McClure and Johnston — would create advisory panels on medical research within the Energy Department. Both bills would subject weapons complex installations to the federal Occupational Safety and Health Act (OSHA) regulations, although Johnston-McClure would phase in such control over five years.

Watkins may partly pre-empt the issue: An advisory commission he created is due to report in March and may recommend transferring the radiation research program to HHS.

The most hotly contested of the external oversight issues likely will be the Senate fight over the two approaches to subjecting the weapons plants to regulation by the EPA and state environmental regulations.

The strong House vote last July against providing the weapons complex with any relief from existing state and federal environmental laws reflected the growing power of environmental politics within both parties.

That fact alone could boost the Senate toward the tougher House version, said Culp of Plutonium Challenge: "If people think this is going to be counted as an environmental vote, that is going to swing people." ■

CAMPAIGNS

Voters' Concerns Are Turning The Political Agenda Green

In Republican-leaning Bucks County, Pa., Democrat Peter H. Kostmayer's party label is not always something to brag about. But the seven-term House member has found another label that helps him fend off his GOP opponents.

Kostmayer regularly reminds voters that he is an environmentalist.

That message, sent out to blue-collar Democrats as well as to affluent Republicans and independents, has played to a broadening audience in recent years. In 1988, when Kostmayer conducted a districtwide poll asking voters what was "the most important issue facing you as an American," traffic came in first and overdevelopment was second, followed by the environment.

Those issues did not strike the same chords 10 years ago, when the county was still largely rural.

"In working-class areas, there is worry about toxic-waste sites and resistance to [a proposed local] incinerator," Kostmayer says. "With the more affluent voters, it's more the preservation of farmland and [of] the rural character of the area."

Kostmayer's continued success in a district where registered Republicans outnumber Democrats is just part of the mounting evidence that the environment can be a potent political issue. As he and others have learned, it is a topic that crosses geographic and demographic lines, appealing especially to the millions of middle-income suburbanites whose votes are coveted by both parties.

"The environment has been transformed from a quality-of-life issue for the affluent to a health-and-safety issue for almost everyone," Democratic pollster Mark Mellman says.

But if there appears to be a national trend toward green campaign themes, candidates also face complex voter demands when confronted with real environmental crises. It is rarely a simple matter for individual candidates, or the major parties, to determine what is the "right side" of the local issues that often drive voter interest in the environment.

By Peter Bragdon and Beth Donovan

Rep. Peter H. Kostmayer of Pennsylvania regularly reminds voters that he is an environmentalist.

Concern over economics, ecology and potential health hazards vary widely from community to community, and shift easily, leaving candidates to negotiate unclear political fault lines.

Clear and Present Danger?

As a voting issue, the environment is most salient where there is a perceived personal threat.

"People will not go into the voting booth and vote for a candidate because he supports saving tropical rain forests," says Ali Webb of the League of Conservation Voters (LCV).

But they will, she says, if the issue is a toxic-waste site in the district.

When an environmental threat is clear, politicians know where to stand on the issue. But if voters cannot discern a difference between the candidates on the environment, one must seem more competent or committed for it to become a voting issue.

In the 1988 Nevada Senate campaign, Republican incumbent Chic Hecht opposed putting a nuclear-waste repository in the state, just as his Democratic opponent, Gov. Richard H. Bryan, did. But Hecht, who developed an image as a legislator prone to mistakes and malapropism, saw that reputation soar when his Senate colleagues moved to put the waste site in Nevada over his objections. Bryan, who promised to be more effective, used the issue to help defeat Hecht in November 1988.

But opposition is rarely so uniform on environmental issues. More typical is the situation in New Mexico, where the state is bitterly divided over government plans to put a nuclear Waste Isolation Pilot Plant (WIPP) in underground salt beds near Carlsbad.

Voters in the quickly growing and prosperous Albuquerque suburbs — near the transportation corridor to WIPP — are increasingly opposed to the facility. But in the southern part of the state, where the economy is relatively sluggish, most voters enthusiastically favor the plant as a potential source of jobs.

The issue has something of a partisan cast in the state, with Republicans tending to favor it and Democrats leaning against it. But even more important than party is geography — GOP Rep. Joe Skeen, who favors WIPP, is from the southern half of the state, while Democratic Rep. Bill Richardson, who opposes it, is from the north.

The issue is complicated further by related problems in Colorado and in Idaho, where nuclear waste slated for the WIPP site is now stored.

Most of the waste is created at the Rocky Flats nuclear weapons facility, 16 miles northwest of Denver. That plant has been buffeted by reports of improper disposal of nuclear and toxic waste, and Democratic Gov. Roy Romer has grown increasingly critical, threatening to close the plant if he is not convinced that it can be operated safely.

But the facility also provides employment in Colorado and arguably provides security for the rest of the country. "It's also a vital link in the national security chain, [and] when you've got 6,000 jobs at stake and a struggling economy, you hate to think about closing it down," said Cindy Parmenter, Romer's press secretary. "But the governor will do it."

In Idaho, where a majority of the waste is temporarily stored, Democratic Gov. Cecil D. Andrus has his own concerns. He does not want his state to become a permanent storage site and won widespread praise in Idaho when he closed the state's border to shipments. The waste is building up at Rocky Flats, and when it reaches storage capacity late this summer, the federal government will face a crisis.

Geography

The geographic complications of environmental issues are most clearly illustrated along the Pigeon River, which flows through North Carolina to Tennessee. When the river passes by Canton, N.C., it is relatively clean and clear. But after it reaches the Champion International Corp. paper mill there, the waters turn brown with allegedly toxic pollution.

Tennessee politicians downstream consider the mill a threat to health and recreation. Politicians in North Carolina consider Champion International the direct source of more than 2,000 jobs and the indirect source of thousands of others.

In a battle that is more geographic than partisan, Tennessee politicians have urged the Environmental Protection Agency (EPA) to clamp down on pollution at the plant, with some success. Tennesseans have also pushed for waste-discharge standards that strike fear into the hearts of mill workers and North Carolina public officials.

But this year the EPA issued a less stringent wastewater-discharge permit than Tennesseans wanted and kept the mill in business with reduced capacity.

In a strange twist, Champion emerged as a 1988 campaign issue in North Carolina's 11th District. Incumbent Democrat James McClure Clarke, widely praised for environmental work by groups such as the Sierra Club, lined up with other North Carolinians to support the plant. But his opponent in a hard-fought race argued that Clarke's support was suspect because Clarke had endorsed the presidential campaign of Tennessee Democratic Sen. Al Gore.

Worth the Risk

If risk-averse politicians sometimes find it hard to determine the "winning" side of an environmental issue, they also may find it difficult to avoid developing a greener agenda.

In part that is because voters seem less concerned with the political

agenda that dominated recent elections. Unemployment, inflation and fear of the Soviet Union will not motivate people as they did in 1980 or 1984. In the view of politicians and pollsters, voters are freer to focus on a host of "quality-of-life" issues.

"There's an economic-environmental continuum," said Rep. David E. Skaggs, D-Colo. "As long as times are good, people are willing for us to be progressive in our environmental policy."

Others suggest that concern for the environment is not just a result of economic growth. Fear may also be a motivator. "Maybe it is because problems have become so obvious that it is impossible to ignore them," says Leon Lowery of Environmental Action.

In some areas, economic growth actually has helped create conditions that spur environmental concerns. Florida, quickly growing and increasingly Republican, has seen the envi-

---

> ## "As long as times are good, people are willing for us to be progressive in our environmental policy."
>
> —Rep. David E. Skaggs, D-Colo.

---

ronmental issue transformed as the state has tried to absorb millions of new residents lured by warm weather, scenic beauty and economic opportunity.

In the past decade, concerns about an overburdened water supply, clean air and clean beaches have helped build a strong consensus behind some of the toughest growth management laws in the country.

"The noose is getting tighter. You have less room to make errors," says Nathaniel Reed, a prominent Republican and one of the state's leading environmental activists. "Everybody is thinking, 'Time is running out on the good life.'"

Ready to Capitalize

Environmental groups are hoping that the new political climate will help them bring more allies to Congress. Some say they are making a more concerted effort to get involved in con-

gressional campaigns, helping to elect members who are considered environmentally sensitive and to raise the profile of their issues on the campaign trail.

The Sierra Club, one of the few such organizations with a political action committee (PAC) that funds candidates, began the practice in 1982, with contributions totaling about $235,000. That was boosted to about $280,000 in the 1988 cycle, and there is hope that the PAC, which solicits from the Sierra Club's 540,000 members, will significantly boost giving in the next cycle.

But environmental groups have more than money to give. They also claim an army of volunteers and organizers, who, unlike standard financial contributors, can draw direct attention to environmental issues.

The League of Conservation Voters is actively training campaign organizers to dispatch to roughly 20 campaigns next year and points to several races in which it made such contributions in 1988.

According to the LCV, New Jersey Sen. Frank R. Lautenberg, D, got a hand from an LCV field organizer; Republican Sen. Dave Durenberger in Minnesota was helped with a phone bank operation aimed at environmentally oriented Democrats; and Rhode Island Sen. John H. Chafee received help in researching the opposition, canvassing and training volunteers.

But if environmentalists see new opportunities to elect some of their own, the recent attention to their issues presents another challenge.

If more candidates on both sides of the aisle tout environmental credentials, it may become more difficult for these groups to draw public distinctions between allies and adversaries.

As long as candidates like George Bush can win while touting environmental credentials that were highly suspect in the environmental community, politicians may have little incentive to change their behavior.

Environmental activists also must temper their optimism for a green Congress with the realization that it is difficult to apply one standard to all candidates.

In 1988, some environmental groups endorsed Democratic Rep. Wayne Dowdy in his losing Mississippi Senate race against Republican Rep. Trent Lott, not because Dowdy was considered a strong ally — his LCV vote rating in 1987-88 was only 38 percent — but because he would be less of an enemy than the Republican. ∎

For Gore, the Payoff May Be Political

If focused thought could solve the global-warming crisis or elect a president, Sen. Al Gore would be well on his way to achieving both.

Gore, D-Tenn., has carved a role for himself as a leader in raising public consciousness about the environment. That role may have little legislative payoff; the chances of Congress passing sweeping legislation on the matter are minimal. But the political dividends for Gore, an unsuccessful presidential aspirant in 1988, might be more promising.

His approach to educating himself and the public about the environment is enhancing an image as a serious legislator with futuristic vision. "He is demonstrating an international and worldwide grasp of environmental issues," says Ali Webb of the League of Conservation Voters. "Perhaps he's auditioning for another job. If that's so, we welcome the leadership."

Gore's efforts already have earned him top billing on the media's list of experts on the environment, with quotes in almost every story on the topic and appearances on news programs. In addition, this spring, he will chair the first international conference of legislators focused on the global environment. *(Story, p. 28)*

Combine this publicity with the freshly honed image, and it's not hard to envision a "Gore for President" strategy for the 1990s.

Becoming the Expert

An intensive, academic approach to problems is one of the defining characteristics of Gore's political persona, and his approach to the environment is typical. Gore zealously delves into the scientific detail of global warming, wanting to see the problem for himself. In 1989, he traveled to Antarctica and to Great Britain to meet with scientists working to measure the Earth's ozone layer and the warming of the environment.

Almost a decade earlier, when he served in the House, Gore put the same energy into mastering arms control. He read and studied and attended a series of private tutorials on the issue. By the early 1980s, he had made himself one of the nation's leading experts.

Gore's single-warhead-missile proposal was creative enough that it was endorsed in 1983 by the Scowcroft commission, which had been established by President Ronald Reagan to chart the future of U.S. land-based missiles. But rather than leading to the elimination of the more threatening multiple-warhead missile, as Gore envisioned, his idea was simply folded into Reagan's defense buildup. Today, it appears financially dubious.

Like the arms race, global warming is a broad, complex issue. But it is still an abstract notion to most voters. This insulates Gore from interest-group pressures — a real concern in the clean-air debate — but

Sen. Al Gore, D-Tenn.

R. MICHAEL JENKINS

it lessens the electoral salience of global warming.

"This is a tough issue to make political hay with," says Fred Martin, Gore's 1988 campaign manager. "It's not only very complicated, it's also one which doesn't seem to touch people in their daily lives."

But the style with which Gore approaches the issue may capture admirers. When *The New Republic* endorsed Gore for president in 1988, it cited his "intellectual powers" and his "ability to grasp the meaning of new and adventurous technologies."

Issue for the 1990s

Two years ago, when he was campaigning for the Democratic presidential nomination, the environment got little more than a line in a speech. His campaign was almost entirely based on his self-proclaimed moderate-to-conservative record and Southern roots. But he failed to gain a toehold outside his native region.

Today, Gore says he finds audiences in Tennessee and across the country more receptive to discourse on the environment. "In inner-city neighborhoods, in the smallest rural hamlets and everywhere in between people are asking questions and making statements that were unheard of just 12 months ago," he says. "More and more people are thinking that at least in environmental terms the whole world is their back yard."

The problem for Gore and his party is that voters see little difference between the parties on environmental issues. Beginning with the successful campaign ad featuring the polluted Boston Harbor and continuing through his recent Clean Air Initiative, George Bush has identified himself as an environmentalist. By contrast, after a decade of fighting Reagan administration efforts to cut the environmental budget and scale back federal regulations, Democrats find themselves looking for new leaders with fresh initiatives. This vacuum is allowing Gore and a new group of "green" Democrats to emerge.

Like the "Atari Democrats" of the mid-1980s on economic issues, the green Democrats look both to government and to industry for cost-effective answers to environmental problems. While this has a more moderate appeal, it is not clear whether this is the stuff a future presidential campaign can be made of.

For the issue to become a national voting issue, according to Democratic pollster Mark Mellman, "the public has to perceive a difference between the parties. In most areas where the environment is important, Republicans have appeared not very different from Democrats."

Asked about how his party can recapture the issue, Gore responds in expected fashion: "Dig in on the substance, and let the politics flow from there."

—Beth Donovan

CALIFORNIA

In Cradle of Environmentalism, The Political Fight Is Hot

Imagine a state where the retiring Republican governor, a staunch conservative, signs legislation to sharply increase solid-waste recycling. His panel of air quality regulators sets auto-emission standards far exceeding anything being considered by Congress. And the GOP candidate to succeed him makes a campaign issue of his own opposition to offshore oil drilling.

Despite these overtures, state environmentalists decry a lack of progress. They propose a far-reaching ballot initiative to clamp down on polluters, ban harmful farm pesticides and force drastic reductions in carbon dioxide emissions. The front-runner for the Democratic gubernatorial nomination quickly adopts the proposition as the centerpiece of his campaign.

In most states, this scenario would be an environmentalist's vision of the future. In California, that future is now.

"The environment" has been a dominant political issue in California since at least 1969 — the year of a disastrous oil rig blowout off the coast of Santa Barbara. Its importance to the state's politicians, policy makers and bureaucrats has been reflected in myriad regulations — from portentous national moratoriums on oil exploration off the California coast to seemingly uncontroversial state and local bottle-recycling laws.

In the process, California has become both the standard-bearer for environmental regulations and the chief battleground for government, industry and environmental organizations from across the country. And now, interest in the environment from California officials, activists and voters appears to be nearing its zenith.

GOP Gov. George Deukmejian, despite many confrontations with environmentalists over the years, consented last year to a series of new laws and rulings on air pollution and recycling. Under one proposal, sales of gasoline-powered cars in the Los Angeles area would be eliminated within 20 years.

By Bob Benenson

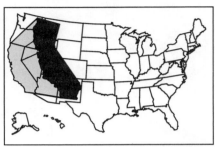

BARBARA SASSA-DANIELS

With Deukmejian retiring after the 1990 election, Republican Sen. Pete Wilson has fueled his effort to succeed the governor by promoting his own environmental credentials, casting himself in the mold of Teddy Roosevelt, the icon of GOP conservationism.

Meanwhile, state Attorney General John Van de Kamp, who is battling former San Francisco Mayor Dianne Feinstein for the Democratic gubernatorial nomination, has positioned himself as the "true" environmentalist in the contest. To prove his standing, he has signed on to what is certain to be the most explosive 1990 ballot issue in California: a sweeping initiative drawn up by a coalition of environmental groups and spearheaded by liberal state Rep. Tom Hayden.

Whatever their outcomes, the impending battles for governor and over the ballot initiative will doubtless ensure California's status as a national trendsetter on environmental issues. "We've had a tradition of being at the cutting edge of environmental issues," said Michael Paparian, executive director of the state's Sierra Club affiliate. "California has been the environmental proving ground."

Critical Mass

It is only natural that California, America's Western nation-state, would run ahead of its 49 counterparts on environmental issues. California is home to about 29 million people, more than a tenth of the nation. Its population is far in excess of also-rans New York and Texas.

California's 50 percent growth rate over the past generation has exacerbated such extant state concerns as smog and garbage disposal, as well as

preservation of the ocean and mountain and wilderness vistas, which drew so many people to California in the first place. The state's bountiful farmlands and wealth of natural resources have also made it an arena for debate on such issues as pesticide use and coastal oil development.

The environment as an issue has a long history in California: The Sierra Club, an environmental organization, was founded in 1892 to defend the recently established Yosemite National Park from ranchers who coveted its grazing lands. But most activists point to the Santa Barbara oil spill as the pivotal event in raising public awareness of environmental issues.

In January 1969, the Santa Barbara Channel was blackened by crude oil that spewed from cracks in the ocean floor caused by drilling at a Unocal Corp. offshore platform. During the weeks it took to stop the flow, more than 3 million gallons of oil seeped out, killing plants, birds, and marine and other wildlife. The oily mess that washed ashore near Santa Barbara also tarred the image of California, historically described as America's natural paradise.

The oil spill energized the then-small community of activists and spurred numerous citizens — many of whom had never given environmental issues much thought — to join ad hoc groups such as Santa Barbara's "Get Oil Out." The issue also provided the first evidence that the environment could be a powerful voting issue: In 1972, the California Coastal Protection Initiative (Proposition 20), which created a state coastal commission to regulate shoreline development, passed by a wide margin.

By the 1980s, California had adopted automobile exhaust emission standards far more stringent than the federal government required. Despite the support of President Ronald Reagan and Deukmejian for offshore oil exploration, a majority of the state's congressional delegation, including many Republicans, has consistently supported limits on drilling. Cities large and small, including Fremont,

Berkeley, San Jose, Santa Monica and San Francisco, adopted solid-waste recycling programs for homeowners and businesses.

But during the same period, the state was flooded with millions of new residents from across the country, Mexico and Asia. And even California's cutting-edge efforts could not stem the tide of problems that accompanied the state's population explosion.

Nowhere have the growth-related environmental problems been more marked than in Los Angeles, the nation's second-largest city. Situated in a pollution-trapping basin between the Pacific Ocean and the San Gabriel Mountains, and heavily dependent on the automobile for transportation, Los Angeles has the worst air pollution among major U.S. cities. In 1988, ozone levels there exceeded federal standards on 180 days, in contrast to only 42 days in New York City. With the garbage landfills serving the metropolitan area rapidly running out of space, and a strong "not-in-my-backyard" sentiment preventing construction of new ones, warnings of a "garbage crisis" in the early 1990s have grown rife.

Other areas of the state were not immune from environment-related pressures. The burgeoning San Francisco Bay region faced land-use and waste-disposal problems similar to those in the Los Angeles area. Population and industrial growth in the San Joaquin Valley, California's agricultural heartland, caused a rise in air pollution and an increase in concern among farmers about lower crop yields.

'Quality of Life'

Over the past several years, these environmental worries have combined with distress over soaring residential prices, gridlocked freeways, cluttered skylines and other symptoms of growth to make "quality of life" a major topic on the California political agenda.

That was evident in 1989, when state and local governments passed a series of landmark environmental laws and regulations. Among these were two proposals, approved by Deukmejian's Air Resources Board (ARB), that have stunning implications for California businesses and individuals.

In August, ARB signed off on a multilayered package of regulations produced by the South Coast Air Quality Management District and aimed at bringing the Los Angeles Basin into compliance with federal air standards by the year 2007. The most

T.H. WATKINS/THE WILDERNESS SOCIETY

California has been a leader in protecting and preserving its scenic areas.

discussed provision calls for 40 percent of cars, 70 percent of trucks and all buses to run on methanol or other "clean fuels" by 1998. By 2008, cars sold in the region will have to use alternative fuels or electricity.

Also under the proposal, paints and aerosol products are to be reformulated to reduce polluting gases; restaurants, bakeries and breweries will have to install special air-cleaning vents and filters. The plan reaches directly into people's back yards: Gasoline-powered mowers and outdoor grills that require starter fluid may be banned.

Then, in December, the ARB issued a plan to drastically reduce polluting automobile emissions statewide.

Under the new rules, in 2000, 98 percent of the cars sold in the state must be "low-emission vehicles," which put out no more than 0.075 grams per mile (gpm) of hydrocarbons — far less than the current standard of 0.25 gpm by 1993.

Earlier last year, trash recycling also received attention. In June, Deukmejian signed an omnibus trash recycling bill produced by the Democratic-dominated Legislature. The law sets up a full-time state board on trash disposal, requires cities and counties to halve their solid-waste flows by 2000, sets up "enterprise zones" for recycling plants and increases state purchases of recycled products.

The state's localities were also busy on the environmental front. In Los Angeles, the City Council passed a measure in November barring most

trucks from city streets during the morning and evening rush hours, and Mayor Tom Bradley announced just before the end of the year a mandatory recycling program for the city's single-family households.

Despite a seemingly epochal movement on their issues, many state environmentalists are dissatisfied with the rate of progress. "The environmental community . . . has been very frustrated in the last decade at the unbelievably slow pace of environmental legislation in California," said Lucy Blake, executive director of the California League of Conservation Voters (LCV).

In the activists' view, the Legislature is timid in confronting powerful business and industry interests that oppose many environmental measures because of their economic cost. And the activists continue to regard Deukmejian — despite his administration's 1989 actions — as an obstacle.

"The governor is very resistant to doing things differently," said Paparian of the Sierra Club. "He has vetoed a number of good bills that have made it through the Legislature."

'Big Green' Ballot Initiative

The LCV, the Sierra Club and four other environmental organizations have proposed a solution to this perceived lack of progress: the 1990 ballot proposition, which has been labeled the "Big Green" initiative.

The measure would create an elected position for a state "environmental advocate," who would have the power to sue polluting businesses and even state agencies. The measure also would ban by 1996 farm pesticides known to cause cancer or reproductive injury, require 20 percent reductions of carbon dioxide emissions by 2000 and 40 percent by 2010, and strictly limit use of such ozone-layer-depleting chemicals as chlorofluorocarbons. The proposition would also create state trust funds for oil-spill cleanups and timber preservation.

The sweeping — and costly — provisions of this proposal guarantee that the initiative will be an electoral battleground this year. In December, the directors of the California Chamber of Commerce voted to oppose the initiative, and several agribusiness groups are organizing to oppose the pesticide provisions.

The business-vs.-environmental faceoff promises, at the least, a replay of an electoral battle in 1986, when the antagonists squared off over Proposition 65. That was a successful initiative restricting toxic chemical emissions and requiring labeling of products, including alcoholic beverages, containing ingredients known to be health hazards.

But the zeal of two Democratic politicians ensures that the 1990 initiative will also be an issue in contests for statewide office this year and perhaps later.

Van de Kamp, who announced his support for the ballot measure even before it was officially unveiled in October, has firmly linked his gubernatorial campaign to the initiative, which he describes as an "environmental bill of rights."

And Hayden — a longtime Democratic state legislator, 1960s radical and chairman of the "Campaign California" organization, which is in the forefront of the initiative effort — has hinted that he is interested in running for the environmental advocate's position in 1992.

Clearly, these Democratic leaders see the environmental issue as a winner in their campaigns for higher office. But high-level Democratic sponsorship is just as likely to be a central issue for opponents of the initiative campaign. Critics are already describing the proposal as the "Van de Kamp-Hayden initiative," in hopes of decreasing its attractiveness to environment-minded voters, especially Republicans, who otherwise hold conservative views on economic and social issues.

Wilson's Dilemma

Nonetheless, the initiative has placed Wilson, the Republican senator and gubernatorial candidate, in a somewhat uncomfortable position. Given the apparent currency of the environment as a political issue, he is wary about disclaiming the initiative. But he will undoubtedly face pressure to do so from business and agricultural interests whose support is crucial to statewide Republican candidates.

Some of these interests already are skittish about Wilson, whose literature highlights his environmentalist leanings, dating to his tenures as a state legislator (1967-71) and as mayor of San Diego (1971-83). In the early stages of his campaign for governor, Wilson has emphasized his longtime opposition to oil exploration on the outer continental shelf off California and his support for various wilderness and scenic-river designations in California.

PAUL CONKLIN   PAUL CONKLIN

A ballot initiative co-championed by state Rep. Tom Hayden, left, has put pressure on U.S. Sen. Pete Wilson.

His positions on offshore oil drilling have occasionally placed Wilson at odds with Republican administrations in Washington. Last July, Wilson joined Democratic Sen. Alan Cranston and 17 House Democrats from California in calling for Interior Secretary Manuel Lujan Jr. to step down from a task force that President Bush appointed on the future of offshore drilling. Wilson said statements by Lujan in support of oil drilling had "severely compromised the credibility of the task force," adding, "The Department of Interior still fails to recognize there are environmentally acceptable alternatives to increased offshore oil drilling."

But while Wilson says efforts such as these have impressed voters in his two Senate campaigns, he is discouraged at winning the support of the state's environmental organizations. "It is almost impossible because they've been very partisan," Wilson said in an interview. During his 1988 campaign, Wilson said, the Sierra Club advised him not to include in his advertisements letters from the organization that were "full of glowing praise about my performance on wilderness issues, offshore drilling issues." He also maintained that the Sierra Club's decision to oppose him in his 1988 Senate contest hinged solely on his opposition to a desert wilderness bill sponsored by Cranston.

Other state Republicans have stated similar frustrations.

Veteran GOP Rep. Robert J. Lagomarsino, whose 19th District centers on Santa Barbara, has long touted what he views as a creditable environmental record: He supports limits on oil drilling and tanker shipping in the Santa Barbara Channel. But in his 1988 re-election campaign against Democratic state Sen. Gary Hart, Lagomarsino — a senior Republican

on the House Interior Committee — was attacked by environmentalist organizations. Environmental Action went so far as to place him on its "Dirty Dozen" list, naming him as one of the 12 worst members of Congress on environmental issues.

Lagomarsino barely held on to win by only 4,000 votes and still fumes over the "Dirty Dozen" listing. He said his analysis showed that his voting record on environmental issues matched that of 44 other House members. He was unfairly singled out because he was accurately perceived as vulnerable to challenge from the popular Hart, Lagomarsino said.

But environmentalists reject such criticisms and say some Republicans seek to be judged by a less rigorous standard. "They think if they support the moratorium on offcoast oil drilling, that qualifies them to be an environmental saint," said LCV's Blake. "Wilson's and Lagomarsino's voting records are very mixed."

Staying Attuned

Most California politicians seem to be adjusting to what they view as a public consensus in favor of a cleaner environment. Even interest groups that oppose many of the environmentalists' specific proposals say they do not quarrel with the movement's goals.

"The business community is much more attuned to the situation," said Kirk West, president of the California Chamber of Commerce. "We urgently want a clean environment. . . . The most egregious polluters should not be defended."

However, West and others say the seeming consensus for stringent environmental regulation may disintegrate when the economic costs begin to hit home, not only to major industries and the state as a whole, but to individual homeowners, drivers, farmers and others. He points out that some organized labor officials have joined with business owners to establish the Council for Environmental and Economic Balance.

There is also the possibility of a backlash against the "lifestyle" impacts as state regulations limit the variety of cars and of consumer products Californians can buy. "When it comes down to not being able to use the backyard barbecue," Lagomarsino said, "a lot of people will be upset." ∎

Part II

Setting Environmental Priorities

*Something must be done soon,
but which problems are the most serious?*

The Problems

The winter's chill may now be in the air, but few will quickly forget the summer of 1988. Record-breaking heat scorched cities across the nation, the sick and the elderly were warned to stay inside away from life-threatening smog, and vacationers steered clear of beaches littered with AIDS-infected medical waste. Scientists warned that a global warming trend and depletion of the planet's protective ozone layer threatened our very survival. Their words seemed prophetic as the season wore on. Erratic weather caused drought in the Midwest and forest fires throughout the West, floods in Bangladesh and a killer hurricane in the Caribbean.

"I think this society crossed a perceptual threshold this summer," says Lester R. Brown, president of Worldwatch Institute, a Washington-based think tank that focuses on global environmental problems. "The issues have moved beyond the hard-core environmental community into the mainstream."

Indeed, this country seems to have begun a third phase of environmental awareness. The first began in 1962 with the publication of Rachel Carson's *Silent Spring*, a wrenching description of how Americans were destroying the land with pesticides and other chemicals. The awakening that Carson's book stirred culminated in 1970 with Earth Day, a nationwide expression of support for laws to save the environment. The 1970s saw passage of the basic environmental protection laws and the creation of the Environmental Protection Agency (EPA) to administer them.

These laws — the 1970 Clean Air Act and the 1977 Clean Water Act and their subsequent amendments — have succeeded in reducing many types of pollution. But they are no longer enough. Environmentalists hope that mounting public concern will provide the necessary support for a new generation of environmental laws. A broad coalition of more than 30 organizations, including the Sierra Club, the Natural Resources Defense Council and the Union of Concerned Scientists, has put together a set of policy recommendations for President-elect George Bush. The "Blueprint for the Environment" contains more than 700 separate recommendations for action.

Even if the new administration accepts the recommendations in toto, it will not be easy to decide what to do first or how to do it. For one thing, the older focuses of national policy, mainly air and water pollution, were easier to deal with than the most serious environmental issues of the 1980s. When the Cuyahoga River went up in flames in 1965, for example, the causes and the solutions were obvious: Industries that dumped flammable substances into the river were required to find other means of disposing of their wastes. Likewise, urban smog could be reduced by

By Mary H. Cooper

forcing the biggest industrial polluters to build taller smokestacks so harmful emissions would be carried downwind or to install "scrubbers" to reduce the amount of pollutants emptied into the air.

Global warming and depletion of the ozone layer, by contrast, require drastic *international* action — and the principals are not just the industrialized nations but the developing ones as well. An important precedent for international cooperation was set in 1987 with the signing of the Montreal Protocol, a 34-nation agreement to limit production of ozone-damaging chlorofluorocarbons (CFCs). But halting CFC production looks easy when compared with slowing the world's production of carbon dioxide, an essential ingredient of any solution to the global warming trend.

Further complicating the job of setting the nation's environmental priorities for the 1990s is public misunderstanding of the problems at hand. As the EPA has discovered, there is a serious mismatch between the actual risks posed by certain environmental problems and the level of public concern over those problems. Hazardous-waste sites, for example, rank high on the list of public concern, and a large portion of the EPA's budget goes toward cleaning them up. But other sources of pollution, such as radon in houses, pose a far greater threat to human health. Yet indoor radon does not even figure on the EPA's agenda.

And as industrial development creates new sources of pollution, as automobiles proliferate, as landfills fill up, each successive step to save the environment becomes more difficult and more costly.

Greenhouse effect: The No. 1 danger

If projections are correct, global warming is today's single most serious environmental threat. Industrial development has been fueled by the burning of fossil fuels — oil, coal and gas — which each year release about 6 billion tons of carbon dioxide into the atmosphere. In tropical regions of the Third World, growing populations burn forests to clear the land for grazing and cultivation, which releases more carbon dioxide into the atmosphere. The gas has accumulated more rapidly than it has been absorbed by natural processes, creating a kind of dirty window over the Earth. Its effect is similar to that of a greenhouse, which allows visible light from the sun to reach and warm the Earth's surface but prevents infrared energy from radiating back into space. To a certain extent, the "greenhouse effect" occurs naturally, and without it life on Earth would be impossible. But human activities are producing so much carbon dioxide that the atmosphere is warming at a faster rate than at any time since the last Ice Age ended 18,000 years ago.

First postulated in 1896 by Svante Arrhenius, a Swedish

chemist, the greenhouse effect was largely ignored until recent years, when advanced computer models allowed scientists to make projections of the Earth's temperatures over the next several decades. They found that carbon dioxide has increased by 25 percent since 1880. Although carbon dioxide accounts for about three-fifths of the greenhouse effect, other gases also play a role, and that role seems to be growing. Methane, emitted by bacteria living in the soil under rice paddies and in the intestines of ruminating cattle and sheep, ranks second to carbon dioxide among greenhouse gases. As the global population continues to grow, herds will get bigger and rice paddies will cover wider areas, producing more methane and, therefore, more global warming from methane. And the impact of CFCs on global warming also is increasing, although the chemicals have less effect today than carbon dioxide. The computer models suggest that by the time the concentration of carbon dioxide reaches twice the level existing before the Industrial Revolution began, global temperatures will have risen by 4-9 degrees Fahrenheit.

The timing of this change is a matter of controversy. Some scientists say temperatures will not even begin to climb until the second half of the 21st century. But others, including James Hansen, the NASA scientist whose testimony last summer focused public attention on the subject, say that last summer's weather patterns marked the beginning of far more drastic changes to come.[1] "The possible link between drought in the United States and global warming may be much stronger than most people realize," says Brown, who is also an agricultural economist. All three severe U.S. droughts since 1950, he points out, have occurred during the 1980s, when the five warmest years for the world on record also occurred. "The odds for that being a coincidence are pretty low."

If Brown is right, the warming trend could spell disaster for the world's food supply. In 1988, the United States for the first time became what Brown calls a "grain-deficit country," as grain harvests fell below domestic consumption. Because U.S. grain reserves are low, he says, "if we were to have another drought next year, exports from North America would slow to a trickle, there would be a frantic scramble among the world's food-importing countries for a very limited supply, food prices would take off, and no one knows where they would go." The global impact, he believes, "could be more traumatic than the oil price hikes of the 1970s."

Although there is some dispute over details, scientists generally agree that the buildup of greenhouse gases is very likely to raise mean global temperatures and cause an increase in precipitation. If they are not countered by unforeseen reactions, these two changes would have wide-ranging effects. Because water expands when heated, ocean levels would rise, a trend that would accelerate with the melting of polar ice caps. By 2050, the sea level may rise by as much as four feet. Flooding of coastal areas, where more than a third of the world's inhabitants live, would cause immense dislocation. The warming trend's long-term effects are even more uncertain. Scientists differ in their assumptions about how fast the oceans will absorb the heat and the carbon dioxide. They also cannot predict with certainty how the global ecosystem will react.

At the same time, some regions would stand to benefit from the change: Vast areas of frozen wilderness in northern Canada and the Soviet Union, for example, would be opened to cultivation as the tundra thawed. On a global scale, however, the winners of global warming would appear to be far outnumbered by the losers.

The United States would be one of the biggest losers, according to a recent EPA study. In California, higher temperatures would increase demand for electricity, worsen urban ozone pollution and dry out the soil, straining scarce water resources. As the sea level rises, San Francisco Bay would spread, pushing salt water as far as six miles farther upstream in the Sacramento-San Joaquin River Delta, with devastating effects on this productive agricultural region. The Southeast would suffer similar problems, with the additional burden of forest die-back from the higher temperatures beginning as early as 2118. The annual cost of meeting higher demand for electricity for air conditioning and other purposes nationwide would reach $33 billion to $73 billion by 2055. In the Midwest, drought would shrink crop yields significantly. Drought also would lower water levels in the Great Lakes, requiring channels to be dredged for ship traffic. This would release pollutants that have settled on the lake bottoms. The EPA's pessimistic conclusion for the country as a whole: "The ultimate effects will last for centuries and will be irreversible. Strategies to reverse such impacts on natural ecosystems are not currently available."[2]

The greenhouse effect poses a greater immediate threat to natural systems — forests, wetlands, freshwater lakes — than to human health, the EPA concludes. This fact alone will make it very difficult to enact measures to slow the trend. And it could take 30 years to *prove* that the emission of greenhouse gases is linked to global warming. By that time, it could be too late to do much more about it than try to adapt. Dikes would have to be built to hold back sea water from heavily inhabited coastlines, additional power plants would be needed to provide air conditioning, and widespread dredging of ports and waterways in drying lakes and rivers would have to be carried out to accommodate ship traffic. The cost of such adjustments in the United States alone could amount to hundreds of billions of dollars. And even these drastic measures would be fruitless in the absence of international cooperation. The United States is the world's largest contributor to global warming, but it cannot stop the trend by itself.

Ozone depletion: A more immediate risk

Close to the Earth, ozone is nothing more than a noxious component of urban smog (*see below*). But the thin layer of this colorless, odorless gas that is suspended 15 miles above the Earth's surface provides essential protection from the sun's harmful ultraviolet rays. No thicker than the cover of a hardback book, this delicate structure is being destroyed by CFCs and halons, another group of gases used in industry.

Discovered in 1930, CFCs eventually found widespread use in automobile air conditioners, refrigerators, fast-food cartons, spray cans, foam cushions and insulation, and as cleaning agents for electronic equipment. Their ozone-destroying capacity was not discovered until 1985. Once they are released, CFCs float upward to the stratosphere and are carried by prevailing winds to the North and South poles. The chlorine atoms present in each CFC molecule that is released into the atmosphere act as catalysts to break apart ozone molecules thousands of times over for about a century.

Ozone depletion poses a more immediate threat to human health than global warming. The sun's ultraviolet rays (UV-B) cause skin cancer and eye damage and weaken the body's ability to defend itself from disease. A half million skin cancer cases are diagnosed each year in the United States alone, the vast majority caused by exposure to sunlight. Although most skin cancers are not life-threatening if treated promptly, about 25,000 cases a year involve a more deadly form called malignant melanoma. UV-B rays can also destroy plankton, the tiny one-celled organisms that are at the base of the ocean's food chain, as well as plant life on dry land, including food crops.

Despite its greater threat to human health, however, ozone depletion is much easier to curtail than global warming. All it takes is to cease producing CFCs and halons. There is a cost: Substitutes for CFCs and halons may not be readily available — and those that are generally cost significantly more to produce. But in the 1987 Montreal Protocol, 34 countries that produce or use CFCs agreed to cut production in half by 1999. Production of three ozone-depleting halons, used mainly in fire extinguishers, will be frozen. The Montreal Protocol has since been ratified by the required 11 signatories and is due to take effect Jan. 1, 1989.[3] If the agreement is honored, emission of ozone depleters will fall by 35-40 percent by the end of the century, the EPA predicts. Unfortunately, scientists found after the protocol was signed in 1987 that stratospheric ozone is disappearing two to three times faster than was previously thought and that the agreement does not go far enough to stop the damage. EPA now estimates that CFCs must be reduced by 85 percent just to hold steady their presence in the stratosphere. Even if ozone depleters are banned, it will take about another century for the CFCs already released to break down.

Acid rain: The distant polluter

While not global in scope like ozone depletion and global warming, acid rain also is an environmental problem that often affects more than the country that produces it. Like the greenhouse effect, acid rain is caused by the burning of fossil fuels. The pollutants involved are sulfur dioxide, emitted mainly by coal-fired electric power plants, and nitrogen oxides, released by numerous sources, including industrial furnaces and automobiles. In the United States, sulfur dioxide accounts for about two-thirds of acid-rain pollution. The rest is linked mainly to nitrogen oxides, which also are greenhouse-effect gases and contribute to urban smog.

Once released into the atmosphere, these pollutants can be swept by wind thousands of miles away from the source and return to the Earth with rain, snow or fog. The polluted precipitation, known collectively as acid rain, changes the pH balance of lakes, rivers and the soil on which it falls. Many animal and plant species cannot survive under heavily acidic conditions. Lakes in large areas of the northeastern United States and southeastern Canada are already sterile. Although deforestation by acid rain has been most pronounced in West Germany and other parts of industrial Europe, forests along the Appalachian range in the Eastern United States also are showing signs of stress.

Acid rain has been a recognized environmental danger for almost a decade. And no issue better demonstrates the

political stalemate that can result when opposing interests come to blows over an environmental problem. The Midwestern utilities that are the source of most acid-rain pollutants have successfully fought legislation requiring them to install expensive technology to cut sulfur dioxide emissions in older, dirtier power plants exempted from the standards set by the Clean Air Act. They are supported by automakers, who would have to improve tailpipe-emission controls if nitrogen oxide standards were tightened. Coal-producing states also have a stake in the issue: Western states that produce cleaner-burning, low-sulfur coal support stricter controls, while high-sulfur coal producers such as West Virginia say such controls would threaten local mining jobs. The utilities have sought to stall legislative action by supporting research into "clean coal" technologies aimed at curbing harmful emissions at the moment of combustion. But these technologies have yet to produce conclusive results, and acid rain continues to fall.

If no further steps are taken to curb acid rain, the Congressional Budget Office predicts, U.S. electric utilities will emit 18.5 million tons of sulfur dioxide in 1995, almost 3 million more tons than they did in 1985. Reducing these emissions by 10 million tons, the budget office estimates, would cost $3.3 billion to $4.7 billion.[4] But environmentalists fear that inaction will mean that acid rain will soon begin to destroy essential tropical forests as well as the woodlands in Western Europe and North America.

Air pollution: A modicum of success

In some respects, the fight against air pollution is one of the environmental movement's biggest success stories. Some cities, of course, are still plagued by various pollutants. The World Health Organization reported recently that two-thirds of the world's urban inhabitants breathe unhealthful air.[5] Milan, for example, has the highest concentration of sulfur dioxide in the world, almost four times the levels found in New York City, while Paris is the worst offender of the U.N. agency's carbon monoxide and lead standards. But the world has come a long way since 1952, when smog killed several thousand people in London.

In the United States, lead has been largely eliminated from the air by phasing out leaded gasoline, while auto-emission standards have cut down on the release of nitrogen dioxide, carbon monoxide and other pollutants each car spews into the air we breathe. Nevertheless, as last summer demonstrated, the battle against air pollution is far from over. In more than 50 American cities, air-quality standards were violated by more than 25 percent.

In addition to lead, the major air pollutants are sulfur dioxide and nitrogen dioxide (the principal ingredients of acid rain), suspended particulate matter (smoke and dust) and carbon monoxide. These pollutants irritate the lungs and may cause cancer and other diseases. Some, such as carbon monoxide, interfere with the body's ability to use oxygen. Ozone, so essential in the stratosphere, is a major pollutant on the ground. It is produced when nitrogen oxides and other pollutants react with oxygen in the presence of strong sunlight. Los Angeles, which has the worst ozone pollution in the country, has introduced more stringent measures to clean up the air, requiring oil refineries and furniture manufacturers to cut their emissions deeply. But even if these strict measures are carried out, the city does not expect to meet its own standards until 2007.

Hot weather is not the only obstacle to cleaner air. Although cars and factories pollute less than they did before the Clean Air Act went into effect, there are more of them. And as the economy and the population expand, the smog will thicken unless further steps are taken to reduce the level of toxic emissions at each source. EPA has come under fire for not doing enough to enforce existing air-quality standards. One such area involves the escape of toxic fuel vapors into the air as gasoline is pumped into cars. These vapors contain benzene, a known carcinogen, or cancer-causing agent. The auto industry says the oil refiners should deal with the problem by installing devices on all gas station pumps. The refiners reply that seals placed inside the gas tanks of all new cars would be more effective. The argument has continued unresolved for six years.

Air pollution indoors is often worse than outdoors

Perhaps the biggest discrepancy between the risks posed by environmental problems and the way the public perceives these threats lies in the area of indoor air pollution. Radon, an odorless, invisible radioactive gas that occurs naturally in some types of rock and soil, has been found in danger-

ously high concentrations in about 200,000 houses in seven states. EPA estimates that about 8 million houses have unsafe levels of radon nationwide.

Radon, which is too diluted to be harmful outdoors, can cause lung cancer if it seeps through cracks in foundations and basement walls and builds to high concentrations in poorly ventilated houses. The EPA estimates that radon alone causes 20,000 deaths a year, more than any other air pollutant. And yet there are no federal regulations to reduce human exposure to radon. The reason is that the EPA does not consider indoor space to be part of its jurisdiction. The agency has thus limited its treatment of radon to issuing guidelines aimed at helping consumers determine at what level of concentration radon constitutes a health hazard. A law signed by former President Reagan in October, 1988 requires the EPA to establish building-code standards to protect against radon pollution by mid-1990. Meanwhile, several states have acted on their own by incorporating radon standards into local building codes.

Radon is not the only health-threatening pollutant in homes. There are a host of others released by such common household items as paints and adhesives, room deodorizers, tobacco and dry-cleaned clothing. Even taking a shower may be hazardous to your health, because hot chlorinated water releases toxic chloroform in steam. Many of the chief outdoor air pollutants, such as benzene, dirty the air inside as well.

Lance Wallace, an environmental scientist at EPA, found that indoor air was as much as 100 times more toxic in one study he conducted.[6] "People spend 90 percent of their time indoors," Wallace says. "Yet indoor levels of pollutants are higher than outdoor levels for just about everything we've ever studied, with the exception of ozone."

Indoor air pollution is especially severe in new buildings, where glues, carpeting and foam furniture exude massive amounts of volatile organic chemicals that can cause cancer and other diseases. And not all indoor pollutants are man-made. Biological contaminants such as pollen and

Air Pollution in the Home

The EPA has found that indoor air pollution can be much worse than the outdoor variety. In the Home the culprits are everything from recently dry cleaned clothes to ordinary disinfectants.

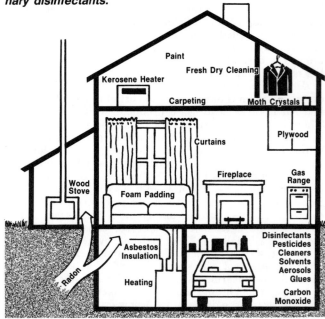

Source: Environmental Protection Agency

animal dander can reach toxic levels inside houses and office buildings when they are distributed by air conditioners and fans. Dirty ventilation systems also provide breeding grounds for molds and fungi that release chemical toxins. The pollution is so bad in some buildings that they cannot be inhabited for months because of "sick building syndrome," which manifests an array of physical symptoms including headaches and nausea.

What will we do with the garbage?

Anyone who tried to go to the beach in the Northeast last summer might place garbage at the top of the environmental agenda of the 1990s. The world may be getting warmer and the sun more dangerous, but solid waste is here for all to see today. American households and industries throw

away more than anyone else in the world. Each one of us, the EPA reports, generates 3.5 pounds of garbage a day; that's a national total of 154 *million tons* a year. Americans throw away enough garbage each year to fill a 30-story building covering 1,000 football fields. An obvious solution to the problem is to throw away less rubbish, particularly bulky plastic items such as disposable diapers and hamburger cartons that have become symbols of our throwaway society. But there are few indications that is about to happen. By the year 2000, the EPA predicts, our annual garbage collection will weigh 193 million tons.

There are three ways to deal with solid waste once it is produced: You can bury it, you can burn it or you can recycle it. In the past, the first two approaches have, by far, been the dominant ones. But landfill space is rapidly running out, and garbage incinerators have polluted the air.

According to the National Solid Wastes Management Association, 131 million tons of trash have to be disposed of in landfills each year, and some parts of the country are running out of space. Land is scarce, so new landfills are difficult to create. And even if land is located, there are political problems. "Nobody wants a landfill in his own back yard," explains Michael Sheward, a spokesman for the association. "As existing landfills reach capacity, states are not compensating [and are engaging in] regulatory foot-dragging." Four states — Florida, Massachusetts, New Hampshire and New Jersey — will close all existing landfills within the next decade. In eight other states — Virginia, West Virginia, Kentucky, Ohio, Pennsylvania, New Jersey, Connecticut and Massachusetts — existing landfill capacity is expected to run out before 1994.[7] It's still an open question as to what they're going to do.

For their part, incinerators are getting better. Early ones spewed pollutants into the air, but modern ones are cleaner. Called resource recovery or waste-to-energy facilities, these plants provide a way both to dispose of trash and to generate electricity, and they now account for about 10 percent of the nation's garbage disposal. But they are too expensive for many localities, and environmentalists say these modern plants still pollute the air with toxic ash. Moreover, even if the ash can be prevented from escaping into the atmosphere, it still has to be disposed of. Burning reduces only the volume, not the mass, of the garbage. In fact, incineration can concentrate toxic materials contained in garbage, and the ash product may be too toxic for safe disposal in landfills.

Recycling is a highly cost-effective way to deal with the problem, but it requires us to change our behavior by separating out metal, paper and glass from household trash before it is collected. EPA estimates that only about 10 percent of the country's solid waste is recycled.

Beached whales, fishing bans and algae-choked waterways bear witness to a more insidious kind of waste problem. The Clean Water Act has helped eliminate the most egregious causes of water pollution, what EPA calls "point-source" polluters, primarily factories and sewage treatment plants. Many waterways that once were off-limits to bathers and fishermen are relatively clean today. But some of the biggest polluters have yet to reduce their wastes. Eighteen years after the President's Council on Environmental Quality first advised that ocean dumping be phased out, numerous cities, including Los Angeles, Boston and New York, still dump sludge, or treated sewage, into the oceans. Although sewage is the biggest water pollutant, heavy metals, plastics, long-lived chemical compounds such as PCBs and DDT, pose daunting obstacles to the cleanup process. Dredging the bottoms to remove toxins, for example, may do more harm than good by stirring them into circulation again.

In addition, today's biggest polluters are harder to identify and monitor. So-called "non-point" polluters range from inadequate city storm sewers that overflow after downpours, carrying spilled toxins and raw sewage into streams and rivers, to farmers and even suburban gardeners whose pesticides are washed hundreds of miles away to kill plant and animal life in the coastal estuaries and harbors where many inland pollutants come to rest. According to the Wilderness Society, a conservation group, animal and plant life in the nation's 445 wildlife refuges are being killed off not only by hunting and development, but by

toxic runoff from farms and industries located far upstream. "Migrating waterfowl are landing in poisoned marshes, development is destroying vital wetlands, and dams and irrigation projects are choking off essential sources of water," it declared in a recent study that described the gradual extinction of life in 10 refuges.[8]

Not all harmful runoff is contaminated by toxic chemicals. Nitrogen and phosphorous fertilizers that stimulate plant growth on farms are lethal when they make their way downstream. Nitrates carried by acid rain also are contributing to the problem. While stimulating the growth of vast mats of algae on the water's surface, these chemicals choke off the oxygen necessary for the survival of marine life. In some places, pollutants continue to kill after they reach open water. A large area extending from the mouth of the Mississippi River into the Gulf of Mexico, once prime fishing grounds, now is known as the "dead zone." Likewise, pollution in the Chesapeake Bay and numerous other coastal estuaries is killing off once plentiful fish and shellfish.

As bad as water pollution and the garbage crisis are, Americans are more concerned about hazardous waste. Toxic-waste dumps have been the focus of attention since 1978, when hundreds of families were forced to abandon their homes built atop a toxic dump in Love Canal near Niagara Falls, N.Y. In 1980, Congress set up the EPA-administered "superfund" to pay for the cleanup of the most harmful dumps, where industries had deposited such lethal compounds as dioxin and polychlorinated biphenyls, or PCBs, used in the manufacture of electrical equipment. But progress has been slow. There are still 1,177 hazardous-waste sites on superfund's "national priorities list" of the worst toxic dumps. Because the production of hazardous wastes continues at a faster pace than the EPA's ability to clean them up, the list is expected to keep growing.

Nuclear waste: It doesn't go away

The nuclear industry poses a special environmental problem because it both uses and disposes of highly toxic and long-lived materials. The partial meltdown at Three Mile Island, Pa., in 1979 and the explosion at Chernobyl in the Soviet Union in 1986 underscored the risks to human health posed by nuclear power plants. After taking off as a result of the energy crisis of the 1970s, new construction of commercial nuclear power plants has virtually ceased because of safety concerns and cost overruns. Meanwhile, proposals to shut down existing nuclear power plants have been the subject of more than a dozen referendums around the country, including an unsuccessful bid to close down Massachusetts' two plants in the November election.

This fall, similar concerns have arisen over several of the 17 plants that produce nuclear weapons and fuel for nuclear-powered warships. Unlike commercial reactors, most of the nuclear-weapons facilities are old, some dating back to the Manhattan Project of the early 1940s that produced the first atomic bomb. The Rocky Flats nuclear-weapons facility near Golden, Colo., was closed Oct. 8 after three people there were exposed to plutonium, and three reactors at the Savannah River plant in South Carolina have been closed since early this year over safety concerns. Workers went out on strike Oct. 7 at a plant in Fernald, Ohio, over reports of chronic leakage of radiation. (The health effects of low-level radiation over long periods of time are largely unknown, but acute exposure to low doses of radiation can cause leukemia and other cancers, while larger exposures can cause "radiation sickness" and death.)

Although commercial nuclear power plants are regulated by the Nuclear Regulatory Commission, the Department of Energy has jurisdiction over the weapons facilities. The Justice Department has ruled that the EPA cannot enforce its nuclear safety and hazardous-waste regulations at these plants because they are run by the Department of Energy, another agency of the executive branch. The department estimates that it will take $200 billion to decommission and clean up the tons of toxic waste it has produced over the past four decades, far more than it cost to build the nuclear arsenal in the first place.

The Solutions

As the EPA rankings make clear, there is no single standard by which to rank these myriad environmental problems and come up with a neat list of priorities for lawmakers to act on. Even if policy makers decide that human health is more important than ecological welfare, for example, some scientists say the worst-case scenario is not a foolproof standard on which to base policy. Take, for example, global warming. "If the worst possible outcome came about, we'd all bake and be left in limpid pools," says Paul R. Portney, director of the Center for Risk Management at Resources for the Future, an environmental research organization in Washington, D.C. In his view, concentrating on the worst-case scenario "leads us sometimes to ignore things like everyday, common, garden-variety air pollution, which in the worst case may not be as bad as some other things, but day in and day out may be causing serious losses to society."

Nevertheless, the consensus in the scientific community seems to be that the most urgent problem is the greenhouse effect and global overheating. "Climate change needs definitely to be first on anybody's agenda," says Frederic Krupp, executive director of the Environmental Defense Fund, a citizens' interest group based in New York City. While its effects on human health and the ecosystem are less certain than, say, acid rain or indoor air pollution, the potential damage this trend could cause places it at the top of most environmental scientists' list of priorities. "Although the effects are delayed and will not be here for a while, if we're going to avert it we have got to act in the next decade," Krupp adds. "If we don't solve this one, all the other things that environmental and conservation groups have worked for all these years will go down the drain."

Of course, any meaningful policy aimed at halting global warming would require global cooperation, and that could take years to accomplish. The Montreal Protocol offers a hopeful precedent, but the scope of that agreement, to cut production of a single class of chemicals, pales when compared with the multifaceted approach required to combat the greenhouse effect.

Nevertheless, as the biggest producer of greenhouse gases, measures taken by the United States alone would both slow the warming trend and provide essential leadership for global action. In addition, placing global warming at the top of the environmental policy agenda offers an additional benefit: The most effective ways to stop it also would help solve other problems related to the environment, the economy and energy policy. "There is no one

At a Glance

Name	Description
Greenhouse Effect	Excessive amounts of carbon dioxide, methane and other gasses are acting like a greenhouse, trapping the sun's warming rays inside the atmosphere. Scientists warn that a global warming trend could cause flooding and drastic shifts in weather patterns within decades.
Stratospheric Ozone Depletion	Chlorofluorocarbons (CFCs), compounds with a variety of industrial uses, are eating a hole in the thin layer of ozone located 15 miles above the earth. The ozone layer shields the earth's surface from the sun's harmful ultraviolet rays.
Acid Rain ‡	Air pollutants washed to earth by rain, snow and fog raise the acidity of the soil and bodies of water where they fall, killing trees and other land vegetation, as well as fish in affected lakes.
Air Pollution ‡	Despite the reduction of some air pollutants, notably lead, since passage of the 1970 Clean Air Act, urban areas remain plagued by noxious smog, especially in the summer months.
Indoor Radon	Radon, a naturally occurring radioactive gas, causes as many as 20,000 deaths a year from lung cancer.
Other Indoor Air Pollution	The EPA has found that indoor air can be as much as 100 times more polluted than outdoor air, even in urban areas with heavy outdoor pollution.
Municipal Garbage	Americans are throwing away more trash than local facilities can accommodate. Landfills are nearing capacity, while modern incinerators and recycling programs remain controversial.
Hazardous Wastes	Chemicals seeping out of storage containers contaminate the water supply.
Nuclear Wastes	Antinuclear sentiment, bolstered by accidents at the nuclear power plants at Three Mile Island and Chernobyl, has built further with recent reports of radiation leakage from nuclear weapons facilities.

‡ This EPA category includes acid rain and air pollutants other than hazardous pollutants in the same category.

policy that by itself is going to make a huge difference," says Dan Lashof, an environmental scientist at the EPA who is preparing a list of policy options for release in the next couple of months. "But by doing a lot of things that move you in the direction of reducing emissions, you can have a large impact."

Greater energy efficiency is the first step

"Climate change is the issue that is going to completely resurrect the need for energy efficiency," Krupp predicts. Once the catchword for a whole set of measures aimed at reducing the United States' dependence on costly foreign oil after OPEC's oil price rises in the 1970s, energy policy was largely dismissed as a concern of hand-wringing environmentalists when gasoline again became available and

What Causes the Problems

Causes	Effects †				Obstacles to Solutions
Industries and vehicles burn fossil fuels to produce carbon dioxide, which is also released in large amounts by tropical deforestation. Methane, a product of anaerobic respiration, is emitted by cattle and sheep and also is released by organisms under the surface of rice paddies. Methane's release is increasing with the global population.	O	X	H	H	Curtailing the greenhouse effect requires a global commitment to take drastic measures — all to solve a future problem whose effects are uncertain. In the United States, the biggest producers of greenhouse gases, industries and consumers, have shown little interest in adopting existing alternatives to fossil fuels. Halting tropical deforestation may mean halting rural development in poor countries. Curbing population growth remains controversial.
In 1987, 34 industrialized nations agreed to reduce CFC production, but more recent findings suggest this agreement does not go far enough to halt ozone depletion.	H	M	H	H	Further CFC reductions require renegotiation of the 1987 Montreal Protocol.
Sulfur dioxide released into the atmosphere by coal-burning industries, chiefly older electric utilities using high-sulfur coal.	L	H	H	H	Midwestern states with older electric power plants and high-sulfur coal producing states, chiefly West Virginia, have blocked legislation to curtail burning of high-sulfur coal.
The main culprit remains combustion of fossil fuels by industries and vehicles producing carbon monoxide, ozone and other contaminants.	L	H	H	H	Efforts to clean the air are hindered by urbanization, which brings more industries and automobiles into smaller areas and worsens local air pollution. Industries resist taking costly measures to curb their production of pollutants.
Radon can seep through cracks in foundations and basement walls and concentrate to harmful levels, especially in air-tight, energy-efficient houses.	H	M	O	L	Because EPA's mandate does not cover indoor air, detection and correction of radon pollution is up to the individual homeowner. Repair costs average $1,000-$1,500 per house.
Tobacco smoke, paints, solvents, dry-cleaned clothing, car exhaust, solid air fresheners, insulating material and pesticides are among scores of known indoor pollutants.	H	H	O	L	There is no single government agency that has jurisdiction over the myriad substances that contribute to indoor air pollution. As is the case with radon, it is largely up to individuals to solve the problem.
Our throw-away society generates more trash than any other in the world. At the same time, much of this garbage is composed of plastics and other materials that do not break down easily.	M	M	M	M	Authorities regularly encounter the "not-in-my-back yard" syndrome when seeking new sites for landfills and incinerators. The public resists recycling as a time-consuming nuisance.
Sources include hazardous waste storage tanks, burned wastes and hazardous waste incinerators.	H	L	M-L	M	Although Congress established a "Superfund" to clean up old hazardous waste sites, progress has been slow. More than 1,000 such sites remain on Superfund's priority list.
The wastes from nuclear power plants and nuclear weapons factories are both highly toxic and long-lived.	H	M	L	L	Nuclear power, a smokeless energy source, offers a solution to the greenhouse effect, acid rain and air pollution. But in addition to the risks related to human error in plant operations, there is no risk-free way to dispose of radioactive wastes.

† O=None.   L=Low.   M=Medium.   H=High.   X=Not Rated.
   The ratings are by EPA.

prices fell. This time around, the impetus will be environmental as well as economic. "One of the nice things about investing in energy efficiency is that you get four birds with one stone," says Brown of Worldwatch. "You cut down on carbon emissions, you cut down on acid rain and air pollution, and you increase energy security."

Energy efficiency also offers a financial incentive. According to William R. Moomaw, the global-warming project director of the World Resources Institute, the United States spends 11 percent of its gross domestic product on energy, while Japan and West Germany spend just 5 percent. "That's one of the reasons we're not competitive," he says. "We're spending all this money pouring energy into a leaky energy system, so our products are more expensive than they have to be and we don't have the capital to invest in other technology."

There are a number of steps that could be taken to increase energy efficiency in the United States, but implementing them can present its own set of problems — political and, sometimes, environmental:

● **Make appliances more efficient.** The United States spends about $4 billion a year on heating, lighting and air conditioning buildings. Moomaw estimates that sum could easily be halved with existing technology and that the investment would more than pay for itself by the year 2000. Appliances such as furnaces and water heaters already use less energy without curtailing output as a result of congressionally mandated efficiency standards. The same notion applied to lighting, heating and air conditioning would be the fastest and cheapest way to cut carbon dioxide emissions, according to EPA estimates.

● **Make automobiles more efficient.** More stringent fuel-efficiency standards for automobiles would have a similar effect. Lashof estimates that fuel consumption could be cut in half with existing technology. But recent developments do not bode well for greater auto efficiency. Big cars are back, and demand is high for gas-guzzling trucks and four-wheel-drive vehicles. Meanwhile, the Department of Transportation announced in October that it was scaling back fuel-efficiency requirements for the 1989 models of American-made cars and trucks from 27.5 to 26.5 miles per gallon of gasoline.

● **Use more efficient fuels.** Fuel-switching offers another weapon against global warming. Natural gas produces half as much carbon dioxide as coal when burned, and new technology is making gas even cleaner to use. But the United States is richer in coal deposits than any other fossil fuel, making such a change politically difficult. Since 1973 the United States has shifted away from natural gas toward coal. By switching to existing advanced gas turbine technology, Lashof estimates, utilities could cut carbon dioxide emissions by a factor of three and eliminate sulfur emissions altogether, thereby helping to solve both the global warming trend and acid rain.

● **Use nuclear power.** Nuclear power plants produce no greenhouse gases. There are 105 nuclear reactors now providing electricity across the United States. Another 416 nuclear reactors are in operation in 26 countries, providing 16 percent of the world's electricity. But accidents at Three Mile Island and Chernobyl heightened concern over the potentially disastrous effects of this smokeless energy source. (*See p. 67.*) Current research into safer nuclear technology than the current generation of light-water reactors is not expected to yield results for at least one or two decades.

● **Use alternative fuels.** Meanwhile, the technology exists to generate electricity from a variety of non-fossil energy sources. Direct solar power and wind power, for example, emit no greenhouse gases. Photovoltaic cells are already being used by utilities in California to transform solar energy into electricity to meet peak demand for air conditioning in the summer months. Because the cost of photovoltaics is falling, direct solar energy could be widely used within a decade, Moomaw predicts. Wind power, which already produces 1500 megawatts of electricity in California, is also well suited to Hawaii and the Great Plains. "We need to have a multiplicity of solutions that are tailor-made for the locations," Moomaw says.

The scope of the solutions must be worldwide

Increased energy efficiency would be the single most effective means of combating most environmental problems, encompassing global warming, acid rain and urban air pollution. But other steps also rank high on environmentalists' list of priorities. One is to have a further reduction in chlorofluorocarbon emissions. Since 1976, non-essential use of CFCs — in aerosol sprays, for example — has been banned in the United States. Further reductions are mandated by the Montreal Protocol. But these ozone-depleting chemicals are still widely used for refrigeration, air conditioning and making foam cushioning. Scientists agree that the protocol should be amended in the light of recent findings that the ozone hole is growing faster than previously thought. Because substitute chemicals exist and only about a dozen industries produce CFCs worldwide, further reductions in their use should be relatively easy to accom-

plish. "It's not like shifting to renewable energy sources or heavy investments in energy efficiency, which amount almost to a restructuring of the global economy," Brown points out.

Brown also underscores the need to divide the tasks involved in environmental protection on an international scale. He suggests that while the United States and other industrialized nations should place energy efficiency at the top of the policy agenda, developing nations should concentrate their environmental policy efforts on effective birth control campaigns. The world population, now at more than 5 billion, is expected to double in the next century, placing great strain on natural resources. In the view of many environmentalists, efforts to control greenhouse gas emissions will depend on the success of efforts to curb population growth, especially in the developing world, where 90 percent of the population increase is expected to occur.

Developing nations also need to do more to stop deforestation. About 20 percent of the excess carbon dioxide in the atmosphere is being released in Brazil, Indonesia and other developing countries whose growing populations are burning forests to clear the land for cultivation. Not only does "slash-and-burn" agriculture add more carbon dioxide to the atmosphere from the fires, it also reduces the planet's ability to soak up the gas. Trees absorb huge amounts of carbon dioxide. They act as sponges, soaking up carbon dioxide and converting it into oxygen and wood. Multilateral institutions such as the World Bank have come under fire for encouraging this expansion by providing funds for Third World development. The bank has begun to change, however, and it recently began to provide incentives for reforestation. But the burning continues, especially in tropical countries, which lose some 18,000 acres of forest land each year.[9] In Brazil alone, an area the size of West Germany is expected to go up in flames this year, despite President José Sarney's October decree to slow deforestation.

The industrial world can lend a hand. One innovative step was taken in October by AES Thames, a private firm that is building a 180-megawatt coal-powered facility in Connecticut. The company has agreed to plant enough trees in Guatemala to absorb the carbon dioxide that the new plant will emit into the atmosphere. The project, devised with the help of World Resources Institute, will also help Guatemala restore its depleted forests and preserve threatened animal and plant species. If the project succeeds, the company has agreed to include similar tree-planting schemes in its future building plans.

Some scientists say regulation isn't enough

Scientists may agree on the general goals of environmental policy in the 1990s, but they differ widely on how to reach them. One alternative is to continue with the "command and control" approach embodied in the basic environmental regulations of the 1970s. These laws set limits on the amount of air or water pollutants industries and individuals may discharge into the environment, with EPA and other government agencies assigned to monitor and enforce the limits.

Supporters of the traditional regulatory approach to environmental problems point to the successes of EPA's cleanup efforts over the past 18 years, such as the deep reduction of toxic lead in air and water. But many scientists say the biggest threats to the environment today are too widely dispersed to be effectively monitored on a case-

Should reliance on nuclear power be increased to meet energy needs and to protect the environment?

YES writes **HERBERT H. WOODSON,** dean of engineering at the University of Texas at Austin.

Since 1987, electricity demand has been growing at a rate of over 4 percent a year — more than double the rate of just a few years before. Unfortunately, plans for adding new generating capacity have not kept pace with increasing demand.

Some regions of the country, particularly New England, are already facing tight electricity supplies. To help meet the demand, utilities have intensified their conservation and energy efficiency programs — adding to the impressive gains of the last 15 years. Since 1973 there has been a 40 percent growth in the U.S. economy with only a 2 percent growth in total energy use. How? Largely by increasing our electricity use by 40 percent and using energy more efficiently.

But now we clearly need new supplies of electricity. The question is where it will come from. Renewable energy sources like solar and wind are just not reliable or economically competitive. For all their hope, they generate only less than 1 percent of the nation's electricity.

Nuclear power is the only large-scale generator of electricity that does not contribute either to the greenhouse effect or to acid rain. Fossil fuels are too dirty. Had nuclear energy's 16 percent share of the world's electricity been generated by coal-fired plants equipped with the best scrubbers available, the result would still have been the release of an additional 1.6 billion tons of carbon dioxide, 1 million tons of nitrogen oxides, 2 million tons of sulfur oxides and 150,000 tons of heavy metals, including arsenic, lead and mercury.

Through the increased use of nuclear energy, France cut its emissions of sulfur oxides by 56 percent between 1980 and 1986, nitrogen-oxide emissions from power plants by 60 percent and carbon dioxide by 270 million tons a year. Some areas of the U.S. have seen similar results. A new report by the environmental group Renew America, for example, lists Ohio as the third highest emitter of carbon dioxide of any state — primarily the result of its coal-burning power plants. By contrast, Vermont, which emits the least amount of carbon dioxide, receives 80 percent of its electricity from nuclear energy, the rest from hydro.

Even with nuclear power, America will have to learn to use less energy and to use it more efficiently. But without nuclear power, the U.S. will not be able to solve the tough energy and environmental problems it faces. The next administration should take the lead in encouraging standardized plants and a one-stop license process, so nuclear power can play its major role in providing electricity in an environmentally sound manner.

NO writes **KEN BOSSONG,** director of Public Citizen's Critical Mass Energy Project.

Nuclear power is no solution to global warming or other environmental problems for many different reasons:

Nuclear power costs too much. In fact, of the conventional means for producing electricity, nuclear power is the most expensive, and its costs are rising faster than all other alternatives.

Nuclear power is inherently unsafe. Since the 1979 partial meltdown at the Three Mile Island reactor, U.S. nuclear plants have experienced nearly 30,000 mishaps. The Nuclear Regulatory Commission has esimated that the chance of a core-melt accident at a U.S. reactor may be as high as 45 percent over the next 20 years.

Nuclear power is environmentally hazardous. The plants produce long-lived, highly-radioactive and extremely toxic waste for which there is still no proven safe method of permanent storage or disposal.

There are serious safety shortcomings with each "new generation" reactor concept, too, and all of them would continue to produce long-lived, highly-radioactive waste as do current reactors.

What's more, a nuclear "solution" is unrealistic. To reduce worldwide fossil fuel use by one-half, at least one new nuclear plant would have to be built every other day between 1995 and 2020 — an 11-fold increase over the current rate. Even if such a construction rate were physically possible, it would be too late to avert the current global warming trend.

So what are the solutions to the problem of global warming and our continuing need for energy? First, improved energy efficiency: It is a far less costly, environmentally cleaner and, therefore, more promising option than nuclear power. Secondly, solar and other renewable energy resources: They are getting cheaper and can now or soon will provide electricity at costs lower than new nuclear facilities can.

Even with massive federal support, it has taken 30 years and more than $150 billion to build the current generation of nuclear plants; yet these reactors now supply only 6 percent of the nation's energy supply and have proved to be a consistently unreliable source of electricity. By comparison, since 1974, energy conservation has reduced U.S. energy use by more than 30 percent, and renewable sources now provide 8.5 percent of the nation's energy.

At a time of massive budget deficits, it makes little sense to invest billions more in nuclear power when modest investments in energy conservation, renewable energy and natural gas could reduce carbon dioxide emissions from utilities, industries and homes by 68 percent by the year 2000.

by-case basis. Costs are another sticking point. In 1984, the United States spent $65 billion — almost 2 percent of the gross national product — in environmental cleanup efforts. The federal government paid about a quarter of the bill. With pressure mounting to cut the budget deficit and the trade deficit, the search is on for ways to reduce these costs to both the government and private industry.

This is the same argument President Reagan made when he took office in 1981. His first appointees included staunch opponents of environmental regulation like EPA Administrator Anne M. (Gorsuch) Burford and Interior Secretary James G. Watt.[10] Reagan also created a Task Force on Regulatory Relief — under the direction of Vice President George Bush — to streamline federal regulations, including environmental standards. Although Reagan's deregulatory campaign slowed the pace of the environmental cleanup launched in the 1970s, he failed to change the basic approach of environmental legislation. One bill Reagan signed into law in November directs the EPA to monitor waste from hospitals and other health care providers. Another measure bans ocean dumping of sewage sludge by 1991 and would impose stiff fines on violators.

Some environmental scientists say that stricter enforcement is not the only solution. "EPA has been required to respond only to the appearance of a pollutant in the environment, at which point it is too late," says Barry Commoner, director of the Center for the Biology of Natural Systems at Queens College in Flushing, N.Y. He suggests the laws be amended to shift EPA's focus from monitoring compliance to searching for technologies that would prevent pollution from occurring in the first place. Once ways are found to transform the technology of energy production, Commoner says, industry could be coaxed into adopting them through the federal government bidding process. Take auto pollution. The technology to produce a smogless car exists, Commoner says. If the EPA were a research agency, it could write the specifications for a smogless vehicle that would be written into government purchase orders. Because the federal government buys about $4 billion worth of cars and trucks each year, he says, the auto industry would soon incorporate environmentally sound technology in their fleets. The same technique could be used to hasten the adoption of solar and other renewable energy sources throughout the economy.

But there is greater support today for solutions that rely more heavily on private initiative than on government intervention of any kind. The so-called market approach to environmental protection is the centerpiece of a recent study called "Project 88: Harnessing Market Forces to Protect Our Environment." Sponsored by Sen. Timothy E. Wirth, D-Colo., and Sen. John Heinz, R-Pa., the study recommends several ways to "enlist the nation's entrepreneurial creativity to develop more inventive and efficient approaches to environmental protection."

Project 88, prepared under the direction of Robert N. Stavins of Harvard University's John F. Kennedy School of Government, acknowledges the value of the traditional regulatory approach for some environmental goals, notably lower auto emissions. But it recommends market incentives such as "tradable emission permits" for industrial polluters. Under this approach, the government would simply set an environmental goal and leave it to the private sector to find ways to meet it. A firm could either invest in new technology to reduce its emissions or buy permits or credits from another firm whose emissions fall below the standard.

Commoner, however, rejects this approach as immoral.

"It simply legitimates levels of pollution by encouraging trading rather than reducing" harmful emissions, he says. But even Commoner acknowledges the difficulty of redirecting EPA's mandate in today's political environment. George Bush, who directed the Reagan administration's deregulatory effort, will take office in January as the nation's next president. Concern over the federal budget deficit and the mounting trade deficit also is likely to deter environmental efforts that are seen to be costly to government and industry alike. But whatever approach is adopted in the next generation of environmental laws, many scientists agree that the public is ready to heed last summer's warnings. "It's hard to develop a constituency around a balanced budget," Krupp remarks. "But no one in his right mind wants to leave an uninhabitable Earth for our children and grandchildren."

Notes

[1] Hansen, director of NASA's Goddard Institute of Space Studies, testified June 23, 1988, before the Senate Energy and Natural Resources Committee.
[2] U.S. Environmental Protection Agency, "The Potential Effects of Global Climate Change on the United States," October 1988, p. 7. This draft report was submitted in November for formal review and is due to be presented to Congress in January 1989.
[3] The Montreal Protocol for Substances That Deplete the Ozone Layer was the product of the Vienna Convention, a 1985 agreement within the United Nations Environment Program to cooperate in research, observation and exchange of data on the ozone layer.
[4] Congressional Budget Office, *Curbing Acid Rain: Cost, Budget, and Coal-Market Effects*, June 1986.
[5] See Robin Herman, "Air Pollution Emerges as a World Problem," *The Washington Post*, Oct. 11, 1988.
[6] Lance Wallace, Robert Jungers, Linda Sheldon and Edo Pellizzari, *Volatile Organic Chemicals in 10 Public-Access Buildings*, EPA, November 1988.
[7] *Landfill Capacity in the U.S.: How Much Do We Really Have?* National Solid Wastes Management Association, Oct. 18, 1988.
[8] The Wilderness Society, *Ten Most Endangered National Wildlife Refuges*, Oct. 27, 1988.
[9] See Robert Repetto, *The Forest for the Trees? Government Policies and the Misuse of Forest Resources*, World Resources Institute, May 1988.
[10] Burford and Watt both resigned in 1983 amid scandals over conflicts of interest and mismanagement.

Selected Bibliography

Books

State of the Environment: A View toward the Nineties, The Conservation Foundation, 1987.

The Conservation Foundation, a non-profit research organization in Washington, D.C., assesses current environmental conditions and suggests policies to improve them. Special consideration is given to the conflict between food needs and environmental protection; disposal of hazardous and non-toxic wastes; new risks posed by air pollution; and protection of endangered species.

Articles

Commoner, Barry, "A Reporter at Large: The Environment," *The New Yorker,* **June 15, 1987, p. 46.**

Commoner, director of the Center for the Biology of Natural Systems at Queens College in Flushing, N.Y., explains why environmental protection requires more than filtering pollutants or cleaning up toxic-waste dumps. "In sum, there is a consistent explanation for the few instances of environmental success: They occur only when the relevant technologies of production are changed to eliminate the pollutant," Commoner concludes. "If no such change is made, pollution continues unabated or, at best — if a control device is used — is only slightly reduced."

Main, Jeremy, "Here Comes the Big New Cleanup," *Fortune*, Nov. 21, 1988, p. 102.

The author describes the main environmental concerns of the next decade and suggests that market-oriented incentives for industries to clean up their own acts offer greater promise than regulations. "Congress has been inclined to saddle the nation with laws that are expensive, prone to regulatory and legal hassles, tied to unrealistic goals, and locked into the wrong technologies."

Reports and Studies

Environmental Defense Fund, *Polluted Coastal Waters: The Role of Acid Rain*, April 1988.

The country's estuaries — the waterways, river basins and bays that make up the coastal water system — have gradually become sterile not just because of the tons of chemical pollutants that industries have dumped into rivers and streams for decades. Airborne pollutants falling to the earth in the form of acid rain also have contributed to the loss of fish and shellfish in these waters.

MacKenzie, James J., and El-Ashry, Mohamed T., *Ill Winds: Airborne Pollution's Toll on Trees and Crops*, World Resources Institute, September 1988.

Acid rain and ozone — pollutants produced when industries, power plants and automobiles burn fossil fuels — are killing forests as well as food crops. As recently as a few years ago, such plant damage was limited to the area around a single source of pollution. Today, tree and crop damage is widespread and the sources diffuse.

Moomaw, William R., *Proposed Near-Term Congressional Options for Responding to Global Climate Change*, World Resources Institute, Sept. 9, 1988.

The author, director of the World Resources Institute's climate, energy and pollution program, lists seven steps to slow the growth of greenhouse gases that are expected to cause a potentially devastating warming of the Earth's

temperature. Better fuel efficiency — "the fastest and least-cost strategy for reducing [carbon dioxide] emissions for an economy like ours" — ranks at the top of the list.

Project 88. *Harnessing Market Forces to Protect Our Environment: Initiatives for the New President*, Sen. Timothy E. Wirth, D-Colo., and Sen. John Heinz, R-Pa., sponsors, October 1988.

As its title suggests, this draft report suggests an alternative to the traditional regulatory approach toward environmental protection. Drawn up under the direction of Robert N. Stavins of Harvard University's John F. Kennedy School of Government, the report explains that record federal budget deficits require cost-saving ways to limit the growing sources of pollution. A number of inducements to industry are listed for 13 environmental problems, including global warming and stratospheric ozone depletion.

Repetto, Robert, *The Forest for the Trees? Government Policies and the Misuse of Forest Resources*, World Resources Institute, May 1988.

Government subsidies and other economic policies to foster development are fueling the destruction of the world's dwindling forests. Deforestation, which degrades the soil, kills off animal species and hastens global warming, is especially damaging in the tropics, where 27 million acres of forest land are destroyed each year.

U.S. Environmental Protection Agency, *The Potential Effects of Global Climate Change on the United States*, October 1988.

This draft report to Congress describes what could happen to four regions of the United States if the warming trend many scientists say is under way raises temperatures by 5-9 degrees Fahrenheit. The EPA predicts that there could be a significant loss of coastal wetlands due to a rise in the sea level, increased demand for electricity in the South, heavier ozone pollution, deforestation and accelerated extinction of endangered species. A companion study outlining policy options to combat the greenhouse effect is due for release early next year.

Not in My Back Yard!

Citizens rise up to
stop development projects

Whether it's a halfway house or a nuclear power plant, a landfill or a new highway, citizens are rising up to halt development projects. Although they may say their objections are fiscal or environmental, and many times they are, all too often their real concern is more personal: fear of falling property values.

The record of what has *not* been built in recent years is impressive. Ground for no new nuclear power plant has been broken since 1978. No large hazardous-waste facility has been sited since 1979. No large metropolitan airport has been built in more than 15 years. Controversies over new prisons have prevented their construction, and prisoners have had to be released from overcrowded facilities in some areas.

And those are only the most visible types of projects. Rare is the county in a populated area of the country that does not have at least one controversy over siting a new landfill for solid wastes.

Several years ago, frustrated planners and developers gave this new kind of citizen power a name — NIMBY, for Not In My Back Yard. Now, NIMBY actions have become so common that another acronym has crept into popular lingo. Frank Popper, chairman of the urban studies department at Rutgers University, has coined the term "LULUs" — Locally Unwanted Land Uses — to refer to the types of projects that inspire a NIMBY response.

"LULU blockage has serious, sometimes ominous implications for national economic policy," warns Popper. "It suggests that the country may be suffering from a creeping paralysis in its will to grow and influence its future, that it may be increasingly unable to attain legitimate development goals."

"A generation ago," he adds, "the burden of proof — whether judicial, legislative or political — fell mainly on the opponents of the [development project]. It was as if the [project] had a presumptive right to be built or operated. Today, the burden of proof falls increasingly on the proponents of the LULU. . . . As a result, essential LULUs have been stymied, stalemated, delayed for years."

The story of NIMBY is not a new one. Anyone rich enough to hire lawyers and to influence city hall has always been able to see to it that a factory was not located next to his home. When Robert Moses — the legendary planner who built many of New York's parks and highways between 1924 and 1968 — planned his parkways on Long Island, for example, the rich who lived on the North Shore managed to get the highways diverted from their estates, and the farms to the south were ruined instead.

What has changed is that now it is not only the extremely wealthy who are refusing to accept LULUs in their back yards. Increasingly, the middle class and the poor are taking the same position, and, thanks to changes in state and federal laws, they now have greater power to halt unwanted projects, even if those projects are important for the community as a whole.

In political terms, then, NIMBY heralds a realignment of the forces that govern land use. The "Power Broker" — as Robert Caro appropriately titled his biography of Robert Moses — is dead, and in his place everyday citizens are exercising the power. "It may be impossible to ever have another Moses," says Frank So, deputy director of the American Planning Association. "As metropolitan areas have grown, as civic and citizen groups have grown in influence, the power of government to make decisions has been fragmented tremendously." The result has been that sorely needed projects are being blocked along with the white elephants.

The situation has led people like Douglas Porter to question whether citizens have gotten too much power. Porter is director of development policy and research at the Urban Land Institute in Washington, D.C., which represents developers, planners and real-estate agents. "What is happening in too many places," he says, "is that the people in government who've achieved some measure of education and knowledge of what's going on and how to balance development . . . with environmental concerns are being replaced by citizens who don't understand the issues, who take very one-sided views and don't bother to look at the others, and often are making snap judgments. I think there is a role for citizen protest. And there are extraordinary times when it ought to be exercised. But to achieve the kind of constant use that NIMBY has achieved seems to go right around the whole representative government process."

Kent Portney, a Tufts University professor of political science who has been studying NIMBY, agrees: "I'm not sure I'm ready to say [citizens have] too much power, but I think the power is being used improperly."

That, of course, is the age-old paradox of power: Along with the power to do good inevitably comes the opportunity to misuse that power. If the public has the power to halt unwise projects, it also has the power to halt needed ones. The trick is to find ways to retain the benefits of citizen empowerment while minimizing any detrimental effects.

Fighting city hall and the developers

At bottom, NIMBY doesn't describe a type of protest so much as a motive for protest. It implies that the protesters approve of the project in general, and may even benefit from it, directly or indirectly — they just don't want it in their back yards. It may be nice to have an elementary school in the neighborhood, but not right next door. The community might need halfway houses, low-income housing projects or drug-treatment centers, but few people welcome them into their neighborhoods. Nearly everybody wants better highways and mass transit, but most people would prefer to live a couple of blocks away rather than right on the thoroughfare. Most people are aware of the need for facilities to treat hazardous wastes, but no one

By Patrick G. Marshall

wants to live near one.

Obviously, citizen opposition to land-use proposals is often based on more than narrow self-interest. Many would argue, for example, that nuclear power plants shouldn't be built anywhere. The problem is distinguishing between legitimate protests and pure NIMBY actions. This can be difficult to do, however, because NIMBY activists sometimes cloak their self-interested concerns behind loftier goals: Residents may object to the siting of a landfill in the neighborhood on environmental grounds when their real concern is not environmental at all.

Planners and politicians cite two main reasons for the rise of the NIMBY phenomenon. Not only are people more aware of the dangers of certain types of projects, such as nuclear power plants, they're also more conscious of their own power to stop such projects from being built. According to Porter of the Urban Land Institute, the environmental movement is responsible for much of the change. "The environmental movement has really educated people on how to fight city hall on these kinds of issues," he says. "There's a greater sense . . . [of] how to raise these issues in ways that allow you to influence the political process."

"People have discovered that they can express their interests much more effectively than they ever knew they could," says Israel Stollman, executive director of the American Planning Association. "What has changed is not that there is now an opportunity [for citizens] to express [their views] but that people are using that opportunity more effectively."

The willingness to speak out on these issues may rise from deeper feelings as well. "People fear the future. They feel tyrannized by development on their corners," says Evelyn Munn, a slow-growth advocate who is mayor of Walnut Creek, Calif. "I don't know if it's NIMBY, or just people tired of being pressured and pushed around."

Who is most likely to get involved in a NIMBY action? The California Waste Management Board released a report in 1984 that provides some insight into the participants. The report, compiled by a Los Angeles consulting firm, used survey data to profile those most likely and those least likely to oppose the siting of a waste-to-energy facility in their neighborhood. The study found that those most likely to oppose such facilities — which generate power from burning garbage, agricultural byproducts or other types of waste — were residents of the Western or Northeastern United States, were politically liberal, were professionals with a college education and middle or high incomes, and lived close to an urban area.[1]

It's not surprising that those who live close to urban areas are more likely to oppose development projects: These are the areas that have been experiencing the most growth and development in recent years. The fact that those with a college education are more likely to be involved in NIMBY actions also may help explain the rise of the phenomenon. According to Census Bureau figures, the percentage of Americans aged 25 and older who have completed at least four years of college has nearly doubled since 1970, rising from 10.7 percent to 19.9 percent.

The techniques used by those organizing a NIMBY protest are often the same as those used in the 1960s and '70s to fight for civil rights and women's rights, protest the war in Vietnam or lobby for environmental protections. Today the lessons learned from such struggles are being used by politically sophisticated neighborhood groups to take on developers and city hall.

Citizen lobbyists have succeeded in pushing many state legislatures to pass sunshine laws requiring most meetings of government agencies to be open to the public. Both federal and state laws now require environmental impact reports for most development projects. Many of those laws also require extensive public hearings.

Neighborhood activists have learned to make use of existing tools, such as zoning laws, to fight development projects they don't want. (*See story, p. 76.*) In many cities and suburbs they have managed to secure a voice in the zoning process through neighborhood advisory councils. They've also pioneered the use of new political tools, such as state and local initiatives and referendums. All have given citizens more say in community planning and development.

Environmental laws help NIMBY activists

The link between environmentalists and NIMBY activists is an important one. "There's networking through the environment organizations, the conservation groups," says Porter of the Urban Land Institute. The networking is mostly informal. An environmental group that is opposed to a particular waste-treatment facility may join forces with opponents living near the site, even though the residents may have no broader environmental agenda. Likewise, someone who is concerned about his property values might contact an environmental group in an effort to build a coalition against a proposed landfill.

"There are people [who] might be called NIMBYs that we've worked with," says Mark Evanoff, a spokesman for the Greenbelt Alliance, a citizen-activists group in the San Francisco Bay area. "They can see behind them that houses are going up on the ridge that they really care about. They call us and find out the basics of organizing and the political process and legal process that one has to go through and they organize the neighborhood."

But citizens opposed to a project on narrow, personal grounds often get more than strategic advice from environmental groups. They also acquire credibility. "[W]hen an environmental group gets involved, you've got that non-self-interested patina of respectability," says Robert Kahn, a Sacramento-based public-relations consultant to alternative-energy developers.

And perhaps the most concrete bequest of the environmental movement to NIMBY is the environmental laws enacted during the late 1960s and '70s at the state and federal levels. The most notable federal law is the 1969 National Environmental Policy Act. NEPA requires, among other things, the preparation of environmental impact assessments for major federal projects, or for any project receiving federal funds. Under NEPA, the impact assessments must:

- Describe current conditions.
- Identify alternative means of accomplishing the objective.
- Enumerate likely impacts of alternatives.
- Identify preferred alternatives.
- Describe the impact of selected alternatives in detail.
- List possible measures to minimize negative effects.

One weakness of NEPA is that it doesn't specify any actual environmental standards that must be met. "A cynical administrator, after stating that the impact of a proposed development would be the end of life on earth as we know it, could then go ahead and approve the project," notes the American Planning Association. "Not only that, but the statement might well be lawsuit-proof, as it would demonstrate that the most adverse potential impact had been considered."[2]

But the act's great strength, at least in the eyes of environmentalists, is that it formalizes a procedure for challenging land-use projects. A person who opposes a project, whether for environmental or other reasons, can delay it by challenging the environmental-impact report. And in some cases the cost of delay is so great to the developer that the project is abandoned at that point. "The environmental-impact process has been institutionalized," says Harvey Kaiser, an administrator at Syracuse University and author of *The Building of Cities: Development and Conflict.* "It's a tool that many people are aware of. By a relatively simple filing of a lawsuit a project can be ground to a halt."

Many states have adopted their own environmental-protection acts, and they often provide broader protections than NEPA. (*See list, p. 74.*) Perhaps because of its varied geography and immense growth strains, California has adopted what some planners say is the most rigorous legislation. The centerpiece is the California Environmental Quality Act. CEQA, like NEPA, requires environmental-impact assessments for projects receiving government funds, but goes further than NEPA in extending that requirement even to private projects involving no federal, state or local government funds.

Laws like CEQA have made it easier to put the brakes on unwise or unneeded projects, but they have also made it more difficult to site facilities that are needed and unobjectionable to most people. And according to Porter of the Urban Land Institute, the environmental grounds for objection are often only a cover for NIMBY — "the excuse, . . . the handle for whatever it is you want to protest against."

Though generally finding California's CEQA legislation "a fairly creditable process," consultant Robert Kahn complains that it gives citizens too much power to block development. "It delays the decisions, it creates a tremendous amount of unnecessary political pressure, it polarizes towns and communities."

As part of the CEQA process, says Kahn, the developer has to pay for "an independent technical evaluation of a project. [The evaluation] must, as part of CEQA, respond to all public comments." And although the developer and the independent analyst are held to a very strict standard of truth, Kahn says, "if you are an opponent, that same standard does not apply. There's no comparable accountability for the opponent. It leads us to a process that becomes too contaminated by misuse."

One example of misuse cited by Kahn involved a power plant in Woodland, Calif., that generates electricity by burning rice straw and rice hulls from nearby fields. "One of the opponents [of the power plant] claimed the cooling tower was going to give people legionnaires' disease," he says. But according to Kahn, the charges of legionnaires' disease were not based on real environmental concerns; they were later discovered to be only a ploy by a local union to put leverage on the developer during contract negotiations. "It was a form of environmental blackmail," says Kahn. "What we're seeing is a truly valid, credible process that's being muddied."

Kahn proposes allowing the independent consultants to dismiss outrageous claims without spending time (and developers' money) responding to every question. "I think there has to be an opportunity for a rough cut and immediate dismissal of outrageous claims," he says. "Let the consultants decide. The city council has no way of knowing whether legionnaires' disease is really an issue, but the consultants do."

Others are not so sure the decision should be left with the consultants. As Israel Stollman of the American Planning Association notes, "When you're developing an impact statement, there is also room for advocacy on behalf of the client. Not everything produces a cut-and-dried answer."

Ballot initiatives are slowing growth

Zoning is still one of the most powerful weapons citizens can use to stop development or control growth. (*See story, p. 76.*) But citizens' frustrations with the zoning process have led to an increasing reliance on the ballot box to settle zoning questions. A handful of towns now require a referendum on any proposed changes to their land-use or zoning laws. This trend has been challenged in the courts, but in 1976, the Supreme Court held that Eastlake, Ohio, a suburb of Cleveland, was within its rights to pass such a measure.

Far more common than laws requiring that all zoning matters be put to the voters are single-issue initiatives, placed on the ballot by the local government or by voters themselves. For example, residents of Portland, Maine, in 1987 resorted to the initiative process to get a measure on the ballot limiting development in the city's booming waterfront district. Despite opposition from the city government, as well as developers, the measure passed by a 2-1 margin.

Slow-growth initiatives are particularly popular in the West. (Of the 23 states that allow initiatives, all but five are west of the Mississippi.) California leads the way. Between 1971 and 1988, there were 69 growth-related initiatives on state and local ballots in California. And the pace is picking up: 28 of those ballot items appeared during 1986 alone.[3]

Most of the West Coast's major cities, and many of the smaller ones, have had growth limitations voted into place in recent years. In 1987 San Diego made an attempt to curb growth by capping the number of new housing units at 8,000 per year. Seattle recently joined San Francisco, Portland, Ore., and a host of smaller cities in placing height limitations on buildings. Seattle's Citizen Alternative Plan, approved by voters on May 16, limits new buildings to 450 feet and limits new construction to 500,000 square feet a year. The measure is expected to reduce the pace of building in the downtown area by as much as two-thirds.

The increased use of initiatives and referendums to settle land-use issues has many politicians and planners worried. "We as planners have concerns about taking [this] approach," says Stollman of the American Planning Association. "On the one hand, we do believe that the power must reside in the people and the people should have an opportunity to express what it is they are after. On the other hand, that sort of expression, if it is applied to a very narrow issue, can produce a result that just doesn't fit into an overall scheme of where the community should be going." Many of the facilities and policies that are put before the voters, Stollman says, "involve engineering considerations, planning considerations, site-design considerations, and many other things that don't lend themselves to solution by a vote."

Critics say one of the disadvantages of putting these issues to a vote, and of NIMBY in general, is that voters don't always consider the regional implications of their decisions. "Things will not get done if everything is settled at the neighborhood level," says Stollman. "There are certain things that have to go past the local level because the community as a whole needs those things."

In 1985, voters in Walnut Creek, Calif., approved a

measure limiting buildings to six stories until traffic in the community improved. But the traffic problems were due to regional traffic moving *through* Walnut Creek, not to commuters going into and out of Walnut Creek. So the height limitation has done nothing to improve the traffic situation. At the same time, the height limitation has complicated the plans of the Greenbelt Alliance, which is trying to secure a greenbelt (an undeveloped ring of land) for the nine counties around San Francisco Bay. The best way to achieve this is to concentrate development in the city center, says group spokesman Mark Evanoff. Walnut Creek's height ordinance runs directly counter to that goal, he says, by encouraging growth to sprawl into the surrounding land. "Basically, we want to see more cooperation among cities to encourage the growth of the city center, and to ensure that there are open lands surrounding the cities."

Similar problems could result from Seattle's new growth limits, concedes Ted Inkley, a leader of the initiative effort. The ideal solution, he says, is to have comprehensive regional planning, "with nodes of growth that are well-served by transit." Unfortunately, he adds, Seattle does not have regional planning.

Like Seattle and Walnut Creek, most areas of the country are without effective regional planning. In an attempt to bring planning from a purely local to a more regional level, some state legislatures have begun to reclaim some of the zoning authority they delegated to local governments in the 1920s and '30s. (*See story, p. 76.*) In some cases, the state exercises its powers through specific legislation. Massachusetts, for example, passed an "anti-snob" zoning law in 1969 that requires some localities to accept apartment units.

A handful of states (Vermont and Oregon most prominent among them) have adopted statewide land-use standards. Oregon's statewide standards require each municipality to produce a master plan that conforms to state requirements aimed at controlling growth patterns. For example, each municipality must establish clear zones within which urban services will be provided and beyond which they will not extend.

Other states have established land-use commissions, but only for special areas, such as New York's Adirondack Park Agency and the California Coastal Commission. But with only a few exceptions, such agencies don't really reduce local zoning authority, according to Dartmouth Professor William A. Fischel. The local governments, he writes, "seldom give up the power to zone and regulate subdivisions." What the regional agencies provide is "a 'double-veto' power to residents who oppose a particular development."[4] Citizens opposed to, say, a proposed marina that has been approved by their local government might be able to stop the project by appealing to an agency like the California Coastal Commission.

Hazardous waste: The classic LULU

According to the National Solid Wastes Management Association, the public now ranks hazardous-waste disposal as one of the nation's most serious environmental problems.[5] But despite increased concern about the hazardous-waste problem, few Americans seem inclined to support additional disposal facilities.

Richard Andrews, a professor of environmental science at the University of North Carolina in Chapel Hill, identified 179 attempts to site hazardous-waste facilities between 1980 and 1986. He says only 22 percent were sited by 1988; 25 percent were rejected and 53 percent were still pending.

NIMBY's Reliance on Environmental Laws

The NIMBY movement would not be as powerful without the federal and state environmental laws enacted during the 1960s, '70s and '80s. The most notable federal law is the 1969 National Environmental Policy Act, which, among other things, requires the preparation of environmental impact statements for projects receiving federal funds. Opponents of a project can sometimes delay it by challenging the environmental impact statements — even if their objections are not really environmental. The states listed below have adopted their own environmental policy acts; those with an asterisk require environmental impact statements. The state laws often provide broader protections than the federal Environmental Policy Act. A few states require environmental impact statements, but have not enacted a broad environmental policy act: Arizona, Georgia, Mississippi, Nevada, Texas and Utah. The following have no environmental policy act or EIS requirements: Arkansas, Colorado, District of Columbia, Florida, Kansas, Maine, Missouri, New Hampshire, North Dakota, Ohio, Oklahoma, Oregon, Pennsylvania, Rhode Island, South Carolina, Tennessee, Vermont and West Virginia.

State	Year Enacted	Last Amended
Alabama	1982	1986
Alaska	1971	1986
California*	1970	1986
Connecticut*	1973	1986
Delaware*	1973	1986
Hawaii*	1974	1986
Idaho	1972	1986
Illinois*	1970	1986
Indiana	1972	1986
Iowa	1972	1986
Kentucky	1968	1986
Louisiana	1979	1986
Maryland*	1973	1975
Massachusetts*	1972	1977
Michigan*	1970	1971
Minnesota*	1973	1984
Montana*	1971	1983
Nebraska*	1971	1986
New Jersey*	1970	1973
New Mexico	1971	1985
New York*	1976	1977
North Carolina*	1971	1983
South Dakota*	1974	1974
Virginia*	1974	1984
Washington*	1971	1985
Wisconsin*	1971	1985
Wyoming	1973	1985

Environmental impact statement required.

SOURCE: The Council of State Governments.

According to Andrews, "The real tests of siting approaches are probably yet to come. Recent surveys of both industry and state officials show expectations of a substantial number of new siting proposals, especially incinerators, in addition to the 94 proposals already pending but not yet resolved." [6]

The Resource Conservation and Recovery Act of 1976 put strict standards on the disposal and treatment of solid and hazardous wastes. But it left it up to the states to decide how they would go about siting waste-disposal facilities. The one constraint, as with the National Environmental Policy Act, was the requirement for public participation in the siting process. The strategies adopted by the states to allow for public participation vary widely. In fact, about the only thing they have in common is that none of them has been particularly effective.

Many states "use public participation only as window dressing," says University of Florida Professor Albert Matheny, and allow "the market to drive the selection process." Matheny cites Ohio as an example of this approach.

Ohio established a blue-ribbon commission in 1980 that, instead of taking the initiative on finding appropriate waste-disposal sites, reviews siting requests from industry. According to Matheny, public participation is kept to a minimum. One of the first tasks facing the commission was to decide whether a disposal facility near Cincinnati should be allowed to continue operating, despite strong local opposition. The site did receive commission approval, says Matheny, but the public felt left out of the decision-making process. As a result, "the public has become mobilized by a statewide network of local opponents," and no new hazardous-waste facility has gone into operation in Ohio since 1980.

When it came time for Florida to choose a site for a hazardous-waste-disposal facility, state officials decided to take a different approach. Florida approved a plan in 1983 that called for extensive public involvement in the siting process. As part of the state's attempt to raise public awareness of the hazardous-waste problem, state officials traveled to different regions collecting hazardous wastes from citizens at no charge. The wastes were analyzed and shipped out of state for disposal, and the citizens were briefed on the wastes and the difficulty of disposal.

But when it came time to make the siting decision, state officials were apparently unwilling to gamble. "The state got chicken when it came to actually allowing the electorate to have some input" on where the plant would be located, says Matheny. "They decided to pull the plug [on public participation], and just go for a site based on a consultant's report exclusively." The result, says Matheny, was all too predictable: "The consultant decided [to put the hazardous-waste-disposal facility] in the poorest, least-populated county of the state. . . . It really upset the people in the area because they [were] already overcome with all kinds of LULUs, prisons and you name it."

New Jersey's strategy for selecting hazardous-waste-disposal sites has attracted a lot of attention. The 1981 legislation setting up the plan calls for siting decisions to be made by a state commission made up of environmental, industrial and political leaders. "The major environmental groups helped to write the act," says Diane Walker, national chairwoman of the Sierra Club's hazardous-waste committee and a member of the task force that wrote the legislation. "Because there was universal recognition in New Jersey that we needed treatment facilities to better handle hazardous waste, there was agreement on the provisions that needed to go into the act. There was support for the act throughout the state." In addition to providing for extensive public hearings in localities being considered as potential sites, the act requires that these localities be provided with funds to hire consultants if they want to challenge the commission's reports. The legislation also calls for strict environmental controls on selected sites, particularly regarding the allowable amounts of groundwater.

New Jersey's approach, though it has not put an end to NIMBY responses in "threatened" communities, has at least prevented what in other states has been a difficult obstacle to overcome: coalitions between NIMBY and environmental groups. "Because of the process, and because the environmentalists recognize the need for these new facilities, there has been no joining of the Sierra Club or any of the other statewide or regional groups with the local groups that have, understandably, opposed facilities," says Walker.

But while the New Jersey approach has minimized opposition, it has also made it very difficult to find a hazardous-waste-disposal site. Only one site has been tentatively designated, and it has not completed the extensive review process specified in the siting legislation. "Over the last year, it's been recognized that the siting criteria have made it difficult to find sites, period," concedes Walker.

Massachusetts has taken still another approach to siting hazardous-waste-disposal facilities. In Massachusetts, a state board mediates between developers who want to site a waste plant and local residents. The purpose of the negotiations, says Tufts University Professor Kent Portney, is to come up with a compensation package to be paid to residents by developers. But Portney says this approach hasn't worked. In every instance where a developer has proposed a facility in the state, public opposition has prevented its construction. "[W]hat the case studies show is that economic compensations simply don't work," says Portney. "Economists argue that everybody has their price, that incentives could be designed to get everybody to accept them, but the problem is they're not within the range of what is economically feasible. People react extremely negatively to them. They do feel that they're trying to be bought off or bribed, and they end up having the opposite effect of what was intended."

Faced with near-universal rejection of hazardous-waste-disposal facilities by localities, states have limited options. As Matheny and his colleague Bruce A. Williams noted in a 1988 evaluation of state strategies for siting hazardous-waste-disposal facilities, "In many cases siting has been 'successful' only when the process has ignored certain groups, such as poor and unorganized interests." [7]

Putting hazardous-waste-disposal facilities and other LULUs in areas that are perceived as having less political clout is common, according to Lois Gibbs. Gibbs is director of the Citizens Clearinghouse on Hazardous Wastes in Arlington, Va., and is a former resident of Love Canal, a neighborhood in Niagara Falls, N.Y., that in 1978 was declared unsafe because of the presence of toxic chemicals. She points to the profiles produced for the California Waste Management board of those most likely and those least likely to resist having a waste-to-energy plant sited near their homes. (See p. 72.) According to the report, those least likely to fight such a facility are middle-aged or older, live in a rural area, have a low income and no college education. "That's the first time it's been put in writing,"

Zoning Laws Help Control Development . . .

Zoning may be the most important tool a community has to control development.

In its simplest terms, zoning is the partitioning of a community into residential, commercial, industrial or agricultural areas. Within these areas, certain types of land uses are permitted, while others are prohibited. Zoning laws determine which areas remain dotted with single-family homes and which are flooded with apartment buildings or low-income housing projects. Zoning laws determine whether a developer can build a supermarket on land that once was a lemon orchard. They also determine whether a homeowner has to worry about a pool hall or an auto body shop opening on the corner, or about smoke from a steel plant wafting into his back yard.

Although zoning broadly categorizes land for residential, commercial or industrial uses, it also may impose other, narrower land-use restrictions. Within residential zones, for example, there may be regulations specifying minimum and maximum lot sizes or limiting the number of dwellings per acre. To help control growth in commercial areas, communities may restrict the square feet or height of buildings, or they may require a certain amount of space between a building and the edge of the property (called setbacks) to ensure adequate sunlight in the area. Subdivision regulations may specify that developers put in roads, sidewalks, sewers, utility poles and even parks.

To get an exemption, or "variance," from some zoning requirements, developers may be required to meet other conditions. For example, a developer who wants to build more apartment units than zoning allows may be given a variance if he agrees to build a wall around the project and to provide attractive landscaping.

It makes sense, given the importance of zoning to the community, that zoning powers have been entrusted to local elected officials. In fact, zoning powers actually reside with state governments. But during the 1920s and 1930s, all the states adopted "enabling" legislation that essentially turned zoning over to local governing bodies. "The creators of the model act [on which the enabling laws were based] conceived of zoning as a local law that would be passed by the local legislative body, administered by the staff, and interpreted by the board of adjustment or appeals. Only changes in the law would then come back to the governing body," explains the American Planning Association's handbook for planners.† Generally, implementation was seen as a matter of routine.

The system may seem rational on the surface, but it doesn't always work as its originators planned. "The designers of the model act did not anticipate the eventual importance of rezoning," notes the APA handbook. "In many communities, virtually every significant development proposal begins with a request for rezoning." Responsibility for granting variances and exceptions to zoning laws belongs to the board of adjustment or appeals, also known as the zoning board. Such boards are comprised of appointed, not elected, officials, and critics charge that board members hold too much power not to be accountable to the voters.

One way to increase accountability, of course, is to require public hearings for any zoning changes. And, according to Dartmouth professor William A. Fischel, that's just what the authors of the early zoning acts relied upon. "To establish a zoning law or to make major amendments, most state enabling acts require at least two public hearings . . . ," Fischel writes. "In the case of rezonings, the [zoning board] and/or the planning commission must make recommendations and hold hearings. Once their recommendation is made, the legislative body must hold hearings before its decision." ††

Despite the public-hearing requirements, history has shown there is still plenty of room for abuse in the zoning process. Virtually every city in the United States has had more than one scandal involving a developer paying someone off in an attempt to get property rezoned. Zoning commissioners may be bribed or pressured to grant variances for land uses that actually require changes in zoning laws. And city council members can be bribed or otherwise coerced into approving such changes. Even where corruption is not a problem, council members may simply be more pro-development than many of the citizens they represent.

Even in areas with strong zoning laws, elected officials can still find ways to dump controversial developments into areas that have less political clout, usually the poorest areas. The officials may feel their jobs are safe as long as only a minority of their constituents are affected by unwanted development.

she says, but these are the demographic characteristics developers always look for when selecting sites for controversial projects. Of the 10 low-level nuclear-waste-disposal sites proposed in New York state, Gibbs says, "every single one" fits the profile of an area least likely to resist the siting. "That historically has been the way that they site these things."

But in recent years even these types of communities have joined the NIMBY movement. The 10 New York communities, for example, have refused to passively accept the sitings, according to Syracuse University Professor Michael Heiman, who has been working with the residents. "They have gotten together in the past year, meeting together every month, seeking joint legal counsel and joint expert witnesses, and they're adopting a not-in-anybody's-back-yard position. They're trying to prevent themselves from being pitted one against the other as the list gets shorter and shorter for where the facility may be located."

Looking for ways to gain consensus

It's not just hazardous-waste facilities that are coming up against NIMBY. Halfway houses, low-income apartments, highway extensions and many other projects — both the questionable and the essential — are being stymied by citizen opposition. And as the protests proliferate, politicians, planners and developers are finding it difficult to come up with effective strategies for combating NIMBY.

Although offering financial compensation hasn't been

... but the Process Is Often Misused

Areas that have borne the brunt of unwanted development have resorted to various strategies to supplement the zoning process, with varying degrees of success. Exercising one's right to protest at zoning board hearings and council meetings is only one option. In some places, neighborhoods are given a formal voice.

Twelve years ago, for example, residents of Washington, D.C., voted to establish Advisory Neighborhood Commissions to increase the public's voice in the zoning process. ANC commissioners were to be elected by neighborhoods and their opinions were to be given "great weight" by the city government in making land-use decisions.

Unfortunately, says ANC Commissioner Clarence Martin, the law does not define what constitutes "great weight." "All the power is concentrated in the mayor's office," Martin says, "and the ANC isn't able to make changes in the community. You can't even get a car towed out of [the neighborhood]."

Martin would like to see members of the city's zoning commission elected instead of being appointed by the mayor. "You have to have some power on the neighborhood level," says Martin. "If it's true that you're placing all the less desirable institutions in a specific community, that community should have the last say in whether it goes there or not."

While zoning may be a community's most powerful means of regulating development and controlling growth, it can also be used as a NIMBY tool itself. One way this is done is through so-called "exclusionary zoning." In its broadest sense, the term means simply to zone *against* something rather than *for* something. But critics say exclusionary zoning is used most often to exclude "undesirable" residents. If a community's residential zoning laws allow for only single-family homes on large lots, for example, low-income families will find it difficult to live there.

Exclusionary zoning "is one of the most subtle forms of using governmental authority and power to foster and perpetuate discriminatory practices," says William Morris, housing consultant to the National Association for the Advancement of Colored People (NAACP).

The courts seldom interfere with local zoning decisions, and in two recent instances, the Supreme Court has pointedly refused to get involved in the issue of exclusionary zoning. In 1975, the court denied standing to non-residents of a Rochester, N.Y., suburb who wanted to contest the community's exclusionary zoning. In 1977, the court turned away a challenge to a zoning ordinance in the Chicago suburb of Arlington Heights that prevented the construction of low-income housing.‡

A handful of states have seen things differently. The Pennsylvania Supreme Court, in a 1965 decision (*National Land Investment v. Cohen*), put the brakes on exclusionary zoning by ruling that communities could not exclude types of housing by setting unreasonably large lot sizes.

And the New Jersey Supreme Court, in a 1975 decision involving the community of Mount Laurel, ruled that zoning regulations "cannot foreclose the opportunity ... for low- and moderate-income housing and ... must affirmatively afford that opportunity, at least to the extent of the municipality's fair share of the present and prospective need thereof." The court also directed the state to come up with a formula for determining a community's fair share of such housing. However, Fischel points out that the decision "is noted widely and approvingly, but in terms of altering zoning practices, it has not yet become [a model]." ‡‡

And for all its good intentions, the 1975 New Jersey decision has had limited results. By 1988, 17 years after the decision, only 2,000 units of low-income housing had been built in 14 communities in the state. And legislation passed in 1985 to ease the process has created a loophole that allows communities to decrease the amount of low-income housing they're supposed to provide. Under New Jersey's 1985 Fair Housing Act, suburbs are allowed to cut their allotment of required low-income housing in half by providing the funds necessary to build the units in cities willing to accept them.

† *Frank S. So and Judith Getzels, eds.,* The Practice of Local Government Planning *(1988), p. 255.*
†† *William A. Fischel,* The Economics of Zoning Laws, *1985, p. 34.*
‡ *Warth v. Selden, 422 U.S. 490, and Arlington Heights v. Metropolitan Housing Development Corp., 429 U.S. 252, respectively.*
‡‡ *Fischel, op. cit., p. 55.*

very effective in getting people to accept hazardous-waste-disposal facilities, some planners believe compensation might be more effective in getting people to accept "lesser" LULUs, such as housing developments or highway extensions. But according to Bob Lake, a professor at Rutgers' Center for Urban Policy Research, if citizens are willing to talk about compensation, their opposition to the project is not that strong in the first place. "What we're beginning to find out is that ... the LULU is either not a concern, so compensation doesn't come up, or there's such opposition that compensation won't do the job."

Another way developers are trying to minimize NIMBY is by taking action to reduce the negative effects of a development, a practice planners call "mitigation." California consultant Robert Kahn described a recent example involving a proposed cogeneration plant in Northern California. The plant was being opposed at least partly on the grounds that it would worsen air pollution in the area. "When it turned out that [the cogeneration] plant was going to put out particulate pollution," says Kahn, the developers proposed replacing residents' wood stoves, which also were sources of particulate pollution, with new wood stoves that had catalytic converters. Kahn says the project's environmental-impact report indicates the new wood stoves will provide a 3-to-1 offset. That is, the new stoves would cut current pollution by about three times the amount that would be added by the new plant.

Some developers and planners say the only real way

around NIMBY is to curb the ability of local citizens' groups to block development and land-use projects. One way, they say, is to give more power to regional governments or planning boards. While nearly every metropolitan area in the United States has some sort of regional planning body, few have any real power. "I don't think, looking at the country as a whole, that the regional mechanisms are adequate," says Stollman. "They are basically advisory, they are efforts to coordinate. They are efforts at mediating problems. But they are not regional decision-makers."

But local officials may not cooperate with efforts that would take power away from them and give it to regional bodies. Gary Binger, planning director of the Association of Bay Area Governments, an advisory council in the San Francisco Bay region, has already encountered this problem. "The comments that we get back from the local elected officials [who attend our sessions] are that 'We definitely need to think more regionally, but when you start talking about a regional level of government, we're out of here.' I don't think we have yet done a very good job of educating them that voluntary kinds of approaches toward regionalism aren't going to get us there."

The one area where regional government actually seems to work is Minneapolis-St. Paul. The Twin Cities Metropolitan Council, established by the state Legislature in 1967, serves a seven-county area that includes more than 2 million people. One reason for the council's power is that the Legislature gave it regulatory oversight in certain areas. It is authorized to prepare a long-range development plan and solid-waste disposal plan to which local communities must conform. It is responsible for a wide range of services, including parks, sewer systems, transit and federally assisted housing programs.

The second key to the council's power is money. It has the authority to issue bonds for capital improvements and to purchase land for parks, landfills and other things. The council is also the conduit through which a portion of property-tax revenues are redistributed throughout the region. Those revenues pay for mass transit and for sewer facilities, which are operated by commissions controlled by the council.

Another important factor in the council's ability to rise above NIMBY pressures is that its members are appointed by the governor, not elected by residents. "The council members are not as subject to parochial concerns," says Guy Peterson, a spokesman for the council. "They're not going to have to answer at election time for allowing a landfill in their county."

Whether other regions are prepared to make the jump and give up powers to an unelected regional government is doubtful. Today, Peterson admits, it might even be difficult to get citizens and politicians in the Minneapolis-St. Paul area to back the idea. "It's often said around here that we probably couldn't set up a metropolitan council again. It was set up under special circumstances [there was a severe sewage crisis at the time and a strong governor, Harold Levander, who backed the idea] that don't come along very often and by a narrow vote in the Legislature at that."

Could the Twin Cities' system be emulated in, say, the San Francisco Bay Area? "Not right now," says planner Gary Binger. "If the people perceive there's a crisis in the way we're governed, it's a possibility. But I don't see it happening in the near term."

Regional governments, particularly those that are appointed, may be even more susceptible than local governments to abuses of power, since they are not as accountable to the local electorate. For example, an unelected regional commission might find it even easier than a local mayor to solve NIMBY problems by concentrating LULUs in areas where citizens are least organized and have the least political power.

One new idea for making the siting process more equitable is to develop a point system for LULUs. The idea, says its originator Frank Popper of Rutgers, is to assign different numbers of points to different LULUs, depending on how unwanted they are. Instead of a state or regional government siting specific LULUs in specific localities, each region would be assigned a certain number of points that must be accommodated. After that, localities could horse trade for which LULUs they would take. One community might agree to accept a hazardous-waste-disposal facility, while another might take two low-income housing projects and a prison.

A major hurdle to establishing such a system would be assigning the points. It would likely prove very difficult to find consensus on just how undesirable various types of LULUs are in relation to each other. But the big advantage of the point system is that voters, when considering the need for facilities in the abstract, would probably be more inclined to accept responsibility for LULUs than when a particular one threatens them personally. The point system would also provide assurance that those who have LULUs inflicted upon them are not suffering alone.

The idea still needs a lot of work, says Popper. In fact, he admits, "It may be totally crazy." Some facilities, such as nuclear plants, about which there is no real social consensus, may not be able to be accommodated in the system at all. And since some facilities cannot be sited just anywhere, because of earthquake faults, prevailing winds, or what have you, certain communities may still have LULUs forced upon them. But at least, says Popper, politically vulnerable regions would not become dumping grounds for LULUs; every region would be required to share the burden.

Some of the projects currently blocked by NIMBY opposition can only be put off for so long. The garbage, after all, has to go somewhere. Sooner or later something will have to be done with radioactive and hazardous wastes. Traffic will come to a screeching halt if communities don't build new roads or improve their mass-transit systems. And if NIMBY keeps governments from addressing these problems until they get out of hand, citizens may be forced to accept solutions that require far greater sacrifices than the proposals now generating so much opposition.

But NIMBY is not likely to go away any time soon. And even its critics admit it's not all bad. Politicians and planners now realize they can no longer take public support for granted, and they are trying to be more sensitive to citizen concerns. In the case of hazardous wastes, NIMBY could have a more concrete legacy, according to Professor Matheny. "[E]ven in its most negative form, NIMBY might have an aggregative good by changing the priorities that the business community brings to its waste-disposal problems," he says. "[B]y making it so damn hard for industries to dispose of the stuff," NIMBY will put pressure on industry to "cure the cause instead of the symptoms."

For the individuals involved, NIMBY is often the first step toward broader social and environmental concerns. "Most of our members start out as NIMBYs," says Lois Gibbs of the Citizens Clearinghouse on Hazardous Wastes.

Impact Fees: Paying for Development

Developers are finding it especially daunting to win approval for new housing developments in areas that have experienced rapid growth, such as California and Florida. For many communities in such states, new housing developments mean not only more people, but more pressure on already-strained city services, from schools and highways to sewers and parks.

Developers have long been required to provide certain on-site facilities, such as sidewalks, curbs, street lights and even school sites, in exchange for being allowed to build. But as growth pressures have increased, communities are requiring developers to pay "impact fees" to cover the costs of the capital improvements that their developments necessitate. "Now, not only does the developer have to build [things like sidewalks], but he may be required to extend a sewer or a water line," says Frank So, deputy director of the American Planning Association. "He may be required to put money into a fund used by the municipality to do major trunk line construction or major water plant or sewer plant construction. It's reaching further and further from the site."

One reason developers are being asked to pay impact fees is that local residents are increasingly opposed to raising taxes or passing bond issues to pay for capital improvements. "Development fees represent one of the safest political options for paying for new infrastructure because, in general, they tax people who are not already local voters — builders and new residents," states a recent report by the Bay Area Council, a San Francisco-based policy group.†

The problem with impact fees, critics say, is that communities may assess them for purposes not related to — or only loosely related to — the new development. "In Florida [impact fees] are being assessed for the construction of shuffleboard courts. In other cities they're being assessed for the purchase of art for public facilities," says Terre Belt, director of state and local affairs for the National Association of Home Builders. "These are things that seem rather indirectly related to that which a new development would necessitate as far as public facilities go."

And Belt says the dollar amount of such fees is climbing dramatically. In certain parts of Southern California, for example, the impact fees amount to $31,000 per single family home.

The courts have recently put some limits on impact fees. In a 1987 case (*Nollan v. California Coastal Commission*), the Supreme Court ruled that there had to be a direct link between the development and the requirements placed on the developer. A city cannot, say, simply impose a fee on a developer and put the money into its general operating fund.

But the exact boundaries around what are acceptable links have not been drawn. The city of San Clemente, Calif., for example, wants to charge a fee of $1,250 on each new home to pay for new parking structures at the beach — parking that will be used by current residents and tourists as well as those moving into the new homes. It is not clear whether the link between the fee and the development is close enough to survive a legal challenge.

* Quoted in the Los Angeles Times, *Feb. 16, 1989.*

"Then they take on the solution and try to push it." Mark Evanoff of the Greenbelt Alliance says this is also the case with his organization. New members often join because of a NIMBY situation, "but often after this first exposure to political involvement they will develop a more regional perspective and work with us on a regional approach to greenbelt protection."

"It really comes down to a profound issue of the notion of community," says Matheny. "We're taught to think in terms of self-interest. We have to be taught to think in terms of community. The only way you can get people to absorb costs so that others might benefit is to see themselves as part of a larger community for which sacrifice is worthwhile."

Notes

[1] California Waste Management Board, *Waste to Energy: Political Difficulties Facing Waste-to-Energy Conversion Plant Siting*, 1984.

[2] Frank S. So and Judith Getzels, eds., *The Practice of Local Government Planning* (1988), p. 191.

[3] See *The New York Times*, May 22, 1988.

[4] William A. Fischel, *The Economics of Zoning Laws* (1985), p. 26.

[5] National Solid Wastes Management Association, *Public Attitudes Toward Garbage Disposal*, May 4, 1989.

[6] Richard N. L. Andrews, "Hazardous Waste Facility Siting: State Approaches," in *Dimensions of Hazardous Waste Politics and Policy*, edited by Charles E. Davis and James P. Lester, 1988, p. 126.

[7] Albert R. Matheny and Bruce A. Williams, "Rethinking Participation: Assessing Florida's Strategy for Siting Hazardous Waste Disposal Facilities," in *Dimensions of Hazardous Waste Politics and Policy, op. cit.*, p. 43.

Selected Bibliography

Books
Davis, Charles E. and Lester, James P., eds., Dimensions of Hazardous Waste Politics and Policy, Greenwood Press, 1988.

This collection of essays by experts in their respective fields provides an excellent overview of the political and technical issues involved in debates over siting hazardous waste disposal facilities. It contains up-to-date information on the siting policies of various states, and a discussion on the psychology of NIMBY and efforts to overcome it.

Fischel, William A., The Economics of Zoning Laws, Johns Hopkins University Press, 1985.

Anybody with an interest in zoning will want to have this book on the shelf. Intelligent and clearly written, it covers everything from the mechanics and history of zoning in the United States to the politics and legal questions surrounding exclusionary zoning.

Heiman, Michael K., The Quiet Evolution: Power, Planning and Profits in New York State, Praeger, 1988.

Heiman, a professor at Syracuse University, provides a trenchant history of land-use planning in the state of New York during this century. His analysis of the political realities of facility sitings and other developments is particularly useful, though it does at times get unnecessarily bogged down with Marxist rhetoric.

Kaiser, Harvey H., The Building of Cities: Development and Conflict, Cornell University Press, 1978.

Kaiser's book, though somewhat dated, provides a great deal of insight into the strains of development and the processes of conflict resolution by examining three emerging communities in the Syracuse, N.Y., area.

So, Frank S., and Getzels, Judith, eds., The Practice of Local Government Planning, International City Management Association, 1988.

Nicknamed "The Green Giant" by planners, this 554-page tome explains the ins and outs of various planning jobs, from transportation planning to filling out environmental impact reports. There are also generous helpings of historical background on zoning, land-use laws, environmental regulations, planned communities and a host of other topics. Virtually all of the material can be understood by non-planners.

Articles

Matheny, Albert R. and Williams, Bruce A., "Strong Democracy and the Challenge of Siting Hazardous Waste Disposal Facilities in Florida," National Civic Review, July/August 1988.

Despite its title, Matheny and Williams range far from Florida in their discussion of problems related to siting hazardous waste disposal facilities. The article was written after, and is critical of, Florida's abandonment of its emphasis on attaining citizen consensus through education programs.

Popper, Frank J., "The Environmentalist and the LULU," Environment, March 1985.

This article presents a clear discussion of the role environmentalists often play in the opposition to Locally Unwanted Land Uses, or LULUs.

Reports and Studies

California Waste Management Board, Waste to Energy: Political Difficulties Facing Waste-to-Energy Conversion Plant Siting, 1984.

This report discusses the reasons for public opposition to the siting of waste-to-energy plants, and attempts to draw a profile of those most likely to join the opposition, as well as those least resistant to plant sitings. The report is remarkable not so much because it's the best of its kind as because it is the *only* published government report that uses demographic data to profile NIMBY-prone people.

America Turns to Recycling

*States and communities finally have
rediscovered the benefits of recycling*

Recycling is back — and this time it may be here to stay. Recycling is no longer just a self-conscious exercise in environmental virtue. Now it's an urgent necessity. The rising costs of waste disposal and the undiminished opposition in many communities to siting new landfills or building new incinerators have seen to that. And so recycling's praises are being sung now, not just by environmentalists, but by virtually everybody.

At least 13 states have enacted some form of recycling legislation. (*See story, p. 82.*) Nearly four in five Americans say they have voluntarily recycled newspapers, glass, aluminum, motor oil or other items in recent years.[1] Businesses, too, are jumping aboard the recycling bandwagon. Last July, for instance, a group representing the plastics industry proclaimed "The Urgent Need to Recycle" in a 12-page advertising insert in *Time* magazine.[2] To be sure, businesses may be as much concerned about warding off any new government requirements that waste be reduced or recycled as they are about solving the nation's solid-waste problem. And some business efforts may be little more than public relations ploys. But, whatever their motives, many companies have indeed committed themselves to recycling.

The Procter & Gamble Co., for instance, has begun putting its Spic and Span cleanser in bottles made entirely of recycled plastics. The company is also embarking on an experiment to recycle disposable diapers and turn them into such products as plastic flowerpots and insulation. Even fast-food restaurant chains are discovering the virtues of recycling. McDonald's has announced plans to recycle plastic containers and other food packaging from 100 of its restaurants in New England. The $16 million program, launched in conjunction with the National Polystyrene Recycling Co., a consortium of plastics producers, will eventually be expanded to McDonald's restaurants around the country.

But it may take more than businesses' growing interest and the public's strong support to turn recycling into as large a reality as its more ardent proponents wish. For one thing, the demand for recycled products may not be enough to take care of all that could be supplied. The most dramatic illustration of this involves recycled newsprint. As a result of the increased efforts at recycling in recent years, the collection of old newsprint rose by 34 percent from 1983 to 1988. But according to Holly Brough of the Worldwatch Institute, actual reuse rose by only 5 percent. The demand for recycled newsprint was just no match for the swollen supply of old newspapers.

As the supply mounted, some East Coast dealers who once paid $30 or more for a ton of old newsprint began charging cities to haul the paper away. "Just when it seemed newspaper recycling was hitting its stride," Brough writes, "volunteer recycling projects have suddenly disbanded, supermarkets refuse to accept newsprint, and

curbside collectors send much of their newspaper loads straight to the dump." Cities may still find it cost-effective to recycle, but Brough worries that the recent collapse of the market for recycled newsprint could cause "lasting damage" to recycling. "More than 1,000 curbside recycling programs in 35 states and the public's carefully cultivated recycling habit are now in jeopardy," she writes.[3]

To help correct the situation and stimulate demand for recycled newsprint, some states have begun prodding newspaper publishers to buy more. Connecticut, for example, enacted a law last summer requiring that 20 percent of the newsprint bought by Connecticut publishers, or by out-of-state publishers who sell papers in Connecticut, must contain a specified amount of recycled fiber by 1993; by 1998, 90 percent of the newsprint must contain recycled fiber. (*See story, p. 85.*)

The federal government is also apparently moving, after more than a decade of inaction, to encourage paper recycling. The Environmental Protection Agency (EPA) issued guidelines for federal procuring agencies, effective last June, requiring them to buy newsprint made of at least 40 percent recycled fiber.

For many years, the federal government didn't pay much attention to the municipal solid-waste problem. But since 1987 — the year the wandering garbage barge *Mobro* made its hapless voyage — there have been signs of change. Last February the EPA adopted an "Agenda for Action" that included the goal, to be reached by 1992, of managing 25 percent of the nation's municipal solid waste by recycling (including composting of yard waste) and "source reduction," that is, preventing waste in the first place by product redesign or other means. Currently, only 11 percent of the nation's waste is recycled; 9 percent is burned (with or without energy recovery) and 80 percent is put into landfills.[4]

Recycling enthusiasts believe recycling can take care of much more than just 25 percent of the nation's municipal solid waste. Neil Seldman, director of waste utilization at the Institute for Local Self-Reliance in Washington, D.C., contends that 75 to 85 percent of the waste could be recycled. But many experts believe such estimates are not realistic. Japan, often cited as doing far better than the United States in recycling, takes care of no more than half of its waste that way. And a recent report by Congress' Office of Technology Assessment says that Japan's recycling rate may be as low as 26 to 39 percent.[5] "[A]nything over 50 percent . . . is just really not feasible," says Marian R. Chertow, director of the Program on Solid Waste and the Environment at Yale University's Institution for Social and Policy Studies.

Some communities in the United States have set extremely ambitious recycling goals. Seattle, for instance, hopes to recover 60 percent of its waste by 1998. But for the nation as a whole, recycling even 25 percent of its waste, as Seattle now does, would be quite an accomplishment.

While it is clear that recycling can play a much larger

By Robert K. Landers

role than it has, it is also clear that recycling is not the whole answer to the nation's municipal solid-waste problem. In fact, as Americans have had to learn again and again, there is no single, national solution to this particular problem. The situation simply varies too much from place to place; even the composition of the waste differs. And while the federal government could help much more than it has, each city or community inevitably is going to have to find its own solution.

Commercial recycling could pay bigger dividends

The amount of recycling being done in the nation has actually grown quite a bit in the past decade, rising from 9.1 million tons in 1975 to 16.9 million tons in 1986.[6]

Of all the recycled materials, paper and paperboard account (by weight) for more than 85 percent, according to a study done for EPA by Franklin Associates Ltd., a Kansas consulting firm. Eight million of the 19.4 million tons of corrugated containers that were discarded in 1986 were recovered, as were 3.8 million of the 12.6 million tons of discarded newspapers. The tonnage of aluminum recovered was much smaller (0.6 million tons, virtually all of it in the form of beer and soft-drink cans), but the percentage recovered (25 percent) was a few points higher than for paper and paperboard. (See table, p. 84.) About one in five beer or soft-drink bottles was recovered, but the total (1.1 million tons) amounted to less than 9 percent of all the glass thrown away.[7]

Although the amount of recycling has grown since the mid-1970s, so, of course, has the total amount of municipal solid waste, from 125.3 million tons in 1975 to 157.7 million tons in 1986. And while politicians and the press, in addressing the subject of recycling, tend to focus on the recovery of materials from the waste generated by households, that waste accounts for only about half of the nation's municipal solid waste. The rest comes from the commercial sector — business, industry and institutions. And in large cities — where the problem of what to do with all the refuse is now most acute — waste generated by the commercial sector is even more significant. For example, 85 percent of the municipal solid waste in the Connecticut town of East Lyme is residential, but 64 percent of the waste in the city of Seattle is commercial.[8]

Thus, the larger cities that were among 15 communities the Institute for Local Self-Reliance cited as being at the forefront of recycling activity were recovering materials mostly from commercial waste. Seattle, for instance, recovered 125,853 tons (or 29 percent) of its commercial waste in 1987 but only 44,430 tons (18 percent) of its residential waste. In smaller communities, on the other hand, targeting residential waste was more effective, and they generally had higher rates of materials recovery. Residential waste represents most of their total waste generated. The community with the highest recovery rate — 50 percent — was Woodbury, N.J., a town of 10,500 people, which has required residents to separate their paper, glass, metal, aluminum and yard waste for curbside collection since 1981.[9]

In Woodbury's case, composted yard waste represented two-fifths of all the recovered materials. Nationwide, yard waste accounts for nearly one-fifth of municipal solid waste, and EPA is hoping that composting more of it will provide a big boost toward reaching the 25 percent overall recovery goal. Already, a number of states have banned some or all yard waste from landfills, and more than 540 composting facilities are in operation in the country.[10]

Targeting yard waste is one way that a community

Many States Going for Recycling

At least 13 states and the District of Columbia have enacted some form of recycling legislation.

Oregon was first off the block. Its law, which became effective in 1983, required municipalities with populations over 4,000 to provide curbside collection of source-separated materials at least once a month.

Rhode Island's legislation, effective in 1986, required residents to separate solid waste into recyclable and non-recyclable components before being brought to state-owned disposal facilities. The state is also compelling businesses to submit detailed plans for waste reduction and recycling.

New Jersey's law, enacted in 1987, required all 567 municipalities in the state to adopt mandatory recycling ordinances. Counties had to submit plans for coordinating collection and marketing of at least three materials to be source-separated, while municipalities within the counties had to enact ordinances requiring residents, businesses and industry to source separate the materials designated in the county plan and to provide for collection of them.

According to Virginia McCoy, a legislative analyst for the National Soft Drink Association, the other states that have enacted some type of recycling legislation are Connecticut (effective in 1987), Florida (1988), Illinois (1989), Louisiana (1989), Maryland (1988), Minnesota (1989), New York (1988), North Carolina (1991), Pennsylvania (1988) and Washington (1989).

New Jersey has set a goal of recycling 25 percent of its waste. Other states have also set recycling goals, the highest being 50 percent in the state of Washington. However, as a recent study by Congress' Office of Technology Assessment (OTA) points out, "how recycling is defined and which portions of the [municipal solid-waste] stream are included in calculating the percentage affects the recycling rate figure." †

In many states, OTA reports, municipal solid-waste plans have been revised recently or are in the process of being changed. "State activities in general are in a state of flux. Almost every state in the country has several pieces of legislation related to [municipal solid waste] pending or recently passed. In some states the flurry of activity is almost too fast to follow."

† Office of Technology Assessment, U.S. Congress, Facing America's Trash: What Next for Municipal Solid Waste?, October 1989.

without the resources to immediately undertake curbside collection of residential waste could step up its recycling. Another is to target some forms of commercial waste, because in many cases larger quantites of easily recycled materials can be found in commercial waste. For example, the California city of Sunnyvale, located in Silicon Valley, found that 70 percent of its refuse was coming from business and industry, and that one-fourth of all its waste consisted of corrugated containers. Armed with this knowledge, city officials began to encourage businesses to set up recycling programs.

If measured by volume rather than weight, the amount of space corrugated cardboard takes up in a city's landfill is often greater than the amount taken up by residential waste. "The commercial sector can be made responsible for separation of high-value items from the commercial stream, such as cardboard and office paper," Chertow says, and at little expense to the city involved. "The yield in volume could be at least 20 percent of the waste stream, and could be much more depending on the mix of businesses." [11]

In some states, commercial recycling now is mandatory. Rhode Island, for instance, is requiring businesses to submit detailed waste reduction and recycling plans. The state provides technical assistance and a "market of last resort" for recycled materials. Over a six-month period, commercial-waste recycling in Rhode Island increased 22 percent.[12]

The commercial sector also has a crucial role to play when it comes to preventing waste in the first place. It's up to industry, after all, to redesign products so that they last longer, contain less toxic substances and are more easily recyclable. "Of course, it helps if there's consumer demand for products like that, but consumers can't demand [them] unless they know that they're available," says Howard Levenson, a senior analyst in the Office of Technology Assessment (OTA) and project director for the recent OTA study, *Facing America's Trash: What Next for Municipal Solid Waste?* "It's industry that has to make decisions about [product] design, and right now there's not much in the way of incentives for industry to do that."

Government could conceivably provide some incentives in the form of grants, awards and procurement specifications. So far, however, the nation has made little progress in waste prevention and the prospects for the future are unclear. For one thing, waste reduction is not always as simple as it is sometimes made to appear. Containers and packaging, for instance, "are mentioned frequently as potential targets for waste prevention efforts [and] are a large and visible part of [municipal solid waste]," the OTA study observes. But, besides appealing to customers, containers and packaging often help to protect public health and safety, and to deter theft. Attempts to cut down on containers and packaging would have to take those functions into account.[13]

There are also behavioral and cultural obstacles in the way of reducing the generation of waste in the United States. Americans consume a lot and demand convenience, and, at least in the past, they've tended to take their seemingly bountiful resources for granted. Americans may indeed be somewhat concerned now about the environment and ready to separate materials out from their trash, but they may not yet be ready to radically change their way of thinking and, indeed, their way of life.

Urban garbage problem recognized a century ago

Concern about the environmental implications of municipal garbage disposal did not originate with the environmental movement of the 1970s. According to historian Martin V. Melosi, it dates back to at least the 1880s. The Industrial Revolution was turning America into an urban nation, and industrial cities were suffering "an environmental crisis characterized by crowded tenement districts, chronic health problems, billowing smoke, polluted waterways, traffic congestion, unbearable noise, and mounds of putrefying garbage."[14]

The first efforts many cities made to deal with the crisis were to find sources of pure water and to build modern

---

What Is Recyclable?

At present, approximately 11 percent of all U.S. solid waste is recycled.

Recyclables

Materials:
- **Paper** (Newspapers, corrugated boxes, office papers, mixed papers)
- **Plastics** (Milk, soft drink and other containers)
- **Glass** (Bottles and jars)
- **Aluminum** (Cans and other aluminum products)
- **Steel** (Appliances and other steel products)
- **Wood** (Pallets, lumber, etc.)

Compost:
- **Leaves, grass and brush**
- **Food wastes**
- **Some other organic materials, such as paper contaminated with food**

Nonrecyclables

- **Wastes heavily contaminated by food residues, household chemicals, or dirt**
- **Composite materials, e.g., aseptic boxes made of paper, foil and adhesives, plastic-coated paper, furniture and appliances (other than their metal content)**
- **Miscellaneous organics, such as street sweepings**

Source: Environmental Protection Agency.

---

sewer systems. But they came to recognize that the refuse problem, initially considered "a mere nuisance," had serious implications for the environment and could not be ignored. "Heaps of garbage, rubbish, and manure cluttered alleys and streets, putrefied in open dumps, and tainted the watercourses into which refuse was thrown," Melosi writes.[15]

Recognition that the "garbage problem" was serious led to altered attitudes and to efforts to solve it. The traditional view that refuse collection and disposal were the responsibility of individuals yielded to the view that they were the responsibility of the community. Citizen groups and civic organizations started protesting against the inadequate collection and disposal methods that prevailed. Those methods reflected an "out of sight, out of mind" philosophy. "Much of the refuse was simply removed from [one] location to create a nuisance or health hazard in another," Melosi relates. Dumping of refuse on land or in water was the most common practice.

But even in the late 19th century, many cities also tried to recycle some of their wastes. This was done by using organic wastes for fertilizer, animal feed, road surfaces and landfill. Using the wastes for agricultural purposes seemed to give "cities the means of ridding themselves of unwanted materials while at the same time converting a liability of urban life into an asset for the countryside," Melosi writes. But, as some present-day recyclers have discovered anew, demand for recycled materials didn't always match the supply. "[The] quantity of refuse was so great that cities could not give it away, let alone sell it to farmers, as had been the earlier custom. [And the] cost of transporting refuse from cities to countryside and the rapid decomposition of organic materials meant that only farms close to

Only 11 Percent of Nation's Waste Is Recycled

Of all the recycled materials, paper and paperboard account for more than 85 percent. The tonnage of aluminum recovered is much lower, but the percentage recovered is slightly higher.

	Amount generated (millions of tons)	Amount recyled (millions of tons)	Percent recyled
Paper and paperboard	64.7	14.6	22.6
Glass	12.9	1.1	8.5
Ferrous metals	11.0	0.4	3.6
Aluminum	2.4	0.6	25.0
Other nonferrous metals	0.3	0.0	0.0
Plastics	10.3	0.1	1.0
Rubber and leather	4.0	0.1	2.5
Textiles	2.8	0.0	0.0
Wood	5.8	0.0	0.0
Food waste	12.5	0.0	0.0
Yard waste	28.3	0.0	0.0
Other	2.6	0.0	0.0
Total	157.7	17.0	10.8

SOURCE: Franklin Associates, Ltd.

urban centers could use the wastes for feed or fertilizer." [16]

Since urban wastes in the late 19th century "were diverse as well as plentiful, no universally accepted methods of collection and disposal had developed," Melosi says. Besides the organic wastes (garbage, manure, human excrement, dead animals), there were also tons of coal and wood ashes, street sweepings, wastepaper, cans and other discarded items. The diversity meant that cities, in disposing of their refuse, had to contend with "very basic and often perplexing questions." For instance, should solid wastes be separated in the homes and business establishments for ease of disposal? Could some of the material be salvaged or recycled? Is it more economical to dispose of separated or mixed refuse? [17]

One person who tried to answer such questions was Col. George E. Waring Jr., who was appointed New York City's street-cleaning commissioner in 1895. According to Melosi, Waring initiated "the first practical, comprehensive system of refuse management in the United States." Waring, who was appointed by reform Mayor William L. Strong, rejected the "out-of-sight, out-of-mind" principle as being neither "economical," "decent" nor "safe." Waring "realized that refuse was diverse in type, requiring various methods [of disposal] to achieve success," Melosi says. "His goal was to collect household refuse quickly and efficiently, to recover whatever economic value the discarded material might have, and to dispose of the remainder in ways appropriate to its composition. . . .

"His most ambitious project," Melosi continues, "was to devise a program for efficient collection of household and commercial wastes. 'Source separation,' which had been advocated for years but never attempted on a large scale, was attractive to him as an answer to New York's collection problem. The rationale for the system was that mixed refuse limited the options for disposal while separation of wastes at the source allowed the city to recover a portion of its costs of collection through the resale of some items and the reprocessing of others." [18]

Waring's plan for "primary separation" required householders and businesses to keep garbage (organic waste), rubbish and ashes in separate containers until the Street-Cleaning Department collected them. Mayor Strong in 1896 assigned 40 policemen to explain the separation plan to every householder and businessman in the city. Despite this educational effort, there was "considerable public resistance" to the plan. In an ironic twist, New Yorkers had come to think of sanitation programs as a municipal, not a personal, responsibility. Those who resisted, however, were sometimes fined and even arrested. "Despite the initial unpopularity of the plan," Melosi writes, "by 1898 it had proved to be fairly successful and was receiving much acclaim from city leaders, if not from an obdurate public." [19]

Establishing a successful system for utilization and disposal of refuse proved more difficult, however. Nevertheless, Waring succeeded "in reducing the amount of waste New Yorkers dumped in the ocean. Until Waring's time the city's dry waste was dumped 10 miles beyond Sandy Hook, where the tide was supposed to carry it out to the open ocean." The debris that washed up on the beaches of Long Island and New Jersey attested to the method's failure.

Waring didn't think any one disposal method held the full solution to the city's waste problem. Incineration, he argued, "in its best form and under proper guidance may be accepted as good, from a sanitary point of view, and as being practically free from offense. At the same time, cremation means destruction and loss of matter which may be converted into a source of revenue." Adds Melosi: "If there was any consistent element in [Waring's] disposal plans, it was to recycle or utilize waste economically to recover some of the money the city invested in disposal." [20]

The father of modern refuse management advocated or attempted various programs of resource recovery or waste utilization that matched specific types of refuse with appropriate disposal methods. In January 1898, he established the first rubbish-sorting plant in the United States. He also devised methods for utilizing garbage, ashes and street sweepings. "Although he never became interested in waste cremation, he was enthusiastic about experiments in garbage reduction that coincided with his philosophy of utilization of waste," Melosi says. During Waring's tenure as commissioner, New York City had a garbage-reduction contract with the Sanitary Utilization Co., which "extracted grease, other liquids, and dry residuum (for use as fertilizer) from the city's waste at its plant on Barren Island. Waring also encouraged further experimentation to find more efficient and economical methods of reducing waste and utilizing the by-products. Eventually he hoped that this process would also be placed under municipal control." [21]

Waring died in 1898 and Strong was turned out of office. Tammany Hall returned to power, and much that Waring had accomplished was undone or neglected. Nevertheless, his comprehensive approach to the problem of urban waste was imitated in many cities. Indeed, reformers naively saw in Waring's programs a "quick fix" for the

Newspaper Recycling: Supply Exceeds Demand

People who separate out old newspapers from the rest of their trash think that what they are doing is "recycling." But if the old newspapers are never actually put to any new commercial use, then there's been no recycling — just wasted effort. The newspapers, separated and collected, remain what they had been: waste in need of disposal.

That unhappy result has become increasingly common. In part because of mandatory recycling programs in Northeastern states, the supply of used newsprint has come to exceed the demand for it in recent years.

As a result, some states are trying to get newspaper publishers to use more recycled newsprint. Last summer Connecticut enacted a law requiring that by 1993, 20 percent of the newsprint Connecticut publishers use must contain a specified amount of recycled fiber. Florida last year enacted a law imposing a 10-cent tax on every ton of virgin newsprint publishers use. Measures to get publishers to use more recycled newsprint are under discussion in other states.

Publishers are strongly opposed to all this legislation. "Regulating newsprint is regulating newspapers, and it is intolerable in a free society," the American Newspaper Publishers Association declared recently.[†] The trade group claims publishers are doing everything they can to promote the use of recycled paper and the recycling of newsprint.

About one-third of the more than 12 million tons of newsprint used in the United States each year is actually recovered and put to a new use. About half of the recovered newsprint is recycled into newsprint; the other half is used for other paper and paperboard products.

Newsprint mills in the United States produced 5.8 million tons of newsprint in 1987, and about 23 percent, or 1.4 million tons, was made from old newspapers. Total U.S. production of newsprint supplied less than half of total U.S. demand; 8.9 million tons were imported, primarily from Canada.

Making newsprint out of old newspapers, provided they are clean, requires only that the paper be deinked to produce a slush pulp; the rest of the process is similar to paper-making that starts directly from logs. "The

virgin fiber process has a lower raw material cost but higher operating costs (particularly for power)," says Fred D. Iannazzi, president of Andover International Associates, of Danvers, Mass., which recently studied the economics of recycling old newspapers.

"However," Iannazzi added, "the quality of newsprint made from 100 percent [old newspapers] is somewhat inferior to that produced using virgin fiber." According to Iannazzi, the quality difference can be avoided by using old newspapers as a partial substitution rather than a 100 percent replacement for virgin fiber.[††]

Although production of recycled newsprint is theoretically more economical, the outlook for much increased production is not good. "Although the current economics appear to favor [old newspapers] over virgin pulp as the fiber stock for newsprint," Iannazzi says, "industry history, investment philosophy, and mill locations favor continuing with the traditional pulpwood feedstock."

Most recycled newsprint mills are located close to major metropolitan areas to reduce the costs of transporting collected newspapers. Most virgin fiber mills are located close to the sources of wood pulp. Transporting large quantities of old newspapers to these mills for use instead of wood pulp isn't likely to be cost-effective.

Future construction of recycled newsprint mills is likely to be hampered by projections that U.S. and Canadian capacity to produce newsprint will soon exceed the demand for it. Within the next few years, nine new newsprint machines, seven of them in Canada and each with a capacity of producing about 200,000 tons per year, will become functional. According to a recent study by Congress' Office of Technology Assessment, most of the new newsprint machines will use virgin fiber, "mainly because the new machines are additions to current plants rather than developments at new sites." [‡]

† Quoted in The Washington Post, Sept. 26, 1989.
†† Fred D. Iannazzi, "The economics are right for U.S. mills to recycle old newspapers," Resource Recycling, July 1989.
‡ Office of Technology Assessment, U.S. Congress, Facing America's Trash: What Next for Municipal Solid Waste?, October 1989.

waste problem. The ensuing decades revealed that they weren't.

"Investigations of collection practices throughout the country indicated that no single method was practicable in all cities," Melosi writes ". . . The choice of system had to depend on the special conditions of the city, the method of disposal in use, and, with the separation system, the availability and dependability of markets for the by-products." Advocates of source separation were most persuasive in cities in which garbage reduction was a major means of disposal. Critics argued that combined-refuse collection was "much easier for the householder, less complicated for the collection team, and cheaper for the city." Surveys

done between 1902 and 1924 indicated that most cities practiced at least some source separation. Cities that relied on incineration were more likely to use combined-refuse collection.[22]

Waste disposal presented city officials with problems different from those involved in waste collection. Whereas the entire populace was affected by refuse collection, only those people who lived near open dumps, landfills, garbage-reduction plants or incinerators were much affected by waste disposal. Hence, when it came to disposal, city officials in the early 20th century were less worried about public protests and more inclined to select methods that were expedient and cheap, or that promised greater efficiency. Many disposal methods remained primitive. Dumping on land continued to be the main method for getting rid of rubbish and ashes; no one method of garbage disposal predominated.[23]

The first generation of American furnaces and crematories had performed badly, and so although incineration was accepted as a viable method of disposal in theory, it remained controversial for years. Garbage reduction was even more controversial. Critics pointed to the method's limited applicability (because it could handle only garbage, 70 to 90 percent of a city's waste had to be disposed of in other ways) and to its high cost. In addition, markets for grease and other byproducts were not always reliable. The worst problem, however, was the awful stench given off by the reduction plants, in which the huge quantities of decomposing wastes were "cooked."

"While the reduction method failed to attract widespread support in American cities, it did help generate interest in the broader area of utilization of wastes and recycling," Melosi recounts. Experiments in turning waste into "wealth" proliferated in the early 20th century. Machines were invented to pulverize inorganic materials so that they could be used as fill or fertilizer. The incombustible residue from incinerator plants, which had traditionally been used as fill, was tested as a possible improvement on gravel for concrete. Some cities found profit in sorting and reselling items found in rubbish, especially given a growing demand for old rags and used paper by manufacturers of paper products. There were also projects to turn waste into energy.[24]

Although some local experiments were successful, the idea of extracting wealth from waste never found wide acceptance in American cities. It was simply "out of step with certain realities of industrial America," Melosi notes. "The availability of cheap energy sources — wood, coal, petroleum, and electric power — made the conversion of waste into heat and light seem unnecessary. ... Furthermore, the United States had so many disposal methods available to it that [waste] utilization was inevitably compared with them on a cost-benefit basis. The advent of the sanitary landfill, in particular, undercut several utilization programs by offering a disposal method that seemed to combine both economical and efficient means of disposal." [25]

Problems grow in the 20th century

America's waste problem grew as the country did after World War I. Urban development, a changing economy, scientific and technical advances all contributed to the problem. The rise of the automobile, chemical and electrical industries during the 1920s led to new and diverse products and packaging materials, which eventually wound up in the trash heap. The composition of America's waste changed. (As the automobile supplanted the horse, for instance, horse manure ceased to be an important component.) And the amount of waste increased at a staggering rate. By one estimate, the solid waste expanded about five times as rapidly as the population.[26]

Interest in resource recovery revived during World War II, when it was deemed a patriotic duty. Manufacturers were heavily dependent on scrap or secondary materials, and there was widespread recovery of paper, steel cans and food wastes. The patriotic obligation ended with the war, however. Although the secondary-materials industries continued to function, recycling became less significant and rampant consumption became the order of the day. Pack-

aging of goods took on new significance. "One of the reasons," Melosi says, "was the rise of self-service merchandising through supermarkets and other consumer outlets. This new direction in marketing required packages that would help sell the product or reduce theft or damage of products. For the sake of convenience, non-returnable bottles and cans replaced returnables. The 'throwaway society' was born amid a rising consumerism and the efforts of industry to cash in on it." [27]

As the amount of waste mounted, so did the costs of collecting and disposing of it. In 1940, local governments had spent only $300 million on the task; by the early 1960s, the figure had risen to about $1 billion. The federal Solid Waste Disposal Act of 1965 recognized that the problem had become a national one and declared that federal leadership and assistance were required to find better methods of disposal. In the 1950s and '60s, those involved in solid-waste management had come to regard sanitary landfilling as the most economical method of disposal and one that produced reclaimed land. There was still belief in a single solution to the disposal problem. But doubts about landfills as the solution began to arise. A major problem was acquiring adequate sites. People frequently did not want a sanitary landfill in their neighborhood, and distant landfill sites increased transportation costs.[28] Even so, new municipal landfills continued to be built, about 300-400 a year in the early 1970s. Yet concern was growing, not only about monetary costs but also about environmental ones, such as landfills' possible contamination of groundwater.[29]

Americans were rediscovering the "garbage problem" and viewing it, as their late-19th-century predecessors had, as part of a larger environmental problem. Unlike their predecessors, however, environmentally concerned Americans in the 1960s and '70s were starting to think that the refuse problem was connected with affluence and consumption, and that its solution lay in reducing the generation of waste and in recovering the resources being wasted.

In 1970, the year the Environmental Protection Agency was created, Congress enacted the Resource Recovery Act. It shifted the federal emphasis from disposal to resource recovery — recycling of materials and conversion of waste into energy. The Resource Conservation and Recovery Act of 1976 expanded on the earlier legislation and identified another goal: conservation of resources.

Nevertheless, EPA chose not to play a leading role in dealing with the municipal solid-waste problem. The federal agency preferred to concentrate on hazardous waste and to leave the refuse problem almost entirely to the states and local governments. The federal legislation, however, did stimulate the states to act. They enacted solid-waste-management statutes and created state-level solid-waste agencies. Local refuse was no longer just a local problem.

Starting with Oregon in 1972, a number of states enacted "bottle bills" into law. These mandated that beverage containers be returned to retail stores for refunds of specified deposits. The measures, primarily aimed at reducing litter, had only a modest effect on the municipal solid-waste problem. However, they did make people more aware of the concept of recycling.

As the environmental movement gained momentum, enthusiastic volunteers and non-profit groups established community recycling programs. Their efforts had relatively little impact, however. The recycling field continued to be dominated by the profit-minded, demand-driven second-

Can most solid waste be recycled?

YES *says* **BARRY COMMONER**, *director of the Center for the Biology of Natural Systems.*

Recycling is often regarded as a good thing to do because it conforms with the "no waste" rule of ecology. Guided by this purpose, people are content to do some recycling, perhaps of newspapers, cans, and bottles. A state such as New Jersey is regarded as ecologically well-motivated because it mandates 25 percent recycling.

But this is the wrong approach.

Of course, recycling is ecologically sound, but its purpose is to solve the trash disposal crisis — to provide an alternative to the environmentally hazardous trash-burning incinerators and landfills burdened with their toxic ash. This calls for intensive recycling, a system aimed not at a few targets of opportunity but at the *total* trash stream.

Intensive recycling recognizes that about 90 percent of the trash is recyclable and that much of the remaining 10 percent — plastics, for example — ought to be eliminated from the trash stream.

In this way, intensive recycling becomes the method of trash disposal, eliminating the need for incineration and greatly reducing the toxic burden on landfills.

Can this be done? The answer is yes: we at the Center for the Biology of Natural Systems have just shown, in a pilot test for the town of East Hampton, Long Island, that intensive recycling can recover 84.4 percent of residential trash in the form of marketable products: compost prepared from the household-separated food garbage and yard waste; various grades of paper separated at a materials recovery facility (MRF) from a second household container; aluminum cans, tin cans, and color-sorted glass also separated at the MRF from a third household container. The fourth container holds the non-recyclables, 13.2 percent of the total in our pilot test. This figure, plus misclassified rejects amounting to 2.4 percent of the total trash, leads to the 84.4 percent actually recovered.

Widely adopted, intensive recycling would generate assured supplies of paper, metals, and glass that could be sold to users at a relatively low price, or even given away, because each ton recycled saves the community the high and rising cost of landfilling or incinerating a ton of unseparated trash.

Since manufacturers prefer recycled materials because they are cheaper than virgin products, they will respond by progressively moving toward maximum . . . use of recycled materials, creating, at last, the recycling society.

From EPA Journal, *March-April 1989.*

NO *says* **DAVID W. BIRKS**, *past president of the National Resource Recovery Association.*

Today, every place is somebody's back yard. And the NIMBY [Not in My Back Yard] syndrome is just one of many troublesome public perceptions. There's also the perception that local solid waste managers are giving disproportionate attention to solid waste combustion to the detriment of materials recovery, or recycling. And there's the perception, encouraged by a tiny but highly vocal minority, that we could recycle virtually *all* waste, if only we would try hard enough. Or at least we could recycle enough to make solid waste combustion unnecessary.

Neither perception has much validity. . . .

We [at the National Resource Recovery Association] define resource recovery as *both* materials and energy recovery, because we regard both the materials and the energy in our waste streams as natural resources worthy of wise management. And *resource* recovery is the only mechanism that can move us . . . from the status quo, in which we are predominantly landfill dependent. . . .

In the status quo, somewhere between five and 20 percent of our waste is being recycled. The rest is going to the landfill. Given that status quo, a typical community with a population of a half million that produces 2,000 tons per day of trash today will require a 240 acre landfill . . . by the year 2010.

About half of that trash is potentially recyclable, however. And reclaiming and recycling 80 percent of that, a significant accomplishment, would effectively handle 40 percent of the total waste stream. That's about the most we can reasonably expect to recycle, and we may be decades away from [that]. . . .

[By] recycling 25 to 40 percent of its trash and incinerating whatever is left that is combustible, [the typical community] would then need only enough landfill capacity for its noncombustible wastes (like construction and demolition debris) and for its incineration ash, which is biologically inert. The required landfill is reduced, then, to just about 50 acres. . . .

Recycling and solid waste combustion are compatible techniques which solid waste managers can use in tandem to reduce their dependence on landfills. In fact, they're more than compatible: they're complementary. Removing recyclable non-combustibles from the waste stream prior to incineration improves the waste's fuel value. . . . Recycling more means burning less, which yields fewer total emissions and less ash for landfill disposal. And the improved combustion efficiency attained by burning waste with a better fuel value reduces emissions, too. . . .

From Solid Waste & Power, *June 1988.*

What's in Our Garbage

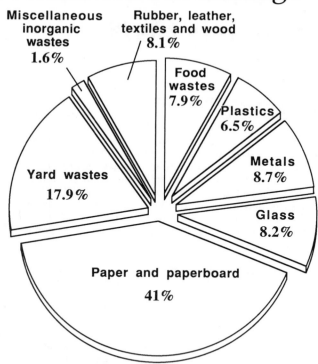

Miscellaneous inorganic wastes 1.6%

Rubber, leather, textiles and wood 8.1%

Food wastes 7.9%

Plastics 6.5%

Metals 8.7%

Yard wastes 17.9%

Glass 8.2%

Paper and paperboard 41%

Source: Environmental Protection Agency.

ary materials industry. Many of the non-profit community programs disappeared before long, but some of the programs managed to find enough financial support from their communities to continue operating.[30] Many cities, a 1974 EPA study noted, "increasingly are viewing resource recovery as both an environmentally and economically desirable alternative to disposal.... Unfortunately," the study added, "this option is most often not available because demand for materials from wastes is nonexistent or severely limited."[31]

Markets for materials are extremely dynamic

The problem of insufficient demand for recycled materials has refused to go away. While it is technically possible to recycle most of the materials that could theoretically be separated out from municipal solid waste, says OTA's Howard Levenson, "there's not enough demand for a lot of that material, in terms of processing it into new products, and [also] a lot of [the material] is of low quality, because either it's low quality to begin with or it gets mixed in with other parts of the trash stream, and that makes it much less attractive to recyclers."

Low quality is not the only reason for insufficient demand for recycled materials. Sometimes the alternative products simply cost less — recycled paper, for instance, often costs more than virgin paper — although primary materials don't always have the advantage. "Markets for materials fluctuate drastically, whether it's recycled material or virgin material," Levenson says. "It depends on where the manufacturers are in relation to the source of the material, and how much transportation costs, and so forth. It's a really complicated situation."

Levenson and OTA elaborated on the complexities of

market conditions in their recent study. The demand for most raw materials, the study points out, "is based on factors far removed from the immediate use of the materials.... For instance, demand for packaging materials depends on the demand for the multitude of products for which packaging is used.... Because demand factors can be in a constant state of flux, with a market having many actors and an increasingly global nature, it is very difficult to externally control or balance the markets for these raw materials, whether primary or secondary."[32]

Nevertheless, it is possible for government to stimulate the growth of markets for recycled materials. Government procurement is one obvious way. In fact, in the Resource Conservation and Recovery Act of 1976, Congress directed EPA to develop guidelines for procurement of recycled materials. EPA, however, did not issue any final guidelines until 1988. Guidelines now exist for procurement of recycled paper products and certain other goods produced with recycled materials.

Many think the government should do a lot more in the way of procurement to encourage recycling. "I think [the federal government] can play an awfully big role there, bigger than anybody else," says Marian Chertow, "and ... that would make a great contribution." But how extensive the federal effort in procurement will actually be remains to be seen. "There are problems with the quality, in some cases, of recycled materials," Levenson says. "There are more problems with cost. And an even bigger problem is just getting procurement officials to think about [buying recycled materials]."

Procurement is not the only thing the federal government could do. In fact, because the Resource Conservation and Recovery Act is now up for reauthorization, a variety of ways in which the federal government might address the solid-waste problem and encourage recycling are under discussion on Capitol Hill. Among the possible measures the government could take are direct subsidies to manufacturers to increase their use of recycled materials, and efforts to promote exports of recycled materials abroad.

But the states have not been content to wait for the federal government to act. At least 23 states have enacted legislation encouraging the purchase of recycled materials or items containing them, and certain states have done better at procurement of recycled materials than the federal government has. Maryland, for instance, gradually raised the amount of recycled bond paper (defined as paper whose content was 80 percent recycled) purchased by the state from 5 percent to 40 percent of all the paper it bought. Certain cities and counties have also adopted procurement regulations. Among them are Washington; Philadelphia; Portland, Ore.; New York City; Anne Arundel County, Md.; and Suffolk County, N.Y.[33]

The federal, state and local governments represent a large potential market for recycled materials. Together, those governments' purchases of goods and services amount to about 20 percent of the gross national product. But as the OTA study observes, "the amount of a product procured by the government will not necessarily have a significant effect on the overall market for the product or on [municipal solid waste] management. For example, one reason for the minimal impact of government procurement programs on paper recycling is that the government consumes only 1 to 2 percent of the nation's total paper." Nevertheless, the study says, consistent procurement policies "could provide economic stimulus for market development and expansion."[34]

Bottle Bills Have Had Litter Impact

Mandatory deposit laws for bottles and cans are now in effect in nine states — Connecticut, Delaware, Iowa, Maine, Massachusetts, Michigan, New York, Oregon and Vermont. These laws generally require the customer who buys soft drinks or beer to place a deposit on the bottles or cans.† The money is refunded when he or she returns them.

Two other states, California and Florida, have adopted modified versions of mandatory deposit or redemption legislation. California's redemption law, adopted in 1987, mandates establishment of "convenience" buy-back centers for recycling. Florida in 1988 adopted a deposit-fee system that affects all types of containers, not just beverage containers. As of Oct. 1, 1992, a disposal fee of 1 cent will be levied on any container sold at retail that is not recycled at a 50 percent rate in Florida. The fee will increase to 2 cents if the 50 percent target is not met by Oct. 1, 1995.

The main purpose of the beverage-container deposit laws — often referred to as "bottle bills" — was to reduce litter, and they seem to have succeeded in meeting that goal. "In general, beverage container deposit systems capture between 70 and 90 percent of the targeted containers and appear particularly effective in reducing litter," Congress' Office of Technology Assessment (OTA) noted in a recent study.†† In states with such laws, total roadside litter decreased between 15 and 50 percent, and beverage container litter decreased by as much as 80 percent.

But such laws have had only modest impact on the municipal solid-waste problem and their effect on recycling has been mixed.

Although bottles and cans are a highly visible part of the municipal solid-waste "stream," they also are a relatively small part. Nationwide, beverage containers constitute 6-11 percent of municipal solid waste, according to OTA. Since most deposit legislation excludes certain types of containers (such as those for wine, liquor or milk), the proportion of municipal solid waste covered by the laws is only about 5 percent. "Curbside programs to collect recyclables can cover a broader portion of [municipal solid waste] and thus have the potential to achieve greater diversion of materials from landfills," OTA observes. "In the past, deposit legislation may have stimulated the development of processing facilities and recycling markets, but curbside and other types of recycling programs also have this potential.'

Although the deposit laws obviously encourage recycling of bottles and cans, they also can have a negative impact on widespread recycling. Aluminum cans are the key factor, because of the high value of recovered aluminum. Marian R. Chertow, director of the Program on Solid Waste and the Environment at Yale University's Institution for Social and Policy Studies, explained the situation by describing the problem facing a man who runs a recycling plant in Groton, Conn., and a similar plant in Camden County, N.J. Connecticut has a bottle-deposit law; New Jersey doesn't. "He tells me that the average revenue per ton in the Camden County plant is about $90, because of the aluminum, [whereas] in Connecticut, the average value per ton is roughly $60. ... The difference between making $90 a ton and making $60 a ton, it turns out, is the cost of making this thing self-sufficient or not. So, ironically, recycling entrepreneurship is much more profitable in states without bottle bills because there are still aluminum cans that come in with the waste."

In the same way and for the same reason, public recycling programs can lose revenues in states that have deposit laws. On the other hand, the total costs to the public sector may be reduced because there is less waste for the municipality to handle. The costs of managing the used beverage-container part of the waste stream are instead borne by the consumer, the retailer and the beverage industry.

† Delaware's law applies to glass only.
†† U.S. Congress, Office of Technology Assessment, Facing America's Trash: What Next for Municipal Solid Waste?, October 1989.

Yet even if the government does extensively stimulate the development of markets for recycled materials, the result is not likely to be a commercial market for every bit of material that could theoretically be recovered from America's municipal solid waste. The most optimistic assessments of recycling's potential role in solving the waste problem — a recovery rate of 80 percent or more — assume that such markets can be found. OTA, in doing its study, tried to assess recycling's potential but refused to make a numerical estimate. "We made a very specific decision not to estimate how much recycling could take place," Levenson says, "because we thought it was counterproductive and didn't mean much, because you have to make so many assumptions about the markets, and as we've seen with newsprint, your assumptions can go drastically awry in a matter of a couple of months. So it seemed to us that the best way to treat this whole issue of the numbers involved in recycling was to say that it's clear that we can do a lot more."

Waste problem still demands more than just recycling

As all but the most extreme environmentalists acknowledge, recycling by itself cannot solve America's solid-waste problem. Even Japan and Sweden, nations that are well ahead of the United States in recycling, use incinerators and landfills. There is little doubt that the United States, too, will have to continue to do so.

But the nation's landfills are filling up. Since 1978, according to EPA, 14,000 landfills — 70 percent of the landfills that were then in operation — have closed. Of the estimated 5,500 landfills in operation last year, EPA projects that only about 3,300 will still be operating in 1993. In New Hampshire, Massachusetts, New Jersey and Florida, virtually all of the currently operating municipal solid-waste landfills will be closed within a decade.[35] States, particularly in the Northeast, have been increasingly transporting their waste out-of-state. New Jersey, for instance, last year exported 55-60 percent of its waste — primarily to Pennsylvania, but also to Ohio, West Virginia,

Connecticut, New York and Kentucky.[36]

As a result of the diminishing landfill space and the increasing amounts of waste generated, there's been a growing interest during this decade in waste-to-energy plants, in which garbage is burned to produce steam or electricity. A 1988 survey by the U.S. Conference of Mayors' National Resource Recovery Association found 107 waste-to-energy plants already in operation. Fifty more facilities were under construction or in advanced stages of planning. Most of the plants were so-called "mass-burn" incinerators in which unprocessed solid waste is fed into a furnace. Of the 107 waste-to-energy facilities in operation in 1988, 82 were mass-burn plants; 39 more mass-burn plants were under construction or in advanced stages of planning.

In the mid-1980s, promoters of waste-to-energy technology predicted that incineration could take care of 40 percent of the nation's municipal solid waste by the turn of the century.[37] Such estimates have had to be revised downward, however. In many cities, mass-burn plants ran into a lot of public opposition. Critics raised concerns about air emissions and the toxicity of the ash produced. Burning refuse reduces its volume, but the ash that is left over contains toxic materials that must be disposed of somewhere. The industry said the potential risks were very small and would be safely guarded against. Nevertheless, since 1985, orders for some 40 mass-burn plants have been canceled, according to mass-burn foe Neil Seldman of the Institute for Local Self-Reliance.[38]

Waste-to-energy technology is still likely to play a significant role in waste management. It's "definitely premature" to write an obituary for mass-burn incineration, says Levenson. "There are certainly more mass-burn incinerators that are coming on line and that are being constructed today, and there are more that are being considered." He thinks mass-burn incinerators may eventually take care of 20 percent or more of the waste stream.

Richard Sweetnam, an analyst who follows the waste-to-energy industry for Kidder, Peabody & Co., a New York investment banking firm, says there is "a lot of optimism" about the industry's future, even though it's currently doing only "fair." The rate of new orders for plants has been well below the levels in 1985 and 1986. That falloff, he says, has to do with the new attention being paid to recycling. "I think recycling is playing a larger part in the equation, and municipalities are deferring plans for incineration in favor of trying to go ahead and get recycling at least started before incineration's considered more actively as an option."

National environmental organizations acknowledge that incineration will have a part in solving the nation's municipal solid-waste problem. "For the substantial amounts of waste that can be expected to remain even after maximum recycling, reliance on landfilling and incineration will continue, so their significant health and environmental risks must be directly addressed," says Richard A. Denison, a scientist for the Environmental Defense Fund's toxic chemicals and solid waste programs. "Proper design of facilities using [the] best available technology is critical. . . . [A]dvanced combustion systems and state-of-the-art air pollution controls, coupled with restrictions on the kinds of waste that may be burned can reduce air pollution significantly. With respect to incinerator ash, provision for chemical or physical treatment and separate disposal of the ash in lined landfills must be integral parts of any incinerator project."[39]

What Happens to Our Garbage?

Currently, only 11 percent of the nation's waste is recycled. Most of the rest is put in landfills.

	Million tons per year	Percent
Material Recycling	17	11
Incineration with Energy Recovery	10	6
Incineration without Energy Recovery	5	3
Landfilling, Other	126	80
Total	158	100

SOURCE: Environmental Protection Agency. Data are for 1986

EPA is supposed to propose regulations for municipal solid-waste incinerators this year. The regulations "will certainly be more stringent," says Levenson. "They'll probably require some kind of best-available technology, such as the use of scrubbers and baghouses [both of which are emission-control devices]." Levenson says it's also possible that EPA may require communities to have recycling programs in place before they can get a permit for an incinerator and require that there be source separation before material goes into the incinerator. Keeping metals such as lead and cadmium, and products and materials containing them, out of the incinerator would reduce the toxicity and volume of the incinerator ash.

Stringent regulations, toughly enforced, might allay people's fears about the hazards of waste-to-energy plants. But that may not make finding sites for such plants much easier. Indeed, as government officials across the country have learned, it's not easy to persuade those who live in the vicinity to accept intrusive facilities — whether it's a mass-burn plant, a new landfill or even a recycling center. It's the NIMBY (Not In My Back Yard) phenomenon, and it's probably the biggest obstacle preventing communities from finding solutions to their waste problems.

Public officials hope that stepping up recycling efforts will help overcome public resistance to siting garbage facilities. At the same time, many experts worry that the public views recycling as a panacea. "Recycling certainly has its place," says Robert Gould, editor of the *Resource Recovery Yearbook*. "But I think a lot of people naively think that if they recycle everything, they won't need landfills and waste-to-energy plants anymore. That's clearly not the case anywhere in the world."[40]

Notes

[1] According to a Gallup Poll conducted in May 1989.

[2] The advertising insert was sponsored by the Council for Solid Waste Solutions, an affiliate of the Society of the Plastics Industry. The insert appeared in the July 17, 1989, issue of *Time*.

[3] Holly Brough, "Why the Recycled Newspaper Bust?" *World Watch*, November-December 1989, p. 31. Worldwatch Institute is a research organization in Washington, D.C., that focuses on environmental, energy, food, population and peace issues.

[4] See Environmental Protection Agency, *The Solid Waste Dilemma: An Agenda for Action, Background Document*, September 1988, p. 1-14.

[5] U.S. Congress, Office of Technology Assessment, *Facing America's Trash: What Next for Municipal Solid Waste?*, October 1989, p. 136.

[6] Franklin Associates Ltd., *Characterization of Municipal Solid Waste in the United States, 1960 to 2000 (Update 1988)*, March 30, 1988, p. 18.

[7] *Ibid., op. cit.*, pp. 17, 21-23.

[8] Theresa Allan, Brenda Platt and David Morris, *Beyond 25 Percent: Materials Recovery Comes of Age*, Institute for Local Self-Reliance, April 1989, p. 13.

[9] *Ibid., op. cit.*, pp. 7, 12, 26-27, 116.

[10] Stated by Jonathan Z. Cannon, EPA's acting assistant administrator for solid waste and emergency response, in testimony July 12, 1989, before House Energy and Commerce Committee's Subcommittee on Transportation and Hazardous Materials.

[11] Marian R. Chertow, *Garbage Solutions: A Public Official's Guide to Recycling and Alternative Solid Waste Management Technologies* (paperback, 1989), pp. 65-66. The book was published by the National Resource Recovery Association, U.S. Conference of Mayors.

[12] *Ibid.*, pp. 13, 66.

[13] Office of Technology Assessment, *op. cit.*, p. 21.

[14] Martin V. Melosi, *Garbage in the Cities: Refuse, Reform, and the Environment, 1880-1980* (1981), p. 16.

[15] *Ibid.*, pp. 20-21.

[16] *Ibid.*, pp. 21-22, 36, 40.

[17] *Ibid.*, pp. 40-41.

[18] *Ibid.*, pp. 50, 69.

[19] *Ibid.*, p. 70.

[20] *Ibid.*, p. 71.

[21] *Ibid.*, p. 72.

[22] *Ibid.*, pp. 156-157.

[23] *Ibid.*, pp. 162, 164.

[24] *Ibid.*, pp. 181-184.

[25] *Ibid.*, pp. 186-187.

[26] Cited by Melosi, *ibid.*, p. 192.

[27] *Ibid.*, p. 210.

[28] *Ibid.*, pp. 194, 199-200, 214, 219-221.

[29] Environmental Protection Agency, *The Solid Waste Dilemma, op. cit.*, p. 2.E-3.

[30] *Ibid.*, pp. 2.B-2, 2.B-3.

[31] Quoted by Melosi, *op. cit.*, pp. 222-223.

[32] Office of Technology Assessment, *op. cit.*, p. 194.

[33] *Ibid.*, p. 331; Chertow, *op. cit.*, p. 55.

[34] Office of Technology Assessment, *op. cit.*, p. 331.

[35] Environmental Protection Agency, *op. cit.*, pp. 2.E-3, 2.E-4.

[36] Office of Technology Assessment, *op. cit.*, pp. 274-275.

[37] Cynthia Pollock, *Mining Urban Wastes: The Potential for Recycling*, Worldwatch Paper 76, April 1987, p. 17.

[38] Neil Seldman, "Mass Burn is Dying," *Environment*, September 1989, p. 42.

[39] "Are Landfills and Incinerators Part of the Answer? Three Viewpoints," *EPA Journal*, March-April 1989, p. 24. Denison contributed one of the three "viewpoints."

[40] Quoted in "Managing Our Waste," *Governing*, September 1989, p. 12A.

Selected Bibliography

Books

Chertow, Marian R., *Garbage Solutions: A Public Official's Guide to Recycling and Alternative Solid Waste Management Technologies*, National Resource Recovery Association, U.S. Conference of Mayors, paperback, 1989.

This work offers a realistic, non-technical look at the roles source reduction, recycling, and composting can play in a community's solid-waste management. The author, now director of the Program on Solid Waste and the Environment, at Yale University's Institution for Social and Policy Studies, was previously president of Connecticut's solid-waste authority, financial manager of San Francisco's solid-waste program, and director of marketing and development for a recycling entrepreneur.

Melosi, Martin V., *Garbage in the Cities: Refuse, Reform, and the Environment, 1880-1980*, Texas A&M University Press, 1981.

In this illuminating history, the author shows that the perception of the refuse problem as one part of an environmental problem centered in cities goes back, not just to Earth Day in 1970, but at least to the 1880s, when industrial cities were suffering "an environmental crisis characterized by crowded tenement districts, chronic health problems, billowing smoke, polluted waterways, traffic congestion, unbearable noise, and mounds of putrefying garbage."

Articles

"Focusing on the Garbage Crisis," *EPA Journal*, March-April 1989, pp. 9-52.

This collection of useful articles includes an interview with Sylvia Lowrance, director of the Environmental Protection Agency's Office of Solid Waste; an explanation of what is in the waste stream; assorted views on recycling, as well as on the question of whether landfills and incinerators are part of the answer to the solid-waste problem; an article on source reduction, and pieces on what various communities are doing. The magazine is published by the Environmental Protection Agency's Office of Public Affairs.

Reports and Studies

Allan, Theresa; Platt, Brenda; and Morris, David, *Beyond 25 Percent: Materials Recovery Comes of Age*, Institute for Local Self-Reliance, April 1989.

A study of 15 communities that are in the forefront of recycling activity. "Cities and states that a few years ago imagined that only 10 to 20 percent recovery levels were possible have now achieved 30, 40, even 50 percent, and are striving for still higher levels," the authors report. "In 1988, Seattle adopted the loftiest goal to date: 60 percent. But even this level may not test the limits. Results from a 100 household, 10-week pilot program in East Hampton, New York, indicated that as much as 84 percent materials recovery was technically feasible."

Office of Technology Assessment, U.S. Congress, *Facing America's Trash: What Next for Municipal Solid Waste?*, October 1989. (OTA-O-424)

A comprehensive, detailed examination of the municipal solid-waste problem and the various ways it can be addressed. Actions taken by local communities or others regarding municipal solid waste are likely to be more effective if they are drawn up in the context of a coherent, comprehensive national policy, the report says. "Congress can provide strong leadership by stating a clear national policy for [municipal solid waste], one that contains clearly articulated goals and sets priorities for action. Such a national policy could set the stage for moving toward a balanced, long-term approach to [municipal solid-waste] problems."

Public Attitudes Toward Garbage Disposal, National Solid Wastes Management Association, May 4, 1989.

Americans currently recycle about 11 percent of their municipal solid waste. This opinion survey found that 70 percent of American adults agreed that "recycling can solve much of the solid waste disposal problem." Fewer than one in four Americans favored building new landfills and only about two in five wanted to build waste-to-energy plants.

Subcommittee on Transportation and Hazardous Materials, Committee on Energy and Commerce, U.S. House of Representatives, *Municipal Solid Waste Disposal Crisis*, hearing on June 22, 1989. (Serial No. 101-37)

——— , *Recycling of Municipal Solid Waste,* hearings on July 12 and 13, 1989. (Serial No. 101-59)

These prints from congressional hearings include testimony from a wide variety of people involved in the search for solutions to the municipal solid-waste problem and the move toward recycling. They include federal, state and local officials, representatives of the solid-waste management industry, environmentalists, representatives of the recycling industry and of many of the various industries affected, from aluminum producers to soft-drink manufacturers.

The Solid Waste Dilemma: An Agenda for Action, U.S. Environmental Protection Agency, February 1989. (EPA/530-SW-89-019)

This report outlines the Environmental Protection Agency's approach to the solid-waste problem and sets a goal for 1992 of managing 25 percent of the nation's municipal solid waste through source reduction and recycling, including composting of yard waste. "We also must work to reduce the risks associated with landfills and combustors, inasmuch as these management alternatives will be necessary to handle most of the wastes," the report says.

Graphics: pp. 84, 87, 89, S. Dmitri Lipczenko.

Free Market Environmental Protection

Bush officials want to offer industries financial incentives to make environmental protection cost-effective

In the nearly 20 years since environmentalists galvanized public opinion with the celebration of Earth Day, the federal government has passed dozens of laws and spent billions of dollars to clean up the environment. With a few notable exceptions, however, the environment still seems to be a mess. Summer smog alerts have become almost commonplace. Toxic wastes continue to leach into groundwater. Acid rain continues to fall. Medical wastes wash up on once pristine beaches. Scientists warn of the threat of global warming — the so-called "greenhouse effect" — caused by burning fossil fuels.

Now Congress and the Bush administration are weighing new campaigns to protect the environment. But even as they do so, the federal budget remains mired in deficit and U.S. industry is under siege from Japanese and European competition. Under current circumstances, says economist Robert N. Stavins of Harvard University's John F. Kennedy School of Government, "if we're going to have environmental protection, we've got to do it at the least cost possible."

The Reagan administration, when it was faced with that problem, opted for slashing EPA's budget, imposing "cost-benefit" tests for environmental protection rules, and promoting private development of resources from federally owned lands. The Reagan approach provoked the wrath of environmentalists, who said the policies only allowed environmental problems to get worse.

For its part, the Bush administration, joined by some economists, environmentalists and industry leaders, say they have a better idea — one that Stavins says is "180 degrees different" from Reagan's brand of environmental deregulation. Arguing that the old "command-and-control" approach embodied in the environmental laws of the 1970s has bogged down in red tape and courtroom battles, they say it's time to let market forces rather than government edict be the driving force behind cleaning up the environment. Congress would still set national environmental standards, they say. But instead of regulating the way factories operate, the government would give businessmen and communities incentives to meet pollution control goals as cheaply and efficiently as possible.

Current laws give federal and state officials authority to fine polluters, and in recent years the threat of legal liability judgments costing millions of dollars has given industry an incentive to do better. On Aug. 15, for example, Alaska sued Exxon Corp. and six other oil companies for unspecified damages, charging negligence in the *Exxon Valdez* grounding that spilled nearly 11 million gallons of crude oil into Prince William Sound. But some businesses have used the current law to their advantage, finding it more profitable to stall action through time-consuming regulatory and legal challenges than to comply promptly with regulations. Economists suggest that market-based policies could provide more powerful financial incentives than the threat of legal action for limiting or preventing pollution.

Not only would such an approach be much less expensive for the federal government, the proponents say, but it might actually work. Current regulatory efforts often pose choices between preserving the environment and promoting economic activity, says Stavins, but "economic-incentive approaches . . . make the market a partner, rather than an adversary, in the search for environmental protection." [1]

Last year, Stavins was commissioned by two U.S. senators — Timothy E. Wirth, D-Colo., and John Heinz, R.-Pa. — to review market-based alternatives to current environmental programs. That effort, known as Project 88, presented the incoming Bush administration with 36 broad-brush recommendations to curb pollution and protect natural resources by taking advantage of economic incentives.[2] Proposed market incentives take several forms, but here are some of the more compelling ones:

● **Imposing taxes or fees on pollution.** The government would charge businesses for each ton or other unit of pollution discharged, setting the fees high enough to encourage businesses to curtail emissions and to develop efficient pollution-control systems.

● **Issuing pollution permits that corporations could buy and sell.** Under this program, EPA would set limits on the amount of pollution a company could legally discharge. Companies that reduced emissions below their allocation could sell their unused emission rights to companies having difficulty meeting their allocation levels. Some companies might find it cheaper to buy emission credits from other companies than to invest in expensive pollution control equipment for aging factories; others might find investing in anti-pollution equipment and selling surplus emission credits to be more profitable.

● **Requiring deposits on hazardous materials.** The government would charge a tax on hazardous materials, then grant refunds for each unit of waste that was recycled or disposed of in proper fashion. The difference between the deposit and refund would amount to a net tax on wastes that companies failed to reclaim. By raising the net tax to higher levels, the government could strengthen incentives for recycling and waste disposal.

● **Ending archaic government subsidies.** The government would repeal existing subsidies that promote destructive harvesting of national forest timber, inefficient irrigation systems, overgrazing on federal rangelands, and other practices that waste public resources and degrade the environment.

In concept, such mechanisms would force businesses and consumers to take costs to the environment into account in day-to-day economic decisions. The devices, in

By Tom Arrandale

Environmental Expenditures

Strong public support for environmental improvement resulted in the adoption during the 1970s of a host of environmental protection laws. These laws, in turn, stimulated significant increases in environmental expenditures by both government and the private sector. During the early 1980s, however, business and government spending on pollution control declined. The decline in government spending was due primarily to changes in spending for sewer system construction, which is the largest single component of government spending on pollution control. Business spending dropped primarily because of declines in new plant and equipment expenditures for pollution control. Total spending increased substantially in the mid 1980s. The slight drop in 1987 was largely the result of declines in personal and business purchases of emission abatement devices on motor vehicles.

billions of constant 1982 dollars

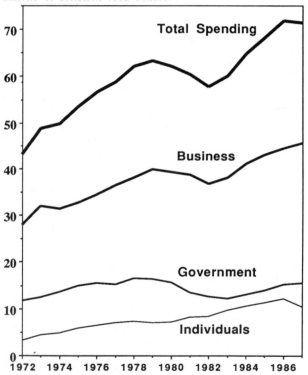

Source: *Bureau of Economic Analysis, U.S. Department of Commerce*

effect, would be a cost for businesses and communities that damage the environment — while offering financial rewards for those that take the strongest cleanup measures. Once in place, economists argue, market incentives would prod polluters to devise innovative ways to control emissions more effectively — and at lower cost — than less flexible federal and state regulations can order.

The U.S. Environmental Protection Agency (EPA), the agency charged with enforcing federal pollution-control laws, has been experimenting with the so-called market approach to environmental protection for more than a decade. Since 1976, the agency has approved the trading of emission rights among factories in industrial zones with heavily polluted air. (*See story, p. 100.*) "Emission trading sounds weird," *Newsweek* contributing editor Gregg Easterbrook wrote recently, ". . . but nearly everyone who studies pollution regulation concludes that what's missing is a positive inducement that works from the bottom up, supplanting the conventional structure of costs imposed from the top down. Emission trading will allow engineers rather than regulators to judge which factories can meet standards most efficiently while adding a profit motive for inventing improved controls." [3]

Current EPA Administrator William K. Reilly, a former Conservation Foundation president, has frequently called for fresh approaches to environmental protection, such as "debt-for-nature" swaps that forgive Third World nations' international debt in return for protecting imperiled rain forests. At EPA, Reilly has met with Project 88 participants and named an agency task force to study market-based approaches.

So far, the Project 88 approach has met a mixed reception in Congress. Rep. Henry A. Waxman, D-Calif., a leading proponent of tougher air-quality regulations as chairman of the House Energy and Commerce Subcommittee on Health and Environment, has given guarded support to using economic incentives in some cases. But Waxman also warns that he supports market-based controls "only when we can be certain that the measure will not be used by industry to delay or derail pollution reductions."

Many environmentalists and government pollution-control officials are even more skeptical. They worry that market incentives amount to granting industries "licenses to pollute" without producing real improvements in environmental quality. The basic question, they say, is whether the federal government could better protect the environment by devising economic incentives or by strengthening pollution-control laws and enforcing them more vigorously.

Michael McCloskey, the Sierra Club's national chairman, contends that the case for market incentives "really is built around how to save costs to the economy. It's not an argument for how you get more cleanup." Even industry, which has spent 20 years adjusting to the command-and-control system, may be reluctant to junk it in favor of untested market mechanisms. "Project 88 is so vague — 14 pages on air pollution," notes William D. Fay, administrator of a business lobby coalition called the Clean Air Working Group. "I'm not sure we're ready to jettison volumes and volumes of air-quality regulations and proceedings . . . for a 14-page summary."

Nevertheless, market-based incentives seem to have caught President Bush's eye, and they have every indication of holding a prominent place in environmental protection in the future. Take acid rain, for example. The clean-air proposals that Bush sent to Congress in July featured market incentives as part of its strategy for curbing sulfur dioxide and nitrogen oxide emissions from utility plants in Midwestern states. The emissions from those plants are believed to be responsible for acid rain that has devastated lakes, streams and forests in the East, Northeast and Canada. The president's plan, instead of taking the usual command-and-control tactic of forcing the utilities to install costly smokestack "scrubbers," would permit plant managers to choose any emissions-reduction technology they wanted.

For example, they might substitute low-sulfur coal for

Market Forces and Water Conservation

In Western states, market forces already are at work encouraging water conservation. In a predominantly arid region, access to water supplies has always been critical for economic activity. After Congress passed the Reclamation Act of 1903, the federal government built huge dams across the West's scattered rivers and streams to generate electric power and supply low-cost water for irrigated farms and municipal water systems. Federally subsidized projects supplied farmers with cut-rate water that encouraged wasteful irrigation practices. But federal budget deficits have helped bring the dam-building era to an end, and Western states no longer can count on new projects to augment their supplies. As fast-growing cities seeking more water now have started buying farmers' rights, prices have risen and lively water markets evolved across the region. Water's increasing value is creating new economic incentives to conserve scarce supplies and protect them from pollution.

But federal water policies and Western state water laws still present obstacles to using water more efficiently. U.S. Bureau of Reclamation rules have cast doubt on whether many water rights could be bought and sold, and the "use it or lose it" doctrine embedded in most Western state water laws means that farmers risk forfeiting rights if they cut water consumption.

In one pioneering step, proposed by the Environmental Defense Fund, the Metropolitan Water District (MWD) serving Los Angeles last year struck a deal to obtain additional supplies by financing water conservation by Southern California farmers. Under that agreement, MWD will pay $155 million for water-saving investments by the Imperial Irrigation District. In return, Los Angeles will obtain rights to at least 100,000 acre-feet of Colorado River water. Environmental Defense Fund attorneys and economists say the deal sets a precedent for similar water-conserving agreements across the West. In addition to ending wasteful use, more efficient irrigation practices will reduce "non-

point" runoff from fields bearing pesticides and concentrated salts that eventually reach groundwater or rivers.

An acre-foot of water is the quantity needed to flood one acre to a depth of one foot. Equal to 325,851 gallons, an acre-foot of water is enough for one family of five for a year.

With Congress no longer willing to fully fund construction of new dams and aqueducts, the U.S. Bureau of Reclamation and the Army Corps of Engineers are shifting their missions away from building new projects to managing existing water delivery and flood control systems.

But continuing subsidies still allow California farmers to pay as little as $10 for water to irrigate an acre of cotton, while Los Angeles pays $600 for the same quantity. Some Denver suburbs now pay more than $2,500 for the right to use an acre-foot of water.

The Project 88 report called on the U.S. Interior Department to clear away regulations that present obstacles to marketing rights to water that federal projects supply to farmers. Environmental Defense Fund officials Tom Graff and Zach Willey have called for a thorough overhaul of federal water policies that encourage wasteful uses that contribute to water pollution.

As one step, Graff and Willey recommend that EPA scrap existing technology-based water-pollution regulations and replace them with tradable discharge permits. Under their plan, EPA would set a total discharge limit for each river basin, then issue marketable permits to communities, firms, farms and other facilities that release sewage, discharge industrial wastes or serve as the source of "non-point" runoff to its waters. To improve water quality in the basin, EPA could periodically purchase and retire discharge permits.†

† Zach Willey and Tom Graff, "Federal Water Policy in the United States — An Agenda for Economic and Environmental Reform," Columbia Journal of Environmental Law, 1988 Vol. 13, No. 2, p. 346.

the high-sulfur coal now used. Plants that exceeded their required reductions would be allowed to trade or sell unused emissions permits to other plants. The Project 88 report concluded that "a market-based approach to acid-rain reduction could save us $3 billion per year, compared with the cost of a dictated technological solution."

Command and control: Regulations and red tape

Public concern for the environment has been growing steadily since 1962, when Rachel Carson published *Silent Spring*, a plea to curb the use of the pesticide DDT. Many Americans came to believe that industry would not control air and water pollutants or conserve natural resources unless the federal government forced it to. On Earth Day, April 22, 1970, millions attended environmental teach-ins and anti-pollution rallies around the country, a dramatic testimonial to public sensitivity to environmental degradation — and to the potential political power of the environmental movement.

President Nixon responded with an executive order cre-

ating the Environmental Protection Agency on Dec. 2, 1970, which immediately assumed the existing environmental responsibilities of other departments and agencies. Congress quickly gave EPA responsibility for several new laws, including the landmark Clean Air Amendments of 1970, which set limits on auto pollutants and strengthened air-quality standards, and the Water Pollution Control Act Amendments of 1972, which expanded the government's powers to clean up the nation's waters. In later years EPA was also given authority to control noise, pesticides and other toxic substances, provide clean drinking water and clean up toxic contaminants.

In writing the environmental-protection laws, Congress opted for a strategy that required polluting facilities to obtain federal permits that set limits on the amount of pollutants they could release into the environment. In granting a permit, EPA and state environmental agencies usually directed plant managers to install smokestack "scrubbers," filters or "the best available technology" to reduce or eliminate harmful emissions.

But drafting and enforcing federal environmental standards proved to be exceedingly difficult. It often took the Environmental Protection Agency years to come up with pollutant standards, and it was often many more years before state governments drew up implementation plans that EPA found acceptable.

From the beginning, EPA has been pulled by competing political pressures: Environmentalists pressure the agency to punish polluters, while businesses want to reduce red tape. Business interests complain that EPA often imposes tougher requirements on new facilities than on older ones, a practice critics say encourages firms to keep operating outmoded plants while discouraging investments that would make U.S. companies more competitive in world markets. Critics also argue that the current system favors existing pollution-control methods but gives companies little incentive to develop superior emission-control equipment with greater long-term pollution reductions.

EPA's enforcement efforts have often bogged down in detailed regulation drafting, lengthy administrative proceedings, courtroom hearings and negotiations. Take the case of Kennecott Copper Corp. Kennecott closed a Nevada copper smelter in the 1970s after a court upheld EPA regulations requiring the facility to install equipment to control sulfur dioxide (SO_2) emissions. Kennecott subsequently persuaded the state of Nevada to revise its air-quality implementation plan to allow firms to control SO_2 emissions through tall smokestacks or production cutbacks, then went to court to force EPA to accept the state's decision. The suit was successful, and the court annulled the EPA regulations.

EPA's regulatory efforts have also been subject to congressional meddling. For instance, in the 1977 amendments to the Clean Air Act, Congress ordered EPA to require electric utilities to install costly emission scrubbers on all new coal-burning power plants. Congress was responding in part to pressure from Eastern coal companies and the United Mine Workers, who wanted to preserve jobs in Appalachia's high-sulfur coal mines by preventing firms from complying with sulfur dioxide emission limits by burning low-sulfur Western coal.

In an unlikely political alliance, environmental groups joined with Eastern coal interests in lobbying for the scrubber requirements. Environmentalists said the scrubbers would ensure the maximum possible reductions in emissions from each new power plant, including those built near low-sulfur coal deposits in Rocky Mountain states with nearly pristine air, and would reduce demand for Western coal extracted by destructive strip-mining techniques. But what really happened, according to Yale University Law School scholars Bruce A. Ackerman and William T. Hassler, was "an extraordinary decision that will cost the public tens of billions of dollars to achieve environmental goals that could be reached more cheaply, more quickly, and more surely by other means."[4]

The scrubber decision was not unusual. When Congress passed the major environmental laws during the 1970s, cost was not often a consideration. But by the 1980s cost had become a major concern. Between 1983 and 1987, the United States spent $336 billion on pollution control, according to the Bureau of Economic Analysis in the U.S. Department of Commerce. In 1987 alone, total expenditures for pollution control amounted to over $71 billion (in constant 1982 dollars). Private industry paid more than 60 percent of the bill, government more than 20 percent and consumers paid the rest. (*See graph, p. 94.*)

Pollution Control: How the Money Was Spent

The great bulk of the expenditures for pollution control have gone for activities that directly reduce pollutant emissions. Critics of the current "command-and-control" system say environmental quality would be better if more money had been spent on monitoring how well environmental regulations and equipment were working.

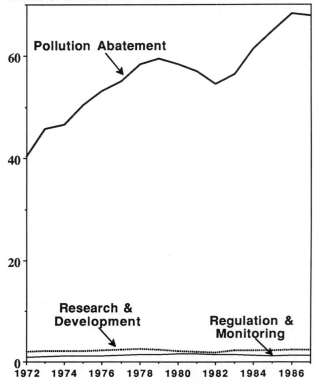

billions of constant 1982 dollars

Source: Bureau of Economic Analysis, U.S. Department of Commerce

Such expenditures might have been acceptable if they worked, but critics contend that what the government bought for all that money was not much at all. What happened, the critics say, is that early on EPA officials, instead of making tough political judgments, defended proposed regulations against industry challenges by trying to marshal scientific data on pollution effects.

But that task required EPA to make complex scientific and engineering judgments that overloaded agency administrators and invited legal challenges from companies that found it cheaper to go to court than to comply. The resulting heavy workload prevented EPA from dealing with other emerging environmental problems.

It also seemed to prevent the government from keeping track of how well its environmental regulations were working. While committing enormous resources to devise and defend regulations, EPA delegated most enforcement power to state agencies; between 1979 and 1985 the agency spent only 8 to 10.5 percent of its own budget on enforcement actions. The Conservation Foundation reports that by 1984, "approximately 70 percent of EPA's day-to-day responsibilities for environmental enforcement had been delegated to the states." [5]

"Our current environmental regulatory system was an understandable response to a perceived need for immediate controls to prevent a pollution crisis," Harvard Law School professor Richard B. Stewart wrote in 1988. "But the system has grown to the point where it amounts to nothing less than a massive effort at Soviet-style central planning of the economy to achieve environmental goals. It strangles investment and innovation. It encourages costly and divisive litigation and delay. It unduly limits private initiative and choice. The centralized command system is simply unacceptable as a long-term environmental protection strategy for a large and diverse nation committed to the market and decentralized ordering." [6]

Tradable emission permits

Stewart and other advocates of controlling environmental risks through economic incentives would rely on the "invisible hand" of market forces to guide decisions on how the nation should meet its pollution-reduction goals. Through various means, they would set a price on conduct that creates pollution or environmental risk, then let each company or other entity decide for itself how much to pay and how much to reduce emissions.

One way this could be done is with "tradable emission permits." Under this approach, the government would set a national cap on certain pollutants and allocate pollution rights among polluters. A firm could either invest in new technology to reduce its emissions or buy permits or credits from another firm whose emissions fall below the standard. To assure further progress in cleaning up the environment, the government could "ratchet down" overall emissions of pollutants by cutting the total number of permits.

Some economists favor a system in which emission permits would be auctioned off instead of granted free of charge. They say this approach would enable the government to raise substantial revenue for environmental research or for reducing the federal deficit. One study cited in a 1988 article by Stewart and Bruce Ackerman estimates that the sale of emission permits could raise between $6 billion and $10 billion annually. [7]

Robert W. Hahn, a senior staff economist for the President's Council of Economic Advisers, and a colleague have estimated that the EPA's current program allowing limited marketing of air-quality permits has saved industry more than $4 billion in costs without making air quality worse. [8] (*See story, p. 100.*)

President Bush's recommendations for reducing acid rain follow a similar line. Past congressional proposals to combat acid rain would have required Midwestern utilities to install smokestack scrubbers to control sulfur dioxide and nitrogen oxide emissions. In his clean-air bill, Bush proposed steps to force more than 300 electric power plants to cut SO_2 emissions by 10 million tons and nitrogen oxide emissions by 2 million tons. But the White House plan would let utilities decide for themselves how to achieve those reductions. Incentives for meeting the reductions would come from marketable emission permits. Companies that reduced pollutants below their allocation could sell their unused emission credits to firms that were unable to meet their limits.

EPA has released studies concluding that meeting simi-

Spending on Major Pollution Control Programs

During the 15 years from 1972 to 1987, the bulk of the expenditures for pollution control were for water and air, with the remainder going primarily to solid waste. The fall in total pollution control spending in the early 1980s (*see graph, p. 94*) was caused primarily by the large decline in spending on water pollution control.

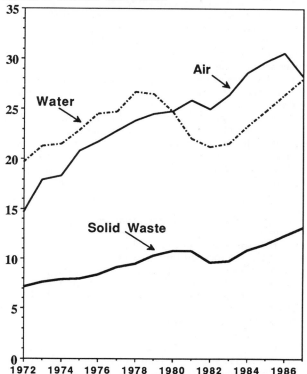

billions of constant 1982 dollars

Source: Bureau of Economic Analysis, U.S. Department of Commerce

lar emissions goals by installing smokestack controls would cost $2.3 billion, while a measure allowing emission permit trading would meet the same goal at a cost of $1.5 billion. A report by ICF Inc., a Virginia-based environmental consultant, suggests that scrubbers would still be the cheapest way for some power plants to comply, and that tighter limits would force even more utilities to adopt smokestack controls. [9] But Bush's plan would let others select less costly alternatives. These might include switching to low-sulfur coal, trying new coal-cleaning technologies, shutting down heavily polluting plants except during peak demand periods, replacing older units with natural gas-fired generators, or offering customers incentives to cut electricity use by buying high-efficiency appliances and lighting fixtures.

The administration program also would grant marketable emission credits to automobile manufacturers that produce vehicles outperforming federal emissions standards and to refiners that surpass clean-fuel standards. "We've provided the goals but we won't try to micro-

Discouraging Destructive Development . . .

Current environmental policy debates focus primarily on using market incentives to encourage steps to control pollution. But some economists also call on the federal government to review current laws and practices that invite environmental destruction by promoting destructive use of the nation's land and natural resources. Those policies grant subsidies or provide government support that artificially encourages wasteful resource development projects that by themselves cannot stand the test of economic efficiency.

Those policies are often holdovers from the era when the federal government was encouraging settlers to convert swamplands to fields, harvest timber and grasslands, and turn other untapped resources into commodities for economic expansion. Those incentives reflect a philosophy that environmentalists say is no longer appropriate to a nation that now values wildlife, wilderness and outdoor recreation.

Previous generations, for instance, regarded wetlands simply as swamps that stood in the way of progress. From colonial times, landowners have drained wetlands, cleared their trees, filled them with soil, and converted them to farm fields and residential areas. Federal flood control and soil conservation programs have provided financial assistance to those efforts. As a result, less than half of the nation's original wetlands are left, and development continues to destroy them at the rate of 458,000 acres a year.

Biologists now see natural wetlands as vital wildlife breeding grounds that purify water supplies and regulate water flows to retard flooding. But landowners cannot profit from those benefits, so they instead alter wetlands to earn economic returns from development. And federal efforts to regulate wetland conversion and to buy them for wildlife refuges meet stiff resistance from development interests.

Bush has endorsed a "no net loss" policy calling for steps to discourage wetland conversion and artificially replace those that are developed. Congress in recent years has repealed tax benefits for wetland conversion and denied federal farm subsidies for "Swampbusters" who drain wetlands for cultivation. The impact of those

changes has yet to be felt, and the Project 88 report called for more comprehensive strategies, including "self-enforcing inducements for people to take account of the full social value of wetlands."

Near major cities, the spread of suburban development also is threatening open spaces provided by farmland. As housing tracts and shopping malls move outward from city lines, farmers can earn more by selling lands to developers than by keeping them in production. Near Brentwood in California's Contra Costa County, a farming region that lies in the path of suburban expansion eastward from San Francisco Bay, farmlands that sold for $6,000 an acre five years ago could be worth $85,000 an acre once they are annexed and zoned for subdivisions. Some Contra Costa County farmers, environmentalists and planners have come up with a plan for the county to buy development rights to about 17,000 acres of prime crop lands, in effect paying landowners to keep the land in farming by making up the difference from what they could earn by selling to developers.

Over the last two decades, several states and some county governments have created tax breaks and bought development rights to provide financial incentives to preserve open space around metropolitan regions. Wisconsin, for instance, grants state income tax credits to farmers who agree to restrict development of their lands for 10 years. The Nature Conservancy and other private groups have protected millions of acres by purchasing them outright or buying conservation easements from owners who agree to keep lands in natural condition. In a 1987 report that the Reagan administration disavowed the President's Commission on Americans Outdoors recommended a national "greenway" program to preserve streamside habitat in fast-growing areas through financial incentives for donations, easements, leases and restrictive land-use covenants.

In managing its own public lands, conservation groups for decades have charged that the federal government encourages destructive resource use without adequately protecting natural values. Producers pay the government fees for access to federally owned resources.

manage them," the president said in announcing the plan. "We will allow flexibility in how industry achieves these goals, but we stand firm on what must be achieved."[10]

Business and environmental lobbyists still are sorting out the president's proposals. While businessmen want more flexible air-quality controls, they are waiting to see how marketable emission permits would fit in the existing command-and-control structure. Among other unanswered questions is whether the government would issue the marketable permits free of charge or auction them off to the highest bidders.

Industry also fears that regulators would defeat the purpose of market-incentive mechanisms by imposing complicated monitoring and reporting requirements. "We're a little skeptical of the agency that's going to be issuing the permits," says William Fay of the Clean Air Working

Group. "Just like the Treasury always interprets the tax laws to raise more government revenue, EPA when it interprets a law always interprets it for more control."

The Edison Electric Institute, a utility industry trade group, and several utilities have criticized Bush's acid-rain plan as harsh, inflexible and too costly. W. S. White Jr., chairman of American Electric Power Company, the nation's largest coal user, predicts that utilities seeking to buy marketable emission-offset credits in order to build new power plants or run older facilities at full power will find that demand outstrips supply. Eventually, White says, "it may become impossible to find additional offsets at any price."

Some influential environmentalists also have serious questions about Bush's acid-rain plan, but they've indicated a willingness to keep an open mind about it. Says the

... of Land and Natural Resources

But in many areas, the government spends far more to manage public lands than it takes in from leasing or selling resources. Commodity production on federal lands in recent years has brought the government between $2.5 billion and $3 billion a year in revenues. But the government has been spending $5.5 billion to $6 billion to manage those lands and share mineral leasing and timber sale revenues with state and local governments.

Except for national parks and wilderness areas, the government manages most of its 700 million acres of federal lands for multiple uses. While Congress directs the U.S. Interior Department and U.S. Forest Service to give equal weight to wildlife and recreation, environmentalists complain that the agencies favor commodity production from mining, logging and livestock grazing. Land managers typically give less weight to hard-to-quantify benefits from wildlife and recreation that show no immediate returns in federal receipts and in revenue-sharing payments to local governments where public lands are located.

Both the Interior Department and the Forest Service lease public range lands for grazing at fees far below what private range lands command; bankers and real-estate agents recognize that access to low-cost federal grazing confers a "permit value" that raises a ranch's worth. Stockmen maintain that the below-market fees are justified by the expense of feeding and controlling livestock on public lands, but environmentalists argue that they provide a subsidy that encourages overstocking of federally owned range.

In recent years, The Wilderness Society and other conservation groups have begun challenging Forest Service timber sales in the Appalachians, the Rocky Mountains and Alaska on economic grounds. After subtracting the costs of preparing sales and sharing 25 percent of receipts with county governments, two out of three national forests actually lost money selling timber in 1985, according to Randall O'Toole, an Oregon forestry consultant. Critics contend that Forest Service accounting practices encourage logging on steep slopes and other sensitive lands while ignoring the growing value of na-

tional forests for wildlife and recreation. O'Toole contends that the Forest Service loses $22 million a year selling timber for logging on six national forests surrounding Yellowstone National Park that produce $20 in recreation benefits for every dollar of timber benefits. "These losses are irrational from a conservation as well as an economic viewpoint," he says.†

Critics say the Forest Service prices its timber through an archaic system that virtually ignores the government's cost of growing trees and offering them for harvest. O'Toole recommends that national forest management be "marketized" by requiring the Forest Service to earn market prices for its timber, halting current practices that in effect subsidize timber sales with federal funds for road-building and planting new trees, and forcing the agency to pay its own way without congressional appropriations.

However, the ranchers and loggers who benefit from those policies are small but well-organized groups that lobby Western congressional delegations vigorously against changes. Congress for years has refused to raise federal grazing fees to market levels, instead imposing a formula that keeps fees low by tying them to ranching costs and livestock prices. And low-cost timber sales provide logs for sawmills that often provide most of the jobs in small towns near national forests. State and local governments dependent on revenue sharing from federal lands also resist proposals that would curtail timber harvests and other economic development.

Wilderness Society economists are studying a proposal that would reduce political resistance to reforms by severing the link between revenue sharing and commodity production, no longer basing local government shares on the amount of timber harvested or minerals extracted. Environmental groups generally remain suspicious that economists' approaches would lead to recreation fees for backpackers, hunters, and others who now enjoy free use of public lands. "Most of these ideas are fairly controversial politically," Hahn observes, "so it will take time [to implement them]."

† Randall O'Toole, "Reforming the Forest Service," Columbia Journal of Environmental Law, 1988 Vol. 13, No. 2, p. 299.

Sierra Club's McCloskey, "I come out as a guarded skeptic, not as a hard-core opponent." And Edward J. Barks, a spokesman for the National Clean Air Coalition, which represents most of the major conservation groups on clean-air issues, says his organization is willing to consider a marketable-permit system, but adds that the coalition insists that pollution standards still be set by the federal government to prevent threats to human health.

William Becker, executive director of the State and Territorial Air Pollution Administrators Association, says an emissions-credit system must be closely monitored to make sure that utility transactions produce overall acid-rain reductions. "There can be good trades and there can be sloppy trades, and the latter will exacerbate the problem we're trying to solve in the first place," Becker says. "It would be ludicrous to allow a Midwestern utility to pollute

more and a Florida utility to pollute less. The result would be more acid rain [in the Northeast]." Even if emissions trading is allowed between existing plants, Becker adds, new plants still should be fitted with state-of-the-art emission equipment to assure maximum control of pollutants.

The Project 88 report: An alternative approach

The debate over Bush's clean-air proposals will test how much Congress is willing to trust market forces to protect the environment. "Whether the clean-air bill is the first of a series [of market-based proposals], it's just too early to tell," says Robert Hahn of the Council of Economic Advisers. But market-approach advocates like Hahn now hold several White House and EPA posts, and the administration now is studying wider use of economic incentives. The Project 88 report suggests that Congress encourage wider

Trading Air Quality Permits

By the mid-1970s, it was obvious that many major metropolitan areas in the country would be unable to comply with the air quality standards that Congress had set in the 1970 Clean Air Act. EPA officials realized there would be unacceptable economic consequences if the agency barred construction of any new factories or other polluting facilities in these "non-attainment" regions.

As a way out of this dilemma, EPA in 1976 devised an "offset" policy enabling businesses that reduced emissions from one facility to earn emission credits they could use to increase emissions from a new facility nearby. Firms could also bank credits for future use, or sell them to other companies wishing to expand their facilities.

Then, in 1979, EPA gave firms more flexibility in reducing pollution from existing plants. It approved a "bubble" policy that allowed existing plants to make major changes in their facilities without complying with all of the standards governing new sources of pollution. Under the bubble approach, as long as pollution from a new source in one part of a plant is offset by reductions in emissions from another part, the plant as a whole would be treated as though it were a single unit enclosed in a bubble.

The goal is not just to allow flexibility for economic reasons. These policies also have been designed to help assure overall improvements in air quality by requiring that offsetting reductions exceed new pollutant emissions. In Los Angeles, for instance, every pound of pollutant produced by a new company must be counterbalanced by reducing emissions somewhere else by 1.67 pounds.

Those who say emissions trading works often cite a 1987 study by G. L. Hester and Robert W. Hahn, a senior staff economist for the President's Council of Economic Advisers. They estimated that EPA's emission trading policies had saved more than $4 billion in pollution control costs with no adverse impact on overall air quality.[†]

But many environmentalists remain skeptical. They contend that the policy prevents the country from achieving the best possible air quality by letting heavy polluters buy credits instead of forcing them to reduce emissions. Critics also complain that EPA has tolerated "paper trades," in which companies claim credits for previously achieved emission cutbacks, for closing outmoded facilities, or for steps they probably would have taken without market incentives.

Not all environmentalists are categorically opposed to emissions trading, however. Daniel Dudek, a senior economist with the Environmental Defense Fund, and John Palmisano, president of an emissions trading consulting firm, contend that EPA's program has demonstrated that "market incentives which enlist the expertise of on-site managers can achieve more pollution control results for less money, now instead of later." But they complain that widespread trading in emissions credits remains "handicapped by bureaucratic inertia and infighting, dogmatic opposition by environmentalists, hostility in Congress, as well as indifference by polluters." [††]

EPA does not require states to permit emissions trades. Even where trading is allowed, advocates acknowledge that companies have been reluctant to participate unless they are forced to buy credits to open new facilities. For one thing, companies fear that the government will tighten air quality standards in the future, denying use of credits companies have saved for future expansion. "Before industry can widely use emissions trading concepts, Congress, EPA, and states must make the rules more certain," Dudek and Palmisano argue.

[†] Robert W. Hahn and G. L. Hester, "The Market for Bads: EPA's Experience with Emissions Trading," Regulation, 1987, pp. 48-53.

[††] Daniel J. Dudek and John Palmisano, "Emissions Trading: Why Is This Thoroughbred Hobbled?" Columbia Journal of Environmental Law, 1988 Vol. 13, No. 2, p. 218.

use of EPA's emissions-trading program by writing authority into the Clean Air Act itself, thus giving businesses greater confidence that credits they accumulate will remain available for future use.

The Project 88 report also advocates extending the marketable-permit system to the federal clean-water program. Instead of just requiring industry to install effluent-control equipment, the report suggests that EPA set overall limits on polluted discharges to watersheds and then issue tradable permits to control pollution levels. While conceding that regulatory approaches may play a larger role, the report also urges combining them with marketable permits as incentives for reducing hard-to-control water pollution from "non-point" sources, such as runoff from farmers' fields and urban streets.

Hahn says the administration also is considering market incentives for removing asbestos from buildings and is looking at recommendations in the Project 88 report for using economic incentives as part of international efforts to control global warming and phase out chemicals that destroy the atmosphere's protective ozone layer.

EPA in 1987 outlined a plan to issue marketable permits as part of its strategy to implement an international agreement to freeze and subsequently reduce use of chlorofluorocarbons (CFCs) and other chemical compounds that scientists have found deplete the ozone layer protecting the earth's surface from ultraviolet radiation. The agency envisions granting tradable permits allowing manufacturers to produce or import specified annual quantities of potential ozone depleters. As annual quotas are cut, permits are expected to rise in value, giving users incentives to replace or recycle the gases where possible and to commit limited supplies for the most essential purposes.

Project 88 suggests applying similar market approaches to reverse global warming, which is occurring, many scientists say, because of a "greenhouse effect" caused by the release of carbon dioxide into the atmosphere when fossil fuels are burned. The report calls for a comprehensive national energy policy to promote alternative fuels; debt-for-nature swaps that would forgive Third World nations' international debt in return for preserving tropical rain forests; and an international system for trading permits to continue emitting carbon dioxide, CFCs and other gases that contribute to the greenhouse effect.

Economists contend that market incentives also can play major roles in forcing safe handling of hazardous substances. As federal regulation of such substances has tightened, the cost of placing hazardous wastes in a dump has risen from about $10 a ton in 1980 to as much as $500 a ton, giving firms an incentive to reduce how much waste they produce and to recycle hazardous materials. And the threat of financial liability may be emerging as a forceful spur for firms to handle toxic materials more carefully. Near Rochester, N.Y., for instance, a Xerox factory paid a $95,000 fine for failing to report that trichloroethylene from the plant was seeping toward nearby residential wells. But more significantly, the company also paid $4.75 million to two families whose wells were contaminated.

Many states have adopted "bottle" laws to reduce solid waste by imposing refundable deposits on beverage containers. Seattle encourages recycling by collecting cans, bottles, newspapers and junk mail for free, but charging $13.55 a month to pick up one garbage can of refuse weekly. West Germany encourages motor oil recycling by charging a levy on new lubricants and using revenues to subsidize development of an oil recycling industry. Norway and Sweden tax new cars and refund the levy to owners when they deliver unusable vehicles to scrap dealers.

Project 88 suggested a similar deposit-refund system for small quantities of hazardous materials that can be transported in containers and dumped just about anywhere. A front-end tax would be imposed on newly manufactured solvents and other products. It would be refunded on toxic wastes that were turned in to designated facilities for disposal or recycling. The tax would encourage producers to substitute less dangerous substances, while the refund would provide an incentive for recycling and disposal. The system would discourage illegal dumping that is nearly impossible to control. Wirth and Heinz have proposed legislation setting up incentives modeled on Project 88 proposals for recycling used motor oil.

Doubts about market approaches

Proponents make clear that economic approaches are not a cure-all for every form of ecological damage. Pollution taxes, permit trading, deposit systems and other proposals can work only for pollution or health risks that can be measured and monitored. Stewart suggests that such devices may be unworkable for managing risks from pesticides, for instance, or from pollutants that become dangerous only if they exceed "threshold" concentrations at a single location. Even the Project 88 report acknowledged that setting more stringent motor vehicle emission standards may be the most effective way to reduce air pollution by automobiles.

Proponents also acknowledge that their ideas face resistance from Congress, environmentalists and regulatory officials steeped in a regulatory system designed to punish, not reward, private-sector actions that affect the environment. A marketable-permit system would require EPA and state environmental officials to monitor permit transactions and emission levels instead of evaluating how industry controls emissions. "Regulators may at first feel that they have less control over the system, because actual pollution-control decisions will be made by polluters, not by the government," the Project 88 report points out. "This, of course, is the whole point of the marketable-permit approach."

So far, state officials and leaders of environmental organizations say they are willing to look closely at proposed market incentives, but skeptics argue that although market incentives may be attractive in theory, they might turn out to be just as difficult to administer as existing regulations. As Rutgers University law Professor Howard Latin put it in a 1985 law review article, market approach theories "represent wishful thinking rather than a realistic appraisal of present environmental knowledge and regulatory capabilities." [11]

Some environmentalists also offer a more fundamental objection to substituting market influences for direct controls on contaminants that threaten human health or the quality of life. Removal of direct regulatory controls would let some industries continue to pollute without taking steps to control emissions as much as possible, they contend, making it more difficult to bring about overall pollution reductions.

Despite its imperfections, environmentalists contend, the existing command-and-control system has improved the environment at a cost that most Americans find acceptable. "Most of us would grant that EPA seems to be badly bogged down right now, but it's an open question whether with good leadership it will be able to generate some progress," says the Sierra Club's McCloskey. Nevertheless, even McCloskey agrees that market approaches offer an appealing vision of "what seems to be an automatic system sending the right signals to all of the actors."

Notes

[1] Robert N. Stavins, "Clean Profits, Using Economic Incentives to Protect the Environment," *Policy Review*, spring 1989, p. 59.

[2] *Project 88, Harnessing Market Forces to Protect Our Environment: Initiatives for the New President*, Washington, D.C., December 1988.

[3] Gregg Easterbrook, "Cleaning Up," *Newsweek*, July 24, 1989, p. 33.

[4] Bruce A. Ackerman and William T. Hassler, *Clean Coal/Dirty Air* (1981), p. 2.

[5] *State of the Environment: A View Toward the Nineties*, The Conservation Foundation, 1987, p. 32.

[6] Richard B. Stewart, "Controlling Environmental Risks Through Economic Incentives," *Columbia Journal of Environmental Law*, 1988, p. 154.

[7] Bruce A. Ackerman and Richard B. Stewart, "Reforming Environmental Law: The Democratic Case for Market Incentives," *Columbia Journal of Environmental Law*, 1988 Vol. 13, No. 2, p. 172.

[8] Robert W. Hahn and G. L. Hester, "The Market for Bads: EPA's Experience with Emissions Trading," *Regulation*, 1987, p. 48.

[9] See Peter Passell, "Selling Rights to Pollute: Bush Backs Idea in Acid-Rain Fight," *The New York Times*, May 17, 1989.

[10] Quoted by Larry Liebert in "Washington Perspective: Bush and the Environment," *California Journal*, August 1989, p. 318.

[11] Howard Latin, "Ideal Versus Real Regulatory Efficiency: Implementation of Uniform Standards and 'Fine-Tuning' Regulatory Reforms," *Stanford Law Review*, May 1985, p. 1267.

Selected Bibliography

Books

Ackerman, Bruce A., and Hassler, William T., *Clean Coal, Dirty Air*, Yale University Press, 1981.

Yale University legal scholars Ackerman and Hassler trace congressional and EPA decisions leading to regulations requiring new electric utility power plants to install smokestack scrubbers. The authors take a critical view of a political process they contend subverted efficient environmental protection to assure markets for high-sulfur Eastern coal mines. "Instead of a solution responsive to the evolving will of a national majority, congressional intervention mixed clean-air symbols and dirty-coal self-interest in a way that invites cynicism about democratic self-government," they write.

Magat, Wesley A., editor, *Reform of Environmental Regulation*, Ballinger Publishing Co., 1982.

The author draws together seven chapters commissioned by Duke University for a 1982 conference assessing different approaches to revising environmental regulations that were commonly discussed in the early years of the Reagan administration. In an introductory chapter, Magat suggests that using economic incentives for environmental protection faces "two substantial hurdles. First, more extensive use of incentive-based approaches would require statutory change before EPA could adopt them," opening up a wide range of conflicting political interests during congressional debate. "Second, the reason for probable congressional inaction is precisely that major wealth transfers would be involved."

Articles

Easterbrook, Gregg, "Cleaning Up," *Newsweek*, July 24, 1989, p. 27.

Easterbrook discusses President Bush's proposal for an emission-trading system to combat acid rain. "Emission trading sounds weird," he writes. "... But nearly everyone who studies pollution regulation concludes that what's missing is a positive inducement that works from the bottom up, supplanting the conventional structure of costs imposed from the top down. Emission trading will allow engineers rather than regulators to judge which factories can meet standards most efficiently while adding a profit motive for inventing improved controls."

Faludi, Susan, "Selling Smog," *California Business*, June 1987, p. 68.

Contributing editor Faludi takes a critical look at emission trading in California under the federal Clean Air Act. Faludi reports environmentalists' complaints that emission trading prevents improvements in air quality: "Cleaner companies make money off their good records, and dirtier companies save money because it is always cheaper to buy emissions-reduction credits than to actually invest hundreds of thousands of dollars in pollution-control equipment. So everyone in the deal walks away happy, unless one happens to be a member of the general public worried that all this swapping of smog is not making our lungs any cleaner."

Latin, Howard, "Ideal Versus Real Regulatory Efficiency: Implementation of Uniform Standards and 'Fine-Tuning' Regulatory Reforms," *Stanford Law Review*, May 1985, p. 1267.

Latin, a Rutgers Law School professor, dismisses proposed market-based incentives for environmental protection as unrealistic and unproven. "Despite its imperfections, command-and-control regulation has fostered significant improvements in environmental quality at a societal cost that has not proved prohibitive," he writes. "... In many environmental contexts, society's real choice may be to rely either on crude regulation or on no regulation."

Main, Jeremy, "Here Comes the Big New Cleanup," *Fortune*, Nov. 21, 1988, p. 102.

Main looks at potential responses to environmentalists' calls for a "third wave" of government programs addressing newly emerging environmental problems. He focuses more than Easterbrook does on economic-incentive approaches. "The third-wave attack demands a fresh, third-wave approach that learns from the errors of the past," Main writes. "... With a more common-sense, market-oriented strategy, the U.S. could get on with the cleanup without drowning the economy in unnecessary regulation and expense."

Stavins, Robert N., "Clean Profits, Using Economic Incentives to Protect the Environment," *Policy Review*, spring 1989, p. 58.

Stavins, a professor at Harvard University's John F. Kennedy School of Government, outlines the conclusions of the Project 88 study he directed for U.S. Sens. Timothy Wirth, D-Colo., and John Heinz, R-Pa. (*See below.*) Stavins argues that economic incentives will be essential if the nation wants to address environmental problems while reducing the federal budget deficit and keeping its industries competitive in international markets. "Incentive-based approaches have an added benefit: They can make the environmental debate more understandable to the general public," he adds. "Because they do not dictate a particular technology, these approaches can focus attention directly on the selection of environmental goals, rather than on complex questions concerning technological alternatives for reaching those goals."

Reports and Studies

"Law and Economics Symposium: New Directions in Environmental Policy," *Columbia Journal of Environmental Law*, 1988 Vol. 13, No. 2, pp. 153-401.

The journal, published by the Columbia University Law School, prints papers that leading advocates of economic incentives presented at an Oct. 1, 1987, symposium.

Project 88, Harnessing Market Forces to Protect Our Environment: Initiatives for the New President, sponsored by Sen. Timothy E. Wirth, D-Colo., and Sen. John Heinz, R-Pa., Washington, D.C., December 1988.

Prepared under the auspices of Wirth and Heinz, the report summarizes arguments for using economic incentives to solve environmental problems. It makes 36 recommendations to President Bush for steps to address acid rain, the greenhouse effect and other emerging problems.

Graphics: pp. 94, 96, 97, S. Dmitri Lipczenko.

INDEX